EXILE AND JOURNEY IN SEVENTEENTH-CENTURY LITERATURE

The political and religious upheavals of the seventeenth century forced an unprecedented number of people to flee from England or remain in internal exile. Among these exiles were some of the most important authors in the Anglo-American canon. Christopher D'Addario explores how early modern authors reacted to and wrote about the experience of exile in relation both to their lost homeland and to the new communities they created for themselves. He analyzes the writings of first-generation New England Puritans, the Royalists in France during the England Civil War, and the "interior exiles" of John Milton and John Dryden. D'Addario explores the nature of artistic creation from the religious and political margins of early modern England, and in doing so, provides detailed insight into the psychological and material pressures of displacement and a much overdue study of the importance of exile to the development of early modern literature.

CHRISTOPHER D'ADDARIO is visiting Assistant Professor of English at Gettysburg College, Pennsylvania.

EXILE AND JOURNEY IN SEVENTEENTH-CENTURY LITERATURE

CHRISTOPHER D'ADDARIO

CAMBRIDGE
UNIVERSITY PRESS

CAMBRIDGE UNIVERSITY PRESS
Cambridge, New York, Melbourne, Madrid, Cape Town, Singapore, São Paulo

Cambridge University Press
The Edinburgh Building, Cambridge CB2 8RU, UK

Published in the United States of America by
Cambridge University Press, New York

www.cambridge.org
Information on this title: www.cambridge.org/9780521870290

First published 2007

Printed in the United Kingdom at the University Press, Cambridge

A catalogue record for this publication is available from the British Library

Library of Congress Cataloging-in-Publication data

D'Addario, Christopher.
Exile and journey in seventeenth-century literature / Christopher D'Addario.
p. cm.
Includes bibliographical references and index.
ISBN-13: 978-0-521-87029-0
ISBN-10: 0-521-87029-1
1. English literature—Early modern, 1500–1700—History and criticism. 2. Exile (Punishment)
in literature. 3. Politics and literature—Great Britain—History—17th century. 4. Literature
and society—Great Britain—History—17th century. 5. American literature—Colonial period,
ca. 1600–1775—History and criticism. 6. American literature—Puritan authors—History
and criticism. 7. Bradstreet, Anne, 1612?–1672—History and criticism. 8. Hobbes, Thomas,
1588–1679—History and criticism. 9. Milton, John, 1608–1674—History and criticism.
10. Dryden, John, 1631–1700—History and criticism. I. Title.

PR438.E95D33 2007
810.9′358—dc22

2006036601

ISBN   978-0-521-87029-0   hardback

Contents

Acknowledgments

Appropriately in writing about journeys and exile, I have myself moved far and often during the several years it took to research and write this study, living in five different cities since the project's inception. I have had the aid of numerous hands and minds amidst these travels. First and foremost, I would like to thank Steven Zwicker for his unflagging support, considerate attention and invaluable advice and insight, without which this study would never have been completed. I would also like to thank Derek Hirst and Joseph Loewenstein for their thoughtful suggestions and advice as they read various chapters through the composition stages. Dan Shea and William Spengemann were kind enough to add their insight to my work on the New England Puritans. I have presented much of this work to the early modern reading group at Washington University – to its members, particularly Matthew Harkins, Sam Thomas, Gavin Foster and Felicia Else, many thanks for your perceptive and helpful comments.

This project was supported by two fellowships – from the William Andrews Clark Memorial Library (through the generosity of Penny Kanner) and from the John Carter Brown Library. In the early stages of the research, I received invaluable assistance from the staffs at these two libraries: Bruce Whiteman and Jennifer Schaffner at the Clark and Norman Fiering at the JCB. Washington University and the Mellon Foundation also provided generous support at various points.

An abridged and earlier version of Chapter 4 appeared as "Dryden and the Historiography of Exile: Milton and Virgil in Dryden's Late Period," in *The Huntington Library Quarterly* 67, no. 4 (2004), 553–72 and is reused with permission.

To my friends and companions in my travels over the past few years, your company has reminded me of the importance and joy that we can derive from conversation and conviviality, no matter the silliness of the dialogue (or the speaker). A special thanks as well to Peter and Tiffany

D'Addario for their hospitality as I completed this project. Finally, my thanks to my closest companion, Kathy, whose love and patience, as well as her willingness to get on an airplane, has enabled me to see the work to completion. May we continue our travels wherever they may take us.

The "remanence" of the past: the early modern text in exile

After a lifetime of wars and conflicts the sixteenth-century Italian writer Matteo Bandello reflected on the disturbances of his native land from exile in Agen, France. Bandello, monk, diplomat, soldier and author, ruminated that, with all of the displaced Italians now living far from their patria, an entire city of exiles could be founded and populated.[1] However, the aging monk does not dwell long on this imagined city, rather letting it fade from the page and from memory. The ephemeral appearance of this city is typical of the imagined geographies of exile, geographies that emerge more often as figments of space and time rather than as realistic, concrete memories. This is not to say that memories do not drive the exile's imaginings; indeed, it is the rupture of departure, and the lingering shadow of the homeland left behind, that gives rise to Bandello's imagined city.[2] Yet Bandello, who left Florence when the Spanish invaded in 1522, does not envision or reconstruct his lost patria in the text, but rather imagines a city characterized primarily by the collective experience of exile, its inhabitants not reminiscing about the lost quotidian particulars of Florentine life, but rather about their various stories of displacement. Almost five hundred years later, Russian exiles in New York City would similarly recreate stories about their exiles as they collected "diasporic souvenirs" that displayed their wanderings while admitting a multiple, transient belonging that lay somewhere between New York City and St. Petersburg.[3] Outside of London, Polish exiles from World War II remained in refugee camps until late into the 1950s, seemingly afraid to forget their displacement, as if this forgetting might mean that they could never go back.

For these exiles, as well as for Bandello, the present is marked by a provisionality necessarily veiled by the rupture of exile, their recreations and memories necessarily piecemeal and complexly layered by the transitory experience of displacement. As they walk in the present, these exiles see, hear and smell both the immediacy of their newly foreign existence and the silhouette of the day before their exile. As the Egyptian émigré André Aciman admits, his New York is the "shadow of the shadow of Alexandria, versions of Alexandria, the remanence of Alexandria."[4] It is this layering of here and there, as well as the sense of provisionality, that often drives the various creations of exiles. The desire to create in exile comes from both the necessity of reorienting oneself somewhere between the lost past and the immediate present, and the need to fashion a peaceful space in which the author can operate away from the unsettled, difficult reality of daily life. Bandello's city of exiles exists only in his imagination, free to be built and peopled however he likes. In many ways, the exilic creation seeks to counter, although never completely successfully, the repeated impressions of provisionality that displacement leaves upon the exile. The Russian exiled poet Joseph Brodsky acknowledges this when admitting that the writer always "knows how willful, how intended and premeditated everything he has manufactured is. How, in the end, all of it is provisional."[5] While the ability to recognize the provisionality that Brodsky elucidates drives the various grand literary constructions of exile, it also adds a poignancy and doubt that serves as a counterpoint to the willfulness of the exilic creation.

The events of the sixteenth and seventeenth centuries in England cast many of Aciman's shadows, shadows of old Englands, across the minds of its exiles. Indeed, by the last decade of the seventeenth century, these Englands lingered in the memories of men and women as various as the second generation New England governor in Boston, John Winthrop, Jr., the converted Catholic at the Jacobite court in St. Germain, Jane Barker, and the exiled and unrepentant regicide in Vevey, Switzerland, Edmund Ludlow. Throughout the century, men and women were forced to recognize that the old England that they had known and to which they had attached themselves was now merely a shadow of a memory that had been indelibly marked by one form of departure or another. So, the memories of George Goring's life of military honor before 1640, tainted by defeat and exile at the hands of the New Model Army, seem to have chased him across the Continent as he eventually drank himself to death, in what the fellow exile Ann Fanshawe would later call a "debauchery beyond all precedents."[6] So, the memories of the high republican rhetoric of the Parliament of 1650 lingered in the ears of John Milton as the poet was inundated in 1660 with the ringing shouts for the return of the Stuarts and the burning of Milton's *The Tenure of Kings and Magistrates*. The "confusions and revolutions" of governments occurred with such frequency, and enacted such wholesale change, that most exiles, excepting the Jacobites at the end of the century, had the opportunity to return to their homeland. Many other prominent exiles, including Edward Hyde, Henry Vane, Algernon Sidney, Edmund Ludlow, and James II and his most loyal Stuart retainers, fled into exile more than once or else returned only to be imprisoned or executed at a later date. For all of these exiles, the disjunctions between "here" and "there" remained constant during their displacements, reinforcing the arbitrariness of their own existence and identities.[7]

We are just beginning to comprehend the psychological, communal and literary terrain of the experience of displacement, mainly because voices from exile are finally being heard and listened to. We only know the story of the first exile, the ancient Egyptian Sinuhe, because he returned to his homeland to communicate his story.[8] In the twentieth century, displacement and exile has become the common fate of groups and individuals too numerous to mention as the ravages of totalitarianism, genocidal ideology, fundamentalism and nationalism have bereft scores of communities of their homes and homelands. Because of the frequency of displacements in the past eighty years, and because of the prominence of the political and literary endeavors of some of these exiles, we have grown increasingly attuned to the experiences and literatures of dispersed communities. Yet we have yet to apply this increased knowledge of and sensitivity to the ruptures of exile to the early modern period, where, particularly in seventeenth-century England, an unprecedented number of men and women were forced to flee England or to remain in an "internal exile," unreconciled to the ruling authority. The broadness of the phenomenon of exile in early modern England has largely gone unrecognized beyond a passing mention in studies that concentrate on one specific community. Yet the conflicting judgments of the 1630s, 1648–9, 1660 and 1688 of what and who "England" and its government represented (and we might also add the judgments of 1641–2, 1653, 1667, and 1680–2) ensured that widely divergent groups were forced from their homes and former ways of life. This study seeks to redress the neglect of the formative psychological, social, affective and literary experience of exile in the lives of these divergent groups. Further, it seeks to outline, at least provisionally, the importance of exile to our understanding of prominent literary, religious and philosophical texts, indeed some of the foundational elements of the early modern canon. In undertaking this study, I wish to emphasize that the experience of exile, of being removed to the margins of the English-speaking world, either geographically, politically or religiously, inflected and influenced in specific ways a series of

English literary traditions and forms, from lyric poetry to political philosophy, from epic to translation.

My move from the experience of exile to the text written in or imagined under the pressures of exile in the previous paragraph should not go unremarked. The studies that follow both examine the experience of exile by reading imaginative texts, and interpret imaginative texts as, crucially, written from one form of exile or another. My approach assumes a particular conception of the written text, one that foregrounds it as a social and cultural phenomenon embedded in the circumstances of its production and consumption, and relatedly as an object that can provide us with a particular knowledge of these circumstances. That is, the written text should be seen both as a social process, an object within the material exchanges of everyday life, and as an immediate and important insight into and formative agent for the social or cultural moment with which it is concerned.[9] I thus view the texts that I examine in the following chapters as both determiners of social and cultural exchange, and also as scripts arising out of the particular effects of banishment from one's home or former way of life. Not only did the text written from a real or imagined exile register the distinct sense of loss, the profound uprootedness, and the novel set of social and political circumstances that attended the author's exile; it also importantly negotiated and attempted to configure these consequences for both the author and his or her audience.

Studying what are social, affective, political and religious experiences through the written word, as I do in the following chapters, draws attention to the centrality of language to the perception of displacement by the exile. Language, crucially, remained the exile's most immediate link to a lost homeland or life that he or she had previously known, the most insistent reminder of the exile's banishment or marginalization. A twentieth-century German exile once expressed the attenuated relationship that the exile maintains with his or her homeland's language: "German, for me, has become a foreign language to which I know all the words."[10] Early modern writers, and we could assume, audiences, also seemed to have been fully aware of the deep effects exile had upon the exiled community's language, as well as the English language's importance to their identity. In *Richard II* for example, upon learning of his banishment from the realm, Thomas Mowbray largely understands his misfortune in terms of the loss of his mother tongue:

> The language I have learn'd these forty years,
> My native English, now I must forego:

> And now my tongue's use is to me no more
> Than an unstringed viol or a harp,
> Or like a cunning instrument cased up,
> Or, being open, put into his hands
> That knows no touch to tune the harmony
> . . . .
> What is thy sentence then but speechless death,
> Which robs my tongue from breathing native breath? (I.3.160–66, 172–3)[11]

Mowbray's lament figures the lost homeland as the loss of his ability to breathe or speak with his native tongue, the silencing of spoken inter-actions in English standing in for his exile generally. Displacement removes the exile indelibly from the living stream of the English language. The English exiles that fled to the Continent were forced to recognize the contingencies of expression as they were removed from the language that they had learned as children, and thus had unconsciously associated with direct reality. It is not without reason that the fall and subsequent ban-ishment of Adam and Eve has also been told as a tale of the fall into human language. The "fruit of that forbidden tree" necessarily entailed the transformation of words from mimetic sacrality to corrupt allegory. Their exile ensured the disjunction between the world as is and the world as represented, a problem of which Milton was all too aware, even as he grappled with the story of that first fall into allegory. The editors of the Geneva Bible similarly immersed themselves in the comforts and diffi-culties of their English translation as they lived in a Swiss canton, far from the interchanges of a Marian England that itself often spoke a language at odds with their own. A constant awareness of the contingency of language would have reminded the exiles at all turns of their banishment or marginalization as they fulfilled their quotidian tasks, and as importantly, those in authority conversed in a language in many ways foreign to them. As much as the nobility and gentry exiled might have been conversant in French or Dutch, those who were banished consistently registered the loss of their native tongue. Ralph Verney, in exile with the Stuarts in the 1640s and '50s, admitted in a letter to his friend back in England that, while he knew French well enough to translate two anti-papist books into French, he still could not speak it easily and relied on servants and others to help him with spoken exchanges.[12] Edmund Ludlow, in the Swiss town of Vevay after the restoration, was thankful that he lodged with a merchant whose wife was English, since they spoke the same language; when he lodged at Dieppe he could only converse with a French doctor in broken Latin.[13]

Beyond the inconvenience that the language barrier posed for English exiles, it also foregrounded a more metaphysical separation from the living exchange of their mother tongue as well as more generally from the past homeland they had known. In the final two lines from Mowbray's lament above, Mowbray conflates the loss of language with a more metaphysical separation from breathing English air. Language, even at this early stage in the formation of a standardized idiom, was a carrier for English traditions and cultural identity, as the phrase "mother tongue" suggests. The upheavals and exiles that ruptured the English nation throughout the early modern period came at a time when growing print production and the move to a vernacular administrative language drove the standardization of English, particularly in and around London, where the print market and political authority lay.[14] But, without placing these exiles in a specific narrative concerning the spread of a uniform language throughout the country, we can recognize that the English language was the medium through which the displacements of exile, however variously defined, were most acutely felt. For Ralph Verney, unfamiliarity with the French language shades over into a distaste for French custom and a yearning for English schooling for his children. Similarly, Ludlow's relief at housing with an Englishwoman with whom he can converse comes alongside a relief over their possession of English beer, rather than the French wine which had so damaged his health.[15] More basically, the removal from the circulation of written materials in and around the print community of London drove the exiles' constant desire for more news from their departed homeland and exacerbated the perception of their displacement from the immediate events of the English nation as well as the living interaction of the English print community.[16]

For interior exiles, such as the defeated republicans who remained in England during the restoration, the experience of immediate removal from the quotidian use of the English language obviously did not occur. Indeed, prominent interior exiles such as John Milton and John Dryden continued to read avidly and were acutely aware of the specific movements of the learned London reading community. However, for these interior exiles the language that they used necessarily remained politically or religiously distant from the discourses of those reconciled to the present authority or even those tacitly accepting of the status quo. Charles Simic, in describing the Romanian exile Norman Manea's increasing alienation under Ion Antonescu's regime, notes that Manea came to find an "unbridgeable gulf between the language he used in public with its canonic certainties and the words he kept to himself."[17]

In the case of those forced into an interior exile by the events of 1659–60 or 1688, the unbridgeable gulf between a language of private thought and public expression would not have opened gradually but widened quickly as they and their compatriots were removed from power and from a public voice. As these men and women sequestered themselves from the active life governed by the present "social contract," and ventured less and less into public spaces to exchange goods and ideas, they also increasingly and consistently recognized the distance at which their language lived from the dominant and accepted modes of discourse.[18] Milton, blind, briefly imprisoned and otherwise sequestered, would have heard keenly the drunken shouts for Charles Stuart around the bonfires that burned calves' rumps in effigy of the Rump Parliament, as well as the reports of attacks on Puritan ministers, the burning of the Commonwealth's arms and the extravagant pageantry of the king's return. A year later, from his house on Jewin Street, Milton would have heard the processions of the hanging carts as the authorities dragged the exhumed bodies of Oliver Cromwell, Henry Ireton and John Bradshaw to the Red Lion Inn and the gallows at Tyburn, around the corner from Milton's residence. Perhaps remembering the vocal support for Richard Cromwell and even the Rump mere months ago, Edmund Ludlow recalled that the "flattering of Charles Steward ... made my eares tingle, and my heart to ake, all thinges running counter to what the providencyes of the Lord had lead to for twenty yeares past."[19] Part of the engaged desperation that can be felt in Milton's *The Readie and Easie Way* should be understood as the desperation of an author grasping at, or holding on to, a language of republican, reasoned citizenship that he knew no longer appealed to or held much authority for his audience (if he still had one).

In light of the events that occurred later in 1660, the second edition of *The Readie and Easie Way* has been seen as the last, desperate plea of the fading hopes of the Good Old Cause on the eve of the restoration. Much of what has puzzled or disturbed critics in Milton's last major publication before *Paradise Lost* is its ability to reconcile a jeremiadic, rigorous independence from common conceptions and opinions with a firm belief in the reasonableness of its proposals, with which everyone should and, to a certain extent, must agree. However, we might see this rhetorical disjunction as an admission on Milton's part of the duplicity of the English language as it turned at the moment of the restoration. In this case, his adherence to a reasoned rhetorical stance at a time when few reasoned in the same way becomes a studied resistance, an assertion of one "way" of meaning when the language of obedience, of deliverance and of providence was being yoked to the fortunes of the soon-to-be Charles II. As Michael Seidel has noted, writing from exile generally necessitates a "willful act of the imagination to comprehend and register the experience of exile and the lost homeland."[20] In Milton's case, and in the case of the other exiles I study here, this "willful act of the imagination" often takes the form of an adherence to idiosyncratic, nostalgic modes of speaking as the discourses of authority change around them. One of the clearest ways in which we can see the "willfulness, exaggeration and overstatement" to which exiles are prone is through their consistently peculiar, yet normative, use of the English language.[21]

When Hobbes vigorously asserted his own refiguring of the body politic and of political language as normative, or when Dryden constructed a model of the icon of imperial poetry, Virgil, for his own purposes, these writers were answering to, and importantly, constructing, the experience of exile. Further, through their presentation of idiosyncrasy – such as in Hobbes's normative rhetoric or Nathaniel Ward's overdetermined Marprelatian neologisms in *The Simple Cobler of Aggawam* – these exiles both insist on their remoteness and distinctness while asserting this remoteness as "true Englishness." As Edward Said has argued, writing from exile often recreates the peripheral as the central as it challenges consensus.[22] Perhaps Shakespeare was reminded of the insistent nationalism of the Marian exiles who had returned from the Continent as he imagined Coriolanus denouncing the plebeians for banishing Rome's true defender and reversing the terms of his own exile:

> You common cry of curs, whose breath I hate
> As reek o' the rotten fens, whose loves I prize
> As the dead carcasses of unburied men
> That do corrupt my air, I banish you! (3.3.120–23)[23]

By refiguring their own marginalization and exile as central, and truly English, exiles react to and seek to comprehend the experience of displacement, the physical, ideological or affective removal from their homeland. Exile is a profoundly disruptive and traumatic experience, one that entails both a sharp break in the quotidian existence of one's life and a removal from that which is most familiar and comforting; it "involves dislocation, disorientation, self-division."[24] As the exile is removed from familiar material, structural and familial surroundings, his or her sense of a coherent identity and continuous history is ruptured. The writing that arises out of this experience, writing such as *Leviathan* or *Paradise Lost*, seeks to heal, reconsider, or even elide these ruptures through the imaginative control of the author both over substance and, more specifically, over language. Drawing on the reflections of Walter Benjamin, Seidel calls exilic creation a "fragile, precious reality of a place where the imagination is sovereign."[25] The self-conscious assuredness of these texts provides a comfortable space within and from which these authors speak.

However, the very self-consciousness of Milton's poetic voice, or, to take another example, of Bradstreet's humble yet confident muse, must not be ignored. The ruptures of exile, the pressures placed on the material and affective lives of these writers through their removal from the familiar, are never fully dispelled by the act of writing; the elision of exile is never fully successful. In fact, we might cite the numerous, and frequent, failed or unfinished creative attempts of early modern English exiles, from the incomplete royalist epics of William Davenant and Abraham Cowley to the unfinished memoirs of the regicide Edmund Ludlow, as evidence of the difficulties, both practical and imaginative, of writing from exile. Even in the grand, created worlds of the early modern exiles examined here, the authors evince a consistent anxiety over the assertiveness of their presence, over the "willful acts" that underwrite their creations. Thus, while Hobbes's authoritarian political philosophy is predicated upon a normative semantics of which Hobbes arrogates control to himself, he also outlines the shaky epistemological basis for all language in his opening chapters. In fact, it is precisely because of his understanding of all language as relative that Hobbes asserts the need for sovereign – and, within *Leviathan*, authorial – control of how words mean. Nervousness over the fixity of language, over its ability to represent accurately, runs through all of the works examined here, and runs parallel to a concomitant desire to assert the author's own, often notably distinct, language as ideal. For many exiles the performative, be it the public gesture, the fashionable garment and posture, or the published written text, becomes an essential method through which identity is created and the disruptions of exile are overridden.[26] As much as early modern English men and women were attuned to the constructedness of all selves, to the extent to which identity was based on performance, we might see in the early modern literature of exile a stark acceptance and enactment of this fashioning of the self. The written text serves as the site for much of this exilic self-fashioning, both because of the availability of writing as an expressive and public form to the literate exile, and because language, even in the early modern period, was a critical carrier of culture.

For seventeenth-century English exiles, the nervousness over semantics and the bold assertion of their own constructed language often came together as they reacted to and attempted to order the experience of exile. Their often idiosyncratic use of the English language arises out of the sudden movement of definitions after each major shift in government, after "loyalty," "obedience" and "honor" leave their possession. The assertion of their own way of meaning often seeks nostalgically to reorient these terms and the English language generally to older, yet now radical, definitions. Similarly, just as the exiled author reaches backward, or perhaps forward, for a language that registers uprooting and loss of an old way of speaking or writing, this author also looks backward as he or she seeks to reconstruct a history and past that comprehends their new status as exiles. Nostalgia, a longing for a return to home, to a return to the way things were, suffuses much exilic writing, from Ovid's *Tristeia* to Milton's *Paradise Lost*, to the poetry of Joseph Brodsky. In her recent exploration of twentieth-century exile and longing, *The Future of Nostalgia*, Svetlana Boym notes that nostalgia, as "a historical emotion, is a longing for that shrinking 'space of experience' that no longer fits the new horizon of expectations."[27] Although Boym places the origins of "nostalgic longing" firmly in the development of modern notions of teleological history and thus after early modern exiles, we can still understand the nostalgic desires of early modern exiles in much the same terms. After all, while a modern history of progress was yet infrequently formulated beyond perhaps Baconian empiricism, notions of providential intervention and protestant reformation, in which the current ruling powers fulfilled God's will in England, identified the defeated parties of 1648–9, 1660 and 1688 as the irreligious opponents to the progress of God's people on earth. As the political tides shifted with war, restoration and revolution, so English history became a contested ground upon which ideological battles were fought. The politics, religion – and narratives – of those in exile were sloughed off as a corruption of God's will and true Englishness. Nostalgia was an expression of a continued attachment to a world, and a way of life, now lost and publicly decried and derided. At the same time, the exiles' turn to history enabled them to control its very terms within their created worlds, thus justifying and ordering the experience of exile both to themselves and to their audience. The turn to history and the past that is so prevalent in all the writers I explore here bridged the gap between a lost homeland, be it geographic or imagined, and the upheavals of exile by denying the gap's historical existence. And, while the nostalgic turn to the past answered to and reflected the insistent memory of a lost world so indelibly part of the experience of exile, it also served a polemical or public purpose, constructing a history that refigures the exiles as central, as the saving remnants of an English nation hopelessly astray.

* * *

This last point, that these texts of exile often anticipated and wrote for a specific public moment, deserves particular emphasis. Diaspora is a term that has increasingly been used to describe specific forms of displacement and community, most often in a postcolonial context. The term, while maintaining its spiritual resonance in its broadly positive assumption of resilience and preservation in the face of loss and migration, has come to identify hybridity, reciprocity and exchange as the markers of the postcolonial, diasporic community. For example, in *The Black Atlantic*, Paul Gilroy discusses the postmodern African diaspora and the dislocations that engendered it by approaching the culture of the Black Atlantic, a culture of creolization and syncretism, from "an explicitly transnational and intercultural perspective," while strongly critiquing the nationalist and "ethnically absolute paradigms" of previous approaches.[28] Similarly, Homi Bhabha, the critic perhaps most responsible for theorizing notions of hybridity in the postcolonial context, argues that in studying the displaced, exiled and marginalized we must begin "focusing on those *interstitial* moments or processes that are produced in the articulation of 'differences.' . . . It is at the level of the interstices that the intersubjective and collective experiences of nationness, community interest, or cultural value are negotiated."[29] It is this notion of the "articulation of 'differences'" that can usefully be deployed in the examination of early modern texts written from exile. Without eliding or downplaying the specific difficulties and freedoms that the displacements engendered by colonization have entailed, we can also understand the texts I examine here, texts written from various forms of exile in the early modern period, as necessarily articulating specific differences with the discourses of authority in and around the print metropolis of London, and from a marginal position. Throughout this study, I have remained particularly attuned to the distances that these exiled texts crossed as they enter back into the London print market, as all of them necessarily did. In *The Black Atlantic*, Gilroy uses the image of ships in motion as his organizing principle, an image that articulately envisions the material connectedness of the diaspora.[30] Much like Gilroy, I wish to foreground the material connectedness of early modern exiles, from those on the shores of New England, to Milton and Dryden living on the outskirts of London, and particularly to foreground their continued reliance upon and engagement with the English language print market and its production center in London. Because of the unique monopoly and Royal charter that the Stationers' Company had on print production in England, the overwhelming majority of books printed in English were produced in and around London.[31] When the exiles that I study here wrote for an English reading public, they wrote with an understanding of the diverse and geographically or ideologically distant print market into which their text would be disseminated.

My analysis of these texts from exile thus understands them as events that cross geographic, linguistic and ideological boundaries, especially as they pass back for entry into the London print market. As such events, these texts had to negotiate, from a marginal position, broad religious or political distances, as well as a distance from the discourses of authority and dominant modes of expression in and around the London print world.[32] Important to my approach to these texts as events is the historical reality that during the seventeenth century, and particularly after the collapse of the licensing act in 1642, England experienced an unprecedented boom in print production and a sharp increase in public interest in current affairs. As recent revisions to Jürgen Habermas's *The Structural Transformation of the Public Sphere* have taken the pains to show, a confluence of conditions – parliamentary and religious upheaval, the outbreak of war, the lapse in licensing, and an opportunistic, materially prepared print industry – led in the 1640s to a quickening print market and rapidly growing readership in contemporary pamphlets and printed materials.[33]

The exiles detailed in the following chapters sorely felt their separation from the living interchange of this burgeoning print market as they remained removed geographically, or, in the case of interior and geographic exiles, removed from claiming an authoritative public voice in this interchange. Yet this separation, certainly intensified by the quickening print market, did not necessarily effect a turn inward, nor did it effect writing that directed itself to an isolated audience of exiled readers or even writing that desired no audience. Indeed, the writers who were successful, who were able to fashion great imaginative works out of the fragments of exile, tended to write with an eye towards not only the exiled world they currently lived in but also the homeland with which they remained engaged and by which they remained haunted. Much of the rhetorical force, the linguistic anxieties and the imaginative innovations found in the texts that follow come from the exiled author's anticipation of and worries over his or her text's release, from a marginal position, into the wide-ranging sympathies of a growing London readership. Whereas the literature of exile has often, and in the early modern period as well, been read as reflecting the dislocation of exile, or perhaps more sophisticatedly, as an allegory of the exile experience, my analyses attempt to delineate the figurations that arise out of the text's movement from exile back to the homeland. It is in anticipation of this crossing that we can most clearly see each of these authors constructing a rhetoric or poetics of exile and distance, an imaginative "articulation of difference" that answers to the disruptions of exile.[34]

In many ways then, my work here has in mind the call of Maureen Quilligan, Margreta de Grazia and Peter Stallybrass to include consideration of the material, of the "object," into our critical discussions about subjectivity and identity formation in the early modern period.[35] As they state in their prefatory remarks to the essay collection *Subject and Object in Renaissance Culture*: "If the subject (or author or painter) is no longer assumed to be prior to and independent of objects, criticism can attend to a dialectic in which subjects and objects reciprocally take and make each other over."[36] Rather than considering the creative act as taking place solely within the psychological and affective worlds of the individual exile, my approach comprehends the literature of exile as intricately related to the continued material connectedness with, yet distance from, the lost homeland that lingers in the exiles' memories and lives on through the familiar objects that made up their everyday lives. Early modern exiles necessarily lived without many of the material objects that had previously surrounded them and had provided a sense of continuity and familiarity, a sense of identity for them. For the "interior exiles" Milton and Dryden, the familiar rhythms and material interactions of their lives before 1660 and 1688 respectively were irretrievably ruptured. As a result of these material conditions, particularly of the material specifics of the English book trade circa 1650–1700, the text in exile exhibits particular strategies that construct and order the dislocations that exile engendered as it crosses back and enters the bookstalls of St. Paul's Churchyard or the stocks of a London bookseller. Once we include the movement and interchange of objects into our account of early modern exile literature, we can begin to move away from, first of all, a limited conception of this complex phenomenon that centers on the individual or the exiled community in isolation; and, second of all, any misconceived assumption that the exile wrote solely, or even primarily, for a "like-minded community of readers" that is coterminous with those in exile.[37]

In concentrating on the exiled text as an event that crosses boundaries as it passes into the hands of a broader readership, I take up two distinct arguments in the two halves of the book with current critical consensus on the writings of these various groups. The first argument pertains to most of the analytical approaches to the geographic exiles I explore in the first two chapters, the New England Puritans and the royalist exiles on the continent. The criticism that has accrued around these two communities of exiles obviously has often widely divergent concerns, encouraged by the clear disciplinary divide coexistent with the great geographic and ideological distance that separated the New England Puritans from the royalists. Yet the two critical traditions work off similar assumptions: that the literatures produced by these groups should be read and contextualized as appealing to a like-minded community of readers, coterminous with the exiled community. As such, the texts produced by John Cotton, Anne Bradstreet, Thomas Hobbes and William Davenant have largely been understood as arising out of and directing themselves towards a limited range of ideological, political or affective concerns that can be broadly labeled respectively "New England Puritan/American" and "royalist."

Let me be more specific in terms of each set of exiles and the respective critical traditions that have grown around them. The study of early American literature, understandably and usefully, has primarily focused on the work of the New England Puritans as the first stirrings of an American literary tradition that extends downward through Jonathan Edwards and Emerson to the full flowering of the American Renaissance in Melville and Hawthorne. Thus, Perry Miller and Sacvan Bercovitch, the two most influential twentieth-century writers on early American literature, both explore the writings of the first settlers of New England with an eye toward identifying what made these works particularly "American."[38] While taking a transatlantic perspective in his *The Puritan Origins of the American Self,* Bercovitch does so in order to outline clearly the "unique qualities of the colonial outlook" and thus identify the origins of an American rhetoric of identity.[39] More recently, Andrew Delbanco and others have expanded Bercovitch's narrative, attempting to explain the ideology and experience of "becoming American."[40] While all of these studies, and Bercovitch's in particular, have invaluably increased our knowledge of early Puritan rhetorical forms and ideology, they also have tended to reinforce the nationalistic disciplinary boundaries institutionally established and physically embodied in the anthologies of "American" literature that begin with Marco Polo, Christopher Columbus or Captain John Smith.

Without derogating the important search for origins that these early Americanists have taken on, my work on the first generation of New England writers concentrates on their productions as exilic "events" with their own conditions of production and consumption. Importantly, these were texts that were printed and read in and around the print metropolis of London, and thus they should be read in the context of their long journey from the shores of New England to the bookstalls of St. Paul's Churchyard and the diverse readers of the entire English print community. In my first chapter, I approach the printed works of Nathaniel Ward and Anne Bradstreet, not to ascertain the specific "American" qualities of their work – the ways in which they prefigure later developments – but rather to delineate the construction of a rhetoric and poetics of distance that arises out of and constructs their English migration to the far shores of the Atlantic. Thus, part of the argument of the chapter emphasizes the importance of moving away from a conception of these texts as "American," a conception, it should be said, that has left Bradstreet and Ward's texts in particular with some odd bedfellows. By conceiving of Bradstreet's *The Tenth Muse* and Ward's *The Simple Cobler of Aggawam* as transatlantic texts written and imagined for a distant audience, I take up the criticism of a strain of Americanists, in particular William Spengemann and, more recently and trenchantly, Paul Giles, who have questioned the accuracy and efficacy of the use of the adjective "American" for the writings of the first generations of New England Puritans.[41] Drawing upon Réné Wellek's attack on the narrow nationalism of much literary scholarship, Giles argues that the categories "American" and "British" literatures "were much more divided and unstable," and that these nationalisms must be "seen as developing as heretical alternatives to one another."[42] Giles's approach rightfully views the early productions of the New England Puritans in a transatlantic context that does not single out the American qualities of these texts against a whitewashed background of vaguely British influence. While my concern does not tend towards the emerging and interdependent nationalisms of both sides of the Atlantic, I do read these texts, much like Giles, as necessarily conceived and consumed in light of the complex rhetorical position in which the New England settlers found themselves as they wrote.

Just as much criticism on "Early American" literature has sought to delineate an American context and, by implicit extension, audience for

these texts, work on royalist literature during the Interregnum has tended
to contextualize the poetry and prose as written for a primarily partisan
audience and as part of a partisan tradition. In the past twenty or so years,
much work has been done on the literature of the English Civil War, thus
reclaiming this critical period in the development of English literature and
ideologies from literary oblivion. Importantly, the work of Nigel Smith,
Lois Potter, David Norbrook, Thomas Corns, and Steven Zwicker especially, has drawn our attention to the ways in which the literature of the
time participated in and reacted to the unprecedented upheavals in the
structures of meaning caused by the Civil War.[43] In this way, these studies
have furthered our comprehension of the act of writing (and relatedly of
reading) during this period of partisan political strife as part of the processes of collective cultural and political production. However, the influence of much of this work has led to a picture of the literatures and
readers of the Civil War split intractably along ideological lines.[44] The
founding premise of many of these studies is to identify and explore the
"literature of republicanism" or "royalist literature" during the years
between Edgehill and the restoration of Charles II. The assumption
that lies behind work such as Robert Wilcher's *The Writing of Royalism*
is that the writers explored wrote exclusively with and for a partisan
political audience who possessed a common, if not a stable or coherent,
ideological system.[45]

My work on the exiled texts of the royalists, and particularly on
Hobbes's *Leviathan*, with its emphasis on the in-betweenness of the act
of writing from exile back into the London print market, necessarily
complicates these boundaries. In Hobbes's case (as well as in
Davenant's, Cowley's and Waller's), even before his return to England
in 1651–2, he wrote with an eye both to the exiled community of the
Stuarts as well as the more diverse community of readers back in England.
Indeed, in the "Preface" to *Leviathan*, after expressing sincere and justified worries over reception of his work, Hobbes notes that he walks a
middle way with his political philosophy: "For in a way beset with those
that contend, on one side for too great Liberty, and on the other side for
too much Authority, 'tis hard to passe between the points of both
unwounded."[46] While Wilcher, for example, argues that Hobbes's
Leviathan declared its Parliamentary sympathies on the eve of the author's
return to England, the "either/or" quality of Wilcher's observations does
not faithfully describe the balancing act that Hobbes envisions here, an
act which later forces him to admit to the "double-edged" nature of
the text.[47] Whereas studies of the "literature of royalism" tend to

assume too readily a lineage and community of royalist propaganda and polemic, my work on Hobbes and the royalist exiles views the text written from exile as an event that lies somewhere between the royalist enclaves on the Continent and the vast, crowded metropolitan print market in England. As such events, these texts evince a particularly exilic anxiety, while at the same time attempting to construct an idiosyncratic rhetoric of distance that often can be called neither simply "royalist" nor "parliamentarian."

In its exploration of the "interior exiles" of Milton and Dryden, the second half of the book takes up a slightly different, although related line of argument, with critical approaches to these two authors' late oeuvres. My analysis of Milton and Dryden's late epics is certainly not the first to read these texts in light of the conditions of political failure and deep disappointment in which each author wrote.[48] The implicit, and at times explicit, methodology behind most readings of these poems, however, has assumed that they were written under a cloud of censorship and that part of the job of the literary critic is to clear away this cloud to reveal the complex allusions to their authors' true political loyalties. Christopher Hill, whose *Milton and the English Revolution* invaluably helped to revive discussion of Milton among his contemporaries, states this methodology most clearly when he argues that Milton's late poetry should be read as "cryptograms to be decoded" from the "great equivocator" for an audience that would have been comprised of "initiates into the secrets of his sub-text, characterized by their sensitivity to the verbal nuances of his poetry."[49] More recent criticism of Milton's epic has tended to be more sensitive about the poem's relationship with its licensor, although it continues to fall back too often on notions of veiled allusion and hidden expression rather than sincere statement. David Loewenstein, for example, while rightfully noting *Paradise Lost*'s concern with the ambiguity of rhetoric and the malleability of political discourse (and as I will argue, the malleability of all language), reverts to reading Satan's crew and their leader as Presbyterians circa 1643–4 at various points in his careful analysis.[50]

Criticism of the last decade of Dryden's poetry has been remarkably fruitful in recent years, but has too often resorted to the siren call of veiled allegory and covert attack. According to many readers of his late poetry, Dryden used his translations to criticize indirectly the Glorious Revolution and Williamite government while alluding to his Jacobite sympathies by drawing on the party's language.[51] For the less careful of these readers, the critical exercise at times seems to be reduced to decoding

Dryden's otherwise politically unintelligible translations, to succeed where the late seventeenth-century censor failed (or perhaps more accurately ignored). Again, as in the history of the critical reception of Milton's poem, more recent readings of Dryden's translations have admitted the multivalent potential for these later works, and their acknowledgment of Williamite readers and potential Williamite uses. However, Paul Hammond, in his careful analysis of Dryden's translation of the *Aeneid* as an attempt to come to terms with his own "internal exile," spends much of his reading applying Jacobite political allegories to the translation, while arguing that Dryden uses the Virgilian analogy as a subterfuge to avoid the charge of seditious writing.[52]

While I do not think that we can deny the impact of censorship on what Milton and Dryden were able to say (even after the lapsing of the Licensing Act in 1695 prosecution for seditious writing remained in practice, albeit without the help of copyright[53]), my work on these interior exiles views their writing after defeat and the removal of an authoritative public voice as legitimate and legitimating attempts to engage with a diverse readership. This is not to implicate Milton and Dryden in a betrayal of their political and religious beliefs, as some have done; however, I do take the other political trajectories that these poems invite seriously, not merely as obfuscation. My analysis sees both *Paradise Lost* and Dryden's translation of the *Aeneid* as arising out of the enormously productive tension between their own attachment to a defeated cause and the dominant modes of expression and discourses of authority. Both authors, as they wrote from their "interior exile," meditated, and at length, upon the nature of their poetic vocation and upon the malleability of language. At the same time, they constructed epic worlds that resisted simple qualification and engaged seriously with various and diverse ideological and affective modes. Both poets become the adjudicating authorities to multivalent worlds in their epics as they attempt to fashion a new poetic voice out of the wreckage of defeat and "interior exile."

There is one more methodological point that needs to be cleared up before I move to the shores of New England. Two years ago, in a book review of a collection, *Letters in Transit: Reflections on Exile, Identity, Language and Loss*, Ian Buruma takes to task the contributors to this collection, specifically Edward Said, Bharati Mukherjee and Eva Hoffman (Charles Simic and André Aciman are excepted as "real" exiles), for invoking the term "exile" for what he considers to be a voluntary and rather comfortable migration. Buruma cites this collection as part of a trend towards the romanticization of exile in the twentieth century through which "exile" has become a metaphor that stands in for "the typical condition of the modern intellectual."[54] Indeed, as Buruma notes in his review, from Theodor Adorno onward, "exile" and alienation have become prerequisites to writing and intellectual work. In *Minima Moralia*, the exilic text par excellence for Said, Adorno argues that a sense of alienation is the only moral perspective from which an intellectual can truthfully write.[55] Similarly, Julia Kristeva argues that, because we are all exiled within language, the visionary intellectual will write from a sense of displacement and alienation in order to question the ossifying structures of meaning: "How can one avoid sinking into the mire of common sense, if not by becoming a stranger to one's country, language, sex and identity? Writing is impossible without some kind of exile."[56] For many of us in the academic world, the twentieth-century conception of the intellectual as exile matches our sense of the place of the university professor in modern society as distant and alienated from the structures of power. This perceived confluence of academic and exile has contributed to the heightened interest in "exile studies" and marginalized voices in the past twenty or so years, as well as the proliferation of studies which use a conception of "exile" to approach texts and writers as diverse as Daniel Defoe and Laurence Sterne, Virginia Woolf and Evelyn Waugh, James Joyce and Vladimir Nabokov, Theodor Adorno and Salman Rushdie.[57]

My use of the term "exile" for the texts I read here is necessarily metaphoric to a degree, as all critical terms used to refer to broad affective, ideological or political experiences are. Yet I have endeavored throughout to construct the term to refer specifically to a particular set of circumstances and a particular rhetorical and affective mode that can be traced through a series of texts that arise out of similar experiences of displacement and marginalization. I have operated under the belief that viewing these four distinct groups of texts as written from either a "real" or "interior" exile enables us to see the poems of Bradstreet, the political philosophy of Hobbes, the epic of Milton and the translations and criticism of Dryden with a clearer sense of their rhetorical emphases and ideological pressures. The use of the term "exile" becomes more problematic, obviously, when I move to the "interior" exiles of the final two chapters, Milton and Dryden; my inclusion of Milton and Dryden, neither of whom ever left the environs of London for a sustained period, would seem to be guilty of just the kind of "romanticization of exile" that Buruma decries in his review and that transforms the traumatic experience of exile into an inexact metaphor for intellectual alienation. Indeed, the history of the phrase "interior exile" has been fraught with controversy since it was first used to identify those who had remained in Nazi Germany yet did not sympathize with Hitler's government. Many of those, most prominently Thomas Mann, who fled out of fear of and anger at the anti-Semitism and violent nationalism of the Nazi party, became quickly and vocally opposed to what they saw as the appropriation of the moral certitude of "exile" by those who, to a lesser or greater degree, accepted and supported the rise of Hitler. Mann famously stated in 1945 that all books written and printed in Germany between 1933 and 1945 should be pulped due to the stench of blood that surrounds them.[58]

Mann's heightened rhetoric arose out of the passions and defensiveness of German exiles after the horrors of the Holocaust, and should be remembered in its context. Yet his strident indignation towards those who remained in Germany can certainly be seen, in a more muted and academic context, in Buruma's annoyance over what he sees to be the appropriation of exile by modern intellectuals. Yet the "interior exiles" I deal with here are decidedly different from modern conceptions of the intellectual as exile such as Kristeva's. These other critical models, including Marxist or Romantic notions of "alienation," or Kristeva's post-structuralist theories on the visionary "exile," can help formulate an oppositional poetics that generally answers to a literature of isolation, even of communal resistance.[59] Yet these models do not speak to the strong sense of displacement that comes with the particular loss of a world that the exile had known until recently; nor do they answer to the continued engagement, and often vehement nationalism, that accompanies this nostalgia. I have therefore remained faithfully and rigorously attuned in each chapter to the exact nature of the authors' displacements from the English homeland they had known, and the exact form that this displacement took as they engaged with a homeland that they had left behind and that had left them behind. Further, because I have construed the "text in exile" as crossing over into a broad and diverse London print market, we can begin to see the same rhetorical forms and innovations as each distant author, be it Hobbes or Milton, Bradstreet or Dryden, imagined and reacted to a wide-ranging metropolitan audience from exile and sequestration. While Dryden and Milton never left the English homeland, they did experience an immediate loss of an entire world that they had known, and a distancing from the accepted modes of discourse. The experience of exile, as I have outlined it here, entails negotiating the dialectical push and pull with this lost homeland, a negotiation that often evokes both nostalgia and continued attachment in both geographic and interior exiles.

I would say that most readers would probably balk more readily at the inclusion of Dryden in a study of early modern exile. In the eyes of modern criticism, Milton would seem a far better candidate for the status of exile, serving in prison for a brief period, blind and forced into, in the words of his nineteenth-century biographer David Masson, "abscondence" in the house on Jewin Street. To be sure, Milton and Dryden did have quite different experiences after 1660 and 1688, respectively, and the phrase "interior exile" applies differently to each author. However, the condition does account for, and explain much of, the psychology and mode of self-presentation in Dryden's late criticism. While Dryden might have had more interaction with and acclaim from the London public in the years after James's abdication than Milton had after the restoration (although this might be argued as a construction of literary history), he certainly perceived of himself, and rightly so, as marginalized in politics and religion. We should not forget that Dryden was ridiculed and derided, and very publicly, for retaining his allegiance to James and to Catholicism after 1688. Dryden seems to have internalized and transformed this ridicule into a consistent stance from which he could pronounce upon politics and matters of literary taste and judgment. Dryden might be the first to admit that this stance was self-conscious, and yet, we might also ask how much our perception of Milton after the restoration has been colored by the author's own heroic and deeply self-conscious presentation of his condition in *Paradise Lost* and elsewhere.

CHAPTER I

Nostalgia and nationalism in New England literature

I would like to begin, as is our convention these days, with a story – the story, aptly for an exploration of exile, of a passage. The early Puritan settlers in America, of course, told many stories about passages, the majority feeding into diverse foundational myths that envisioned a pious passage of legions of conscientious souls to the shores of the New World.[1] Yet, while I am ultimately concerned with this mass movement of individuals whose motives assuredly were untidily complex, I would like instead to begin, somewhat heretically, with the passage of an object. In doing so, I wish to emphasize the transatlantic and the eventual rather than the American and the originary. That is, whereas the story of the movement of a people, the Puritans, can easily resolve itself into the story of the beginnings and evolution of the American way, the story of the movement of objects must describe the complex interconnectedness of the English Atlantic world. Whereas the Great Migration is most often considered, somewhat inaccurately, unidirectional, the migration of objects must comprehend the multilateral and encompass not only the British Isles and New England, but also the Chesapeake, the West Indies, Newfoundland and Hudson Bay, the Azores and southern Europe.[2] It is not surprising that one of the strongest statements for an interconnected and mutually dependent Atlantic world, Ian Steele's *The English Atlantic*, often focuses on the traffic in goods: tobacco, molasses, lumber, fish, and news and information.[3] To begin with the material also reminds us that the experience of migration was not merely driven by the spiritual or the political, but was supported, shaped and driven by the trade in goods and information. As a result, one cannot talk about the experience or ideology of the first settlers in New England without considering the traffic in objects. The early settlers' removal from many of the materials with which they had surrounded themselves in England reinforces the importance of this transatlantic traffic. In many ways, the promotional literature that depicted the natural world of New England to English readers as

22

much the same as their homeland, only better, attempted to allay the fears of just such a material dislocation. The transatlantic trade, especially when it came to writing materials, letters and news, remained the colonists' only connection with the English homeland they had once known.

I would like to begin, then, with the passage of a manuscript.[4] Almost any writing from the early New England settlers that made it into print would have had to make this journey. Prior to the last decades of the seventeenth century, the New England presses (Boston began publishing in 1679) remained primarily the domain of almanacs, session acts and occasional sermons. Even as late as the 1680s, the range of titles produced by Marmaduke Johnson and Samuel Green in Cambridge and John Foster in Boston was remarkably limited, understandably so for such an early market.[5] The colonial New England manuscript would have most likely been written in Boston, or Newton, or even as far as Ipswich or Providence. The possessor of the manuscript would then have sent it to Boston through an Indian runner, a servant or a ship, if that person was not traveling there him or herself. If produced during the 1640s and '50s, the manuscript almost certainly would have made it into the hands of Richard Fairbanks, whose tavern, by a 1639 General Court order, served as the center for incoming and outgoing transatlantic mail. For a fee, Fairbanks would then have sent it out on the next ship bound directly for England, a somewhat monthly occurrence, unlike the trip from London to Boston, which vessels did not attempt in the winter months. The passage eastwards across the Atlantic, the "downhill" part of the transatlantic circuit, would have taken approximately four to five weeks, half the time of the "uphill" trip from London to Boston. Upon arrival at one of the main ports of England, the manuscript would then have been shipped to London if necessary, a shipment that could have waited up to a week for departure. Most often the manuscript would have been taken up by a friend or an interested party in London, or perhaps even carried across the Atlantic by such a person. This party would then have located a publisher in London and given the manuscript over to him. After entering the work in the Stationers' Register and thus gaining copyright to the manuscript, the publisher would have hired a printer to set the manuscript into type and, finally, onto the printed page. Thus, at least six months, and more often over a year, after the manuscript was completed, and after a not insignificant outlay of capital, the work would have appeared in the bookstalls around St. Paul's Churchyard.

The transatlantic journey of our manuscript emphasizes some critical considerations concerning the print productions of early English settlers in North America. Most importantly, the fact that the manuscript went back to England at all plainly identifies the print market of the early Massachusetts Bay Colony as an outlier of the broader English print market centered in London. Colonial works by such authors as Anne Bradstreet, John Cotton and Nathaniel Ward were printed not specifically for their neighbors in Boston or Salem, but for a broader, and importantly, English, community of readers on both sides of the Atlantic.[6] It is significant that the sole avenue that guaranteed copyright for English texts remained the Stationers' Register in Stationers' Hall, London. Printing a manuscript at the early press in Cambridge left no protection from an enterprising stationer on the other side of the Atlantic getting his hands on the text, registering it, and printing it in London, in full compliance with English copyright laws (as perhaps John Sims did with Michael Wigglesworth's extraordinarily popular apocalyptic poem, *The Day of Doom*). While neither English nor New England authors in the mid-seventeenth century could attain anything that we would understand as authorial copyright, English authors, at least, often remained in close proximity to the mechanisms that controlled the printing and dissemination of their texts.

As readers, the colonists had access to printed books primarily through the work, either directly or indirectly, of London wholesalers.[7] Hezekiah Usher became the primary bookseller in seventeenth-century Boston, importing his wares from various London wholesalers upon order. More connected and wealthy New Englanders relied heavily on correspondents in London and elsewhere for their books and news. John Winthrop, Jr. was perhaps the most avid collector of ephemera and occasional literature, maintaining strong connections with several friends in England, including Samuel Hartlib and members of the Royal Society.[8] That Winthrop, Jr. and others were largely successful in procuring books, however delayed, from London is evidenced by the size of their libraries. When Simon and Anne Bradstreet's house burned down in 1666, Simon recorded in his diary that: "Tho: my own losse of books (and papers espec.) was great and my fathers far more being about 800, yet ye Lord was pleased . . . to make up ye same to us."[9] Indeed, the larger colonial libraries, such as Winthrop's, often acted as private circulating libraries, much like their counterparts in England. While these libraries circulated books amongst the well-connected, colonial readers at virtually all social levels displayed an avid appetite for books coming directly from the metropolis, especially as events in the 1640s heated up, and the potential political fruition of the Puritans' hopes came more sharply into view.[10]

In his Marprelate-influenced satire, *The Simple Cobler of Aggawam*, Nathaniel Ward displays this appetite in his effusive praise of Marchamont Nedham, the Parliamentarian pamphleteer. In a lively passage that oscillates between outright flattery and light-hearted invective, Ward invites Nedham to emigrate to New England if he runs into trouble: "to help recruite our pumpkin blasted braines: we will promise to maintain him so long as he lives, if he will promise to live no longer then we maintain him."[11] The sharp prose, with its rustic and rather crude tone, is characteristic of Ward's text; yet this invitation to Nedham, while dressed in the garb of an innocent, country perspective, also displays a familiarity with the personalities and events of the quickening London print market of the 1640s.

In fact, the 1640s represent a particularly fruitful time for the transatlantic production and consumption of books. As much as New England settlers maintained an interest in the rapidly changing political climate in their homeland, certain English readers were looking to the New England colonies, and the religious and social debates on the other side of the Atlantic, for analogues to English upheavals. It should not be forgotten that much of what we know about the Antinomian Controversy of 1636–7 has been gleaned from printed accounts released to a London audience in 1644–6 as English Puritans were attempting to understand and foresee the consequences of their own reforms.[12] John Owen, originally a rather conservative Anglican minister, acknowledged later that John Cotton's justification of the New England Way, *The Keys to the Kingdome of Heaven* (London, 1644), allowed him to see the light of truth in New England's independent stance.[13] Perhaps the most notable example of the metropolitan milieu into which books from New England were published is the exchange between two of the more famous early "Americans," Roger Williams and John Cotton. These two men, who had lived within fifty miles of one another, conducted an extended argument 3,000 miles away in the bookstalls of London. Cotton responded to Williams's *The Bloody Tenet of Persecution* (1644) with his own *The Bloody Tenet Washed* (1647). Williams, in turn, wrote a second book, *The Bloody Tenet Yet More Bloody* (1652), in reply to Cotton's. While the delayed rhythms of this exchange reveal the distance at which these combatants fought their battle, the place in which they fought it, the bookshops of Interregnum London, signals to some extent for whose minds they struggled. Much like Williams and Cotton, colonial authors generally wrote for an English audience that was centered in the metropolis, but stretched, albeit unevenly, to the provincial counties and distant colonies of a budding British empire. The early

American book, at least before 1680 (and this date is overly conservative), was a decidedly transatlantic phenomenon.

These considerations about the book trade in early New England begin to reveal a print world that is not simply a primitive forbear of a future, vibrant American public sphere. Understandably, most work on the literature of the early settlers in New England has attempted to place, at times unhappily, these texts into the chronology of the birth of the American mind. The magisterial work of Perry Miller, and his critical descendent, Sacvan Bercovitch, has impressively charted, in more subtle ways than I can detail here, the complex and unsettled Puritan sense of purpose that evolved (or devolved) into the unique American spirit.[14] Much of the "unsettledness" that drove this sense of purpose could be seen as a consequence of displacement and distance from the familiar. "All nationalisms," Edward Said has noted, "develop from a condition of estrangement."[15] This would also seem to be the story that Benedict Anderson details in his work, as "Creole pioneers" began to differentiate themselves along nationalistic lines in response to the push and pull of indigenous populations and a distant metropolis.[16] My narrative of the journey of the colonial manuscript into printed book instead draws attention to the early colonial text as an event in and of itself. As such, it does not comprehend or presuppose the development of the New England settlements into the northeast corner of a much larger, emerging empire. Of course, the "United States" is a foregone conclusion indelibly in our own minds, but ineffably far from the colonists', at least in the mid-seventeenth century.

To view colonial texts in such a manner, to recall the particulars of the transatlantic book trade in the seventeenth century, then, is to recognize Bradstreet's *Tenth Muse Lately Sprung Up in America*, or Nathaniel Ward's *The Simple Cobler of Aggawam* as not steps in a process towards the American nation, but rather as events with their own conditions of production and discourses of authority. Viewed from such a perspective, these texts do not become interesting depending on their degree of "Americanness." Indeed, the question of labels, of American or English, becomes rather unimportant, or perhaps uninteresting. These were texts that were printed in the metropolis, and read by readers throughout the broad sprawl of the English-speaking world, just as, say, *Paradise Lost* or *Leviathan* was.[17] They participated, albeit in a singular manner, in the complex, rapidly moving exchanges of the English market in books, and should be understood as competing for space within such a market, not as anthologized way-stops worthy of short attention on the road to "American Literature." Rather than springing forth full-grown on the shores of New England, these writings were born out of the difficult, contrapuntal negotiation between New and Old England, out of the interstices between exile and home. Bradstreet's elegies on Sir Philip Sidney and Elizabeth I, and Ward's imitation of the Elizabethan Marprelate tracts, can be understood fully only when placed within this varied world of print. Ward's satire, for example, has always held a rather uneasy and vexing position in the American literary canon and anthologies. Read alongside Thomas Hooker's sermons or Cotton's religious treatises, Ward's extravagant and often ludicrous prose is patently incongruous. Yet, viewed from the perspective of a distant New England author entering into the London pamphlet culture of the 1640s, we can begin to place *The Simple Cobler*, as well as Hooker's sermons and Cotton's treatises, in their proper milieu. The nature of the New England book trade, at least prior to the growth of a fully capitalized and conceivably independent market there, should force us to take such a transatlantic perspective. All of these writers partook in the discourses of a broader English print market, and, while indelibly shaped by the specific concerns of the experiences of the Puritan communities in New England, often drew upon the conventions and topoi of that print market for their rhetorical purchase.

The connectedness of early colonial readers and writers to the London print market cannot be overstated. However, it is also crucial that this perspective should not subsume the New England text under the broad rubric of an "English" print market. Recognizing that the early settlers, and early colonial texts, partook in a necessarily metropolitan print culture should not preclude our also recognizing that these settlers and texts held a particular place in such a market, while also exhibiting the concerns and interests of migration and settlement across the Atlantic. The settlers themselves would have been constantly reminded of their distance from and differences with the homeland each time the newest shipload of books arrived from London. The journey of the colonial manuscript, while emphasizing the colonists' continued connection with the homeland, also emphasizes the contingency of that connection. This passage from New England manuscript to London imprint, or from London imprint to New England reader, was an arduous and unsure one. The colonists' active involvement in the rapidly moving printed exchanges during the middle of the century would necessarily have been uncertain. In general, the lag time between an event in England and news of it in America was at least three and could have been more than eight months.

In the winter, New England settlers would often have to rely on the ever-increasing traffic of ships from Barbados for news, as few vessels attempted the direct route from London during this time.[18] Even at the turn of the eighteenth century, Nathaniel Saltonstall joked to Rowland Cotton six years after Queen Mary's death: "Captain Foster's ship is come lately from England, and, they say, brings news that Queen Mary is certainly dead."[19]

The colonists' distance from the metropolis, as far as news-gathering was concerned, may have been little different in fact from that of a provincial reader in Scotland or northern England, where infrequency of posts almost made up for length of traveling time.[20] Yet many of the readers in New England, and many more of the authors, left behind organized, sophisticated distribution systems, particularly in the Puritan enclaves of East Anglia. In his groundbreaking study of Puritan radicalism, Michael Walzer details the crucial role that dissemination of news, debate and gossip had on the activism of the godly.[21] Networks of Puritans, organized around prominent ministers and gentlemen, kept in touch with current events, seeking to remain informed about the progress of the reformation in England and across the Continent. Many of these information networks, in fact, helped to spread the word about, and recruit for migration to, New England. "Companies" of Puritans who eventually made the journey to the New World formed along the lines of these networks, including those associated with the Earl of Lincoln and John Winthrop.[22] It should come as no surprise then that, even after their departure for the New World, many of the early colonists maintained close ties with correspondents in England who kept them abreast of recent events and sent them newsbooks, broadsides and printed polemics. Yet even the settlers' best efforts at information-gathering must surely have emphasized their distance and dislocation from their former homeland. These feelings, reinforced by a Puritan sense of political engagement, are in part what drove the colonists' insatiable appetite and constant requests for more news from England.

Beyond the contingency of their information connections with the homeland, other, less quantifiable, factors must have contributed to the early settlers' sense of "unsettledness," distinguishing their dislocation from that of those in the remoter areas of England. Although crucial to any account of the migration to and settlement of New England, perspectives such as Steele's that tend to emphasize the material also can minimize the psychological and personal effects of migration. "Subject" and "object," that is, must be seen as mutually dependent; just as the

transatlantic traffic in materials shaped and sharpened the degree of connection with or dislocation from England, so the psychological effects of
displacement also drove the desire for familiar materials from the homeland. The extent to which the New England settlers felt their dislocation
has been the subject of fierce debate amongst historians. To be sure, the
fact that many New England settlers migrated in "companies" made up of
household, neighborhood or parish groups tended to lessen the shock of
their journey across the Atlantic and their displacement from the familiar
environs of England.[23] Yet, without subscribing to the rather reductive
notion of "American exceptionalism," we can admit that the early colonists did not view themselves as typical Englishmen and women, nor did
they consider their settlement in terms that ignored their distance from
the homeland they had left behind. The numerous tracts written in sympathy to England during the 1640s by New England authors offered
prayers to the former homeland, but consistently figured the
New England community as distinct and free from the ills that plagued
England. Further, the inevitable immediacy of the experience of migration and settlement on the shores of a new continent colored the local
concerns and language of these New England texts, despite their attempt
to appeal to a broader metropolitan audience across the ocean.

Not only did the exiles view themselves in particular ways as distinct
from England, but many of the godly, as well as the curious, on the other
side of the Atlantic specially recognized the print productions from
New England in a crowded print market. The "community of saints"
that some of the New England migrants had left behind took a particular
and keen interest in the progress of their brethren's experiment in the
Massachusetts Bay Colony. Early letters back to England in the 1630s
often were written with a larger audience of the godly in mind, and
were circulated through Puritan networks to potential settlers or interested parties. In 1629–30, Francis Higginson wrote a series of three propagandist letters back to his "friends in Leicestershire" that were quickly
disseminated, with the last being hurried into print as *New England's
Plantation* in 1630.[24] Higginson anticipates that his letters will be circulated, opening the first of them with a defense of his rhetorical style for
"any critic that looks for exactness of phrases."[25] Once the majority of
colonists settled in New England, letters continued to flow back to
England, sometimes read aloud at religious services and often receiving
reverential treatment. An "old planter," writing retrospectively in 1694,
reminisced about these letters: "A letter then from New England was
venerated as a sacred script, or as the writings of some holy prophet,

'twas carried many miles, where divers came to hear it."[26] Similarly, in a sermon preached in Taunton, Massachusetts, William Hooke lamented the fate of England:

How doe they (I mean all this while, multitudes of well affected persons there) talke of *New England* with delight! . . . And when sometimes a *New England* man returns thither, how is he lookt upon, lookt after, received, entertained, the ground he walks upon beloved for his sake, and the house held better where he is?[27]

While these characterizations should be understood as attempts to contribute to a saintly mythology of the New England settlement and, as such, surely overstate the reverence with which the letters and visitors were received, the accounts would not have had much resonance without some truth. The particulars of these memories, the transmission and public reading of letters and the entertaining of colonial visitors depict readers in England that publicly recognized the New England settlement as worthy of special attention and that treated any materials or individuals connected to the colony with special care.

Higginson's letters were not the last from New England that made it into print. Indeed, the line between private letter – Higginson's first letter begins with conventions often found on title pages – and public print object was often deliberately obscured.[28] Relations from or about the distant colonies attempted to establish a position of authority and trust by claiming to be direct correspondences from writers who had been "an eye or eare-witness" to the events related. Higginson vigorously asserts such claims in his letters, as does John Wilson in his printed account of the conversion of some native inhabitants.[29] Thomas Shepard's follow-up to Wilson's account, structured as a series of letters between Shepard and John Eliot (a fellow "missionary" and author of the first Bible translated into Wampanoag), becomes so concerned with verifying itself that it stands more as a meditation on the anxieties of publishing from afar than as an account of the native encounter.[30] The claims to being an "eye or eare-witness," sometimes advertised on the title page – indeed, the very conventions of the titles – show these printed texts attempting to clear a space for themselves in a quickening market in printed texts from New England.[31] Understanding the market for news from across the Atlantic, William Wood, in *New Englands Prospect*, dismisses his competition as the uninformed work of men who had never set foot in New England.[32] Distinctions such as Wood's, along with the representation of printed accounts as letters or eye-witness accounts, capitalized on the special reverence or mere curiosity that readers had for texts and news from New England. With a simple place-name and a basic phrase, such as "eye-witness" or "true relation" on the title page and in the preface, these texts took on a different character, updates of God's progress across the Atlantic or curiosities exploring an entirely new world.[33] These texts competed in a broader English print market, and they did so often by identifying themselves as direct accounts from a distant and distinct land, as textual voices from across the ocean.

Central to my understanding of the early texts of the New England settlers then is a comprehension that these texts were complexly informed by the settlers' continued material connectedness to, yet distance from, the English homeland, a homeland that shades their vision, their rhetoric and their ideologies. New England texts display a bewitching blend of the local and the distant, a layering of near and far. Of course, ideologies have a power all their own and do not merely reflect a particular material existence; they also explain it, and at times attempt to deny it. The Massachusetts Bay settlers developed and displayed a specific notion of their endeavor in the New World that at once engaged with their home-land and their particular relationship with that homeland. As the colonists continued to express simultaneously their Englishness and their differ-ence, an ideology particularly suited to and encouraged by their material relationship with England, this ideology became a powerful rhetoric that had its own spiritual and psychological appeal. Much of this appeal lay in the nature of the colonists' exiled state. Separated from local relationships, from the familiar landscape of England, and from many of the materials that made up their daily lives, these men and women were consistently reminded of the precariousness of such terms as "native soil" and "home-land."[34] As a result, they struggled to maintain their Englishness while comprehending their new environment and political autonomy in the New World. Thus, much like other exiled groups, the early New Englanders constantly had their eyes fixed nostalgically on the departed homeland and hopefully on the colony in the New World, on the mother church in England and the new Israel in America, on both Old and New England. They lived somewhere between here and there, never quite fully embracing or denying either.

The literary works of these exiles, their sermons, letters, poetry and satire, respond to and, importantly, order the exile of the colonists on the shores of the New World by negotiating the distance between here and there. Writing was a way to fill the gap between colony and abandoned homeland, not only figuratively, but also often literally as the author

wrote for a specifically transatlantic audience. As they negotiated the
distances of the exile's world, they attempted to develop their various
relationship with their homeland into a more coherent position.[35] This
is not to say that the works of the first generation of Massachusetts
settlers, beyond some of the planned, public statements of the Bay
Colony for an English audience, represent a unified attempt to generate
a coherent ideological structure for the early colony. Together, these
New England authors display a range of differing concerns – from
Anne Bradstreet, a female author seeking the proper tropes for an authoritative and authorized poetic voice, to Nathaniel Ward, an elderly lawyer
and minister soon to return to England, writing in the Marprelate tradition, to John Cotton, a deeply popular and respected English preacher,
attempting to justify the New England Way to detractors he left behind.
Yet the writings of the men and women of Massachusetts Bay do show
remarkably similar patterns and concerns and broad rhetorical and imaginative structures usefully thought of in terms of the contrapuntal nature
of exile.

Many of the distinctive features of these texts arise from the construction of an imaginative world which combines the local immediacy of
New England and the disruptions of exile with the persistent shadow,
embodied by material reminders from the boats of England, of an audience on the other side of the ocean. More specifically, in these authors'
balancing of the local and the distant, they insisted on the particular
Englishness of their perspective, as well as, importantly, their language.
While the rhetorical construction of a "pure Englishness" in the writings
of Cotton, Ward and Bradstreet makes an overt appeal to their distant
audience, it also shows them reconstituting the psychological and material
disruptions of their departure from their homeland into a statement of
their true faithfulness to a different notion of national identity. Much
of this reconstitution, further, takes place in their insistence on the purity
of their use of the English language. As I have noted, concerns over the
status of language, over how words mean, are endemic to exiled authors in
the early modern period. In the case of the Puritan exiles, these concerns
find their most extreme expression, as we shall see, in the intolerance for
dissent and linguistic discord in the authorities and authors of early
New England. The New England writers I explore here also attempt to
overwrite these concerns by presenting themselves as "plain-spoken"
outsiders to their metropolitan audience, as progenitors of a truer
English because of their removal and distance from London. Arising
out of both nostalgic Puritan traditions of a plain style, as well as the

material realities of their exile to the rural extremes of the English-speaking world, this persona justifies their specific brand of the language, and thus in some ways their exile, while overseeing the reception of the text as it made its journey from exile to homeland.

*   *   *

English Puritanism, that peculiar and unique brand of European Protestantism, was largely forged in the tribulations of the Henrician and Marian exiles of the mid-sixteenth century.[36] Early English Protestants such as William Tyndale and John Frith, both of whom removed themselves to the Continent at various points in their lives, were the first early modern English writers to advocate a vernacular Scripture and justification by faith, to deny the authority of the Catholic ecclesia, and to lament the corruption of the pure religious zeal of the early Church. Tyndale's later writings especially emphasize the godly's contract with the divine and a "Puritan" reliance upon Scripture as a moral code for a commonwealth of saints in this world.[37] Their writings would be reprinted and commemorated by the next generation of English Protestants and the Marian exiles, particularly John Foxe. After fleeing to the Continent, these later English ministers, influenced by Calvinist doctrine and armed with their Edwardian prayer books and libraries smuggled over from England (including the works of Tyndale, Frith and other early Protestants), wrote the formative tracts of what would become Puritan theology as polemic against a misguided England. In reading Calvin, and meeting with he and his followers while in the Protestant enclaves on the Continent, the Marian exiles found Calvin's own emphasis on the unsettledness of a flawed human society particularly appealing. Their exile pushed them to form a community based upon opposition politics and spiritual belief rather than upon family, parish or neighborhood. They based these communities upon the natural authority of God's will on earth, and thus envisioned the most important social bond as that between God and man. Freed from any effective jurisdiction, and spurred by the intensely communal experience of collective displacement, writers such as John Foxe, John Bale, and the editors of the Geneva Bible, elaborated a spiritual and political activism, and a godly sense of duty, that could stretch beyond the bounds of what Christopher Hill terms "compulsory communities" such as parish and neighborhood. These bonds would eventually become the cornerstones of a spirituality that linked, voluntarily, the godly throughout the English country.[38]

As the Marian exiles wrote their spiritual community into existence, they also rewrote English religious history to accommodate their oppositionist agenda. Instead of viewing Henry VIII as a Protestant innovator, Foxe and Bale both sophisticatedly argued that pure apostolic Christianity came to England well before the corruptions of Rome, and further, that the Church of England was founded upon an apostolic authority that eventually became corrupted by Popish practices.[39] For example, Bale, writing from his first exile, detailed how Joseph of Arimethea came to England and founded a true Christian religion that came slowly more and more under the control of Rome until Pope Gregory sent "a Romyshe monke called Augustyne, not of the order of Christ as was peter, but of the superstycyouse secte of Benet, there to sprede abrode the Romyshe faythe and relygyon."[40] That the Marian exiles would turn to history in their creation of a community of the godly should come as no surprise. The early Protestant polemicists attempted generally to reorient ecclesiastical history to characterize Rome as a corrupt distortion of divine ordinance. Foxe himself had in part started *Acts and Monuments* to respond to the Catholic claim that the Reformed churches had not existed before Luther. He begins his monumental project with this very point, affirming that "our church was, when this church of theirs was not hatched out of the shell, nor did yet ever see any light" and that

we have sufficient matter for us to shew that the same form, usage, and institution of this our present reformed church, are not the beginning of any new church of our own, but the renewing of the old ancient church of Christ; and that they are not any swerving from the church of Rome, but rather a reducing to the church of Rome.[41]

More to my point, Bale and Foxe's historiography acknowledges and attempts to edit the history of the past in an effort to resituate their marginal community as *the* English way. For exiles, history becomes crucial as a link to a lost, idyllic time and space before displacement. While the Marian exiles waited and hoped and wrote on the Continent, they sought to bridge the gap between themselves and their homeland by denying that gap's historical existence, at least religiously and ideologically. For Bale and Foxe, the history of the English church, and the Christian church at large, is one of constant conflict between the true servants of apostolic authority and the servants of Roman corruption. Because of its apostolic origins and the early "reformations" of Wyclif, England had received a pure church early, and had also attempted to cleanse it of Roman influence earlier than anyone on the Continent.

Now, under the reign of Mary, God's chosen agents of reform were being persecuted and his chosen country was set in ruin. Foxe laments the death of that "godly imp," Edward, "with whom also decayed in a manner the whole flourishing estate and honour of the English nation."[42] Foxe's litany of true Christian and English martyrs, and those persecuted under the devilish, Romish hands of Mary and her servants, thus establishes these men and women, and by association the community of exiles on the Continent, as the loyal followers of Christ, the only true progenitors of an English church. This historiography helped their cause back in England, while also justifying their exile both to themselves and to their English readers. Ultimately, Bale and Foxe's histories perpetuated, on both sides of the channel, the communal identity of the Marian exiles as truly English and Christian (in some ways the two are synonymous in Foxe as he is writing a history of the Christian church and a national history simultaneously) in the face of persecution and displacement.

Thus, from its origins, English Puritanism was Janus-like, forced into and embracing innovative political and social relationships, yet obsessed with the notion of a true and English church, a notion grounded in their own versions of English history. When Elizabeth took power, and the Marian exiles trickled back into England, many of the ministers remained nostalgic for the enclave they had left behind in Switzerland.[43] Others, such as Foxe, embraced their new Protestant queen; Foxe completed his *Acts and Monuments* after his return to England, and closes it with the triumphant accession of Elizabeth to the throne: "what cause have we all Englishmen so to do, that is, to render most ample thanksgiving to the mercifulness of God, who hath granted, conserved and advanced to the seat-regal of this realm, so good, godly, and virtuous a queen."[44] In some ways, the dual nature of the Marian exile, and of exile generally, can help to explain the peculiar and paradoxical place that English Puritanism occupied in the national church and politics in the years to follow. As Patrick Collinson has so meticulously detailed in his multiple explorations of Elizabethan Puritanism, the Puritan gentry and ministers saw themselves as both a privileged group of godly worshipers within a corrupt church *and* participants in a broader national and English reform movement ordained by God.[45] Often, these gentry and ministers would represent themselves as the leaven that would leaven the whole bread, a metaphor that imagined a conservative, slow-moving reform from the inside (necessarily so, since many of these men held prominent establishment positions).[46] The tensions within this position, its rigid adherence to a specifically English religious reform, along with its sense of alienation and aloofness, might be seen as arising out of the exilic origins of its first progenitors.

The first groups of Puritan "companies" who left to settle Massachusetts Bay under John Winthrop's direction in 1629 had inherited this paradoxically alienated yet nationalist vision of their undertaking. The momentous decision to leave made by Winthrop, the Earl of Lincoln, and their followers, signals a profound dissatisfaction with and distance from the mainstream of English society, a dissatisfaction that seems to have become more widespread as the Great Migration quickened in the 1630s.[47] It should be noted that the reasons for leaving England were various, and involved economic as well as religious factors; often the decision to migrate to New England came not out of a specifically Puritan alienation from Laudian reforms, but rather from local influences, such as the decision of a neighbor, a minister, or, more immediately, a patron or employer to depart across the Atlantic.[48] Yet the leaders' deep sense of difference can be seen in their farewell sermons, which railed against a degenerate England, as well as in their successful attempt to transport the charter of the colony with them to Massachusetts, effectively cutting off any administrative interference from the homeland. The decision by Winthrop and others to lead a migration westward certainly came from a sense that the Puritan cause in England had faltered, but its faltering, in many ways, may have been effected by the Puritans' own conservatism and "assimilation into the fabric of English society."[49] Winthrop and Thomas Dudley, the Earl of Lincoln's steward, for example, represented important propertied interests in New England, and went with the Crown's permission to the New World, not only to found a godly community, but also, according to their own representations, to further the cause of England in the burgeoning Atlantic commercial world.[50] The Massachusetts Bay colonists, a rather different set of migrants from those who left Leiden for Plymouth a decade earlier, often included prominent gentlemen and ministers or their servants leaving the mainstream of English society.

To a certain extent, then, the questions that surrounded the exact nature of the New England settlers' relationship with their homeland were ones that they had brought with them from across the Atlantic, and that had been generated by the first Puritan exile.[51] Settlement in the New World, of course, did not dissipate these questions but rather focused and redirected them, giving a more palpable psychological and material immediacy to the contradictions inherent in English Puritanism. Thus, for example, John Cotton had acknowledged a church within a church in his parish at Boston, Lincolnshire, calling the elite godly to prayer with a special ringing of the church bell. Yet it took the specific opportunities and pressures of exile for Cotton to formulate fully his notion of the relationship of the godly to the larger English church, an Independent way that acknowledged a transatlantic English reformation without recognizing a national church. The Great Migration, as I have noted, did not constitute a definitive break with the homeland; indeed, it could not on a material basis. Those who argue for such a break, further, tend to overstate the centrifugal force of Puritanism and the extent to which Puritans felt marginalized from the mainstream of English society under the Stuarts, thus simplifying the complex place of Puritanism in England, and the effects of exile on those that left for Massachusetts Bay.

Far from renouncing their status as English men and women, the English settlers more often sought to fortify their Englishness as they settled in the New World. Recently, numerous historians have emphasized the conservative and retrospective nature of the Puritan migration. Rather than a radical movement to start a new society, the early settlers in New England strove to preserve what they saw as the essential institutions and culture of their homeland. In his social history of four early American communities, David Grayson Allen argues that, in terms of modes of agriculture, governance and elective processes, "the English Puritans who came to settle in New England gave up as little of their former ways of doing things as possible."[52] Indeed, the very character of the migration to Massachusetts Bay aided in the preservation of English institutions. Unlike in Virginia, where mainly unmarried men settled, encouraging dispersed and isolated plantations, in Massachusetts "companies" of migrants associated around gentlemen, ministers or wider kinship networks voyaged on the same ship and eventually settled in the same towns. While some New England colonists reswarmed and moved again after a few years, a great number also stayed in the same area, thus giving a specific and local English character to particular towns.[53] Massachusetts communities were thus able to retain continuity across the Atlantic through already established kinship networks, hierarchies, customs and social institutions.[54]

Just as the character of the migration to Massachusetts encouraged conservatism and preservation of "English ways," so the experience of displacement and exile, in part, deepened this conservatism. Attraction to the familiar comes naturally to those distant from home. As a result, the early colonists sought to replicate settlement patterns, hierarchical relationships and social customs that they had lived under while in England in an attempt to impose a recognizable order upon the chaotic nature of migration and exile. In the colonists' writing, we can also see this imposition of order in the insistence on their continued Englishness in the face of their removal from the homeland. Conspicuously, the New England authors' most vociferous assertion of their Englishness came in the 1640s, when the homeland itself was fighting a war over the identity of the nation. These New England texts, which became something of a genre in the '40s, seem to feel the crisis in English identity just as acutely on the other side of the Atlantic, while also sensing the opportunity to justify and explain their exile as their homeland went through its own transformation. These poems and polemics, lamenting and decrying the state of affairs back in England during the 1640s, suggest a substantial degree of connection between Old and New England.[55] In the tracts themselves, the authors variously assert the settlers' deep ties to their homeland. William Hooke, who issued several sermons of this type, states categorically in *New Englands Teares for Old Englands Feares*: "there is no Land that claimes our name, but *England*, wee are distinguished from all Nations in the world by the name *English* . . . there is no Nation that calls us Countrey-men, but the *English*."[56] Similarly, Anne Bradstreet, in her poetic entry into this genre, "A Dialogue between Old *England* and New, concerning the present troubles, Anno, 1642," begins the poem by positing a maternal relationship between Old and New England and imagines England calling New England "a childe, a Limbe, and dost not feele/My weakened fainting body now to reele?"[57] Bradstreet's evocation of this maternal metaphor links the New World settlement with its Old World origins while extending the notion of the English political body beyond the boundaries of England. The settlers' bodies did not cease to be English upon departure from England, a persistent concern of both the settlers and commentators in the homeland.[58] The recurrence of the body politic metaphor across the Atlantic shows the migrants adapting old ideologies to their new situation, incorporating the tropes central to notions of English community to their novel and unsettled place in that community.

The pattern of adapting ideologies, of revising the local concerns of exile with an awareness of a distant audience, is replicated in the numerous texts on the New England Way, the colonists' own brand of Independent Puritanism. Many of these works, including those by John Cotton and Thomas Hooker, address themselves specifically to an English audience in an attempt to explain and justify the New England ministers' doctrines.[59] These efforts even took an institutional form when the Cambridge Synod convened in 1646, both to specify the New England churches' ecclesiastical platform for a questioning English audience and to delineate their own newly constructed religious community for their local churches. In all of these statements, the authors make significant efforts to denounce separatism, such as that endorsed by Roger Williams or the "Brownists," as heretical and inherently unstable. Thus, in his grand treatise on ecclesiastical policy *A Survey of the Summe of Church-discipline*, Hooker states categorically "that the faithful Congregations in England are true Churches: and *therefore it is* sinfull to separate from them as no Churches."[60] Similarly, Cotton argues in the Preface to the Synod's platform that: "wee, who are by nature, English men, doe desire to hold forth the same doctrine of religion (especially in fundamentals) which wee see & know to be held by the churches of England, according to the truth of the Gospell."[61]

Yet, while the leading New England ministers persistently emphasized their continued participation in the affairs of the Church of England, these same men also repeatedly denied the authority of the English Church in spiritual matters over the individual churches in New England and attacked the notion of a national church. The Cambridge Synod held that churches on both sides of the Atlantic should be "united but distinct," while the printed defense of the colony's actions against the perennial malcontent Samuel Gorton, written by Edward Winslowe, denies the righteousness of national churches altogether.[62] Cotton, the most prolific, and perhaps the best-known, New England minister in England, delicately walked a middle ground between separatism and Presbyterianism in much of his work. For example, in *The Way of Congregational Churches Cleared*, Cotton attacks the separatists for their non-communion with the Church of England, but then goes on to praise, faintly, Henry Ainsworth, the early Brownist leader of the exiles in the Netherlands, as "not unuseful." He then equivocally states: "Though we put not such Honour upon those he calleth Brownists, as to owne them for our Fathers; yet neither do we put so much dishonour upon them, as to heap coals of contumely upon their heads."[63] John Higginson perhaps most succinctly describes the equivocal, contradictory relationship that the colonists felt they held with the Church of England when he bid farewell on the eve of his departure: "We will not say as the separatists were wont to say at their leaving of England, Farewel Babylon! farewel Rome! but we will say, farewel dear England! Farewel the Church of God in England."[64] The repetition of "farewel" lends a muted, poignant tone to Higginson's goodbye; yet the ambiguity of the final farewell, while leaving open the possibility that the migrants were leaving some of their godly brethren behind, also denies that possibility by implying the Church of God in England ends with their departure.

Admittedly, Cotton's almost comically hesitant posture towards Ainsworth, and, more generally, the colonists' advocacy of non-separatism in their printed works, can be attributed to their continuing reliance on and worries about the homeland's involvement with their affairs. It does not seem a coincidence that the vigorous persecution of the separatist opinions of Roger Williams in 1635–6 coincided with reports of the impending arrival of Crown officials sent to rein in what Charles I felt to be the increasingly rebellious and schismatic attitudes of the colonists. The years 1635–6 also saw an original patentee of the colony and supporter of the Stuarts, Sir Fernando Gorges, bring a suit before the crown, with the help of the eccentric Thomas Morton, in an attempt to wrest control of the charter from Massachusetts Bay. Further, Charles became angered, as did public opinion, when John Endicott defaced the English flag because of its cross, which Endicott viewed as a sign of idolatry.[65] Similarly, Hooke's insistence on New England's continued participation in and identification with England and its struggles, apart from compensating for the upheaval that migration entailed, also served the colonists' interests back in the homeland. Massachusetts Bay required continued economic and material support from England, a fact that the leaders of the colony understood all too well. The colonial magistrates rigidly controlled the information that made it back to England concerning the colony, prosecuting those who disseminated negative reports in letters or manuscripts meant for publication.[66] But what I would also suggest is that the very conditions of their position, as peripheral concern and distant cultural and religious outlier of old England, indeed their very isolation from England, allowed the Puritan ministers and elders to maintain their non-separatist stance without seriously undermining their Independent theocracy, or their intolerance of dissenting opinions. The very realities of their distance from England enabled and encouraged a particular understanding of their spiritual community, as independent and pure, without their having to abandon their Englishness wholesale.

The extent to which the colonists employed this rhetoric of "Englishness" to further their own causes back in England can also be seen in the pamphlet exchanges surrounding the Hingham militia case, a dispute over the nature of the authority of the General Court and Standing Council.[67] When the Hingham townspeople, through John Child, brought their case before the London print public in 1647 in order to garner the attention of the London public and the favor of Parliament, they attacked the magistrates on the grounds that the magistrates had not formed a government "according to the Fundamentall laws of *England*." They, thus, asked Parliament to establish the laws of their "native country" because they were "best agreeable to our English tempers."[68] Edward Winslowe, the magistrates' representative in London, replied in print by repeatedly defending the laws of the Bay Colony, arguing that they were as close to the fundamental laws of England as conditions would permit.[69] The specific grounds of this printed debate were determined by the patent, which required such "English" laws from the colony, yet the wider rhetoric of Child and Winslowe, which attempted to sharpen, in the case of Child, or deny, in the case of Winslowe, the "separatist" tendencies of the magistrates, suggests that their appeal to Parliament and their readers rested on the nature of the colony's connection to and similarities with the homeland. Beyond the rhetorical battle that Child and Winslowe waged in the London print market, however, the Hingham militia conflict played out more generally as a debate over the very nature of the Bay Colony's relationship with England. The Hingham petitioners, who worried over both the religious and political innovations of the colony, complained before the General Court in Boston that some "have stiled Foraign the Country and the Laws," and lamented that they desired to continue "to write, that we and ours are *English*."[70] The magistrates had no inclination to deny a connection with England; they merely questioned the nature of that connection as it was shaped by the conditions of the New World. The entire episode instances a crisis in the identification of the colony as English, a crisis, moreover, brought out by the distance of the community from their homeland and fought in the bookstalls of London. It demonstrates the extent to which New England authors kept both sides of the Atlantic in focus, and the extent to which their communal identity was created out of this productive dual focus brought on by the exigencies of migration.

Much like the Marian exiles before them, the first settlers of New England did not merely seek to define themselves as English, but instead sought to redefine Englishness in their own image. And, again much like the Marian exiles before them, they looked beyond the present to past models of Englishness for their discursive authority and communal identity. Nathaniel Ward, for example, chose the voice of the Elizabethan

Marprelate tracts when he composed his polemic against toleration, the New Model Army and King Charles, *The Simple Cobler of Aggawam.*[71] Ward's use of the Marprelate voice ostensibly gains him entry into a metropolitan discourse that had been renewed at the start of hostilities in the 1640s.[72] Yet the cobbler persona, as it reminds the reader of the Marprelate tradition, also evokes a nostalgia for the past through its Elizabethan voice and its attack on the current corruption of English religion and fashion, which are compared unfavorably to old English ways.[73] Ward's nostalgic imitation of Marprelate, along with his vehement attacks against religious innovation, remind us of the traditionalist nature of the Puritan migration and, often, of exile more generally. It also delineates a specifically exilic rhetorical position, one that harkens to an idyllic, lost golden age and historical discourse in an attempt to authorize itself and to resituate the genealogy of ideal Englishness to the margins. In his title, Ward announces his satire's origins from the periphery, in essence co-opting a popular Elizabethan London character and shifting its lineage to New England circa 1645.

Anne Bradstreet, an inhabitant of Ipswich in the 1640s like Ward, also looked back to the Elizabethan era as a locus of poetic authority and an idyllic past. Bradstreet's 1650 collection of poems, *The Tenth Muse Lately Sprung Up in America*, included three elegies that lament the passing of the Elizabethan generation. These occasional elegies, to Sir Philip Sidney, Elizabeth and the French Renaissance poet G. Salluste Du Bartas, describe a golden age of England, "when England enjoyed her Halsion dayes." In the elegy to Elizabeth, Bradstreet asks, "Was ever people better rul'd than hers?/Was ever Land more happy, freed from stirs?/Did ever wealth in England so abound?" (Bradstreet 156).[74] Such forceful lines praising Elizabeth's reign surely meant to compare the Stuarts negatively to the former queen, a sentiment that would not have surprised many readers coming from a book clearly labeled as "American" in origin. What probably would have struck the readers as odd is the form of these poems. Bradstreet chose to include both an elegy and an epitaph, a form generally reserved for those recently deceased.[75] The choice is telling: Bradstreet may have been imitating Joshua Sylvester's elegies on Prince Henry and William Sidney, included with his translation of Bartas and republished in 1631. With Bradstreet's elegies following their models by more than nineteen years, these poems illustrate the long rhythms of exilic consumption and production, rhythms driven perhaps by the material distance of New England from old, but also particularly appropriate to the nostalgic view of history so readily embraced by the displaced.

Of course, elegy is inherently nostalgic, often lamenting a lost purity or innocence embodied in the departed. But Bradstreet's elegies do not use the immediate occasion of a recent death to meditate on the passing of an age. Rather, these poems create the fiction that they are written into an active exchange of poetic skill occasioned by the deaths of Sidney, Bartas and Elizabeth. Repeatedly, Bradstreet expresses her desire to step aside from composing her elegies in order to admire others' forthcoming poems. In "In Honour of Du Bartas," Bradstreet decides "Ile leave thy praise, to those shall doe thee right,/Good will, not skill, did cause me bring my mite" (Bradstreet 153). Similarly, in her elegy to Elizabeth, she admits her skill cannot describe Elizabeth adequately; rather, her "pride doth but aspire,/To read what others write, and then admire" (Bradstreet 157).[76] Temporally, these are strange lines, and they remind us in some ways of the shadows of past cities and past communities that typically haunt the exile's mind. Yet, Bradstreet's shadows are of course imagined and figure forth a lost England that is twice removed from Bradstreet's isolation at her house in Andover. While Bradstreet's expressed humility displays her understanding of elegiac conventions, her caveats also resituate the distant, exiled, author within a nostalgic, but still immediate, community of readers and writers. She essentially draws the past into the present, implying that the true inheritors of Elizabethan Englishness now live on the shores of New England. In the process, Bradstreet, much like Ward, also authorizes her own poetic voice in past ideals, using her connections to Sidney, as a relative, and Elizabeth, as a woman, to ensure that "none dis-allow of these my straines" (Bradstreet 149).

It cannot be ignored that Bradstreet's elegies attempt to reorient poetic traditions to authorize her voice as a female poet, particularly in the elegy to Elizabeth, where she responds to the "carping tongues" who would silence her poetry by calling on the example of Elizabeth: "Let such, as say our sex is void of reason,/Know 'tis a slander now, but once was treason" (Bradstreet 157). Indeed, the concerns of writing from exile and as a woman fascinatingly coalesce in much of her poetry.[77] These elegies evince particular concerns and anxieties that identify Bradstreet's poetry as driven by the exigencies of displacement. Her re-creation of an elegiac Elizabethan poetic world has the same nostalgic tinge as Foxe's valoriza-tion of Wyclif and Ward's appropriation of Marprelate; and, her explicit attempt to bring this nostalgic world into the present redraws the lineage of English poetry and history to include the displaced author. Nostalgia inherently includes both a desire to return and a sense of permanent loss and disjunction with a world that has passed. By calling on Elizabethan forbears, Bradstreet evokes not a direct connection with the homeland that she had left behind, and for whom her works were published, but instead a nostalgic distance from current affairs that connects her with a purer, past era. Paradoxically, Bradstreet's nostalgia denies identification with the homeland to which she writes, while identifying her poetry as deriving from a specifically English inheritance.

Yet, beyond merely looking to the past for a truer version of Englishness, Bradstreet, in her elegy to Elizabeth, also sought a fully realized and authorized femininity for her own poetry. In the lines quoted above, Bradstreet, in a move habitual in her early poetry, reverts to silence in the face of the conventional images of male poetic power and inspiration: "Her personal perfections, who would tell,/Must dip his Pen [and notice the gendered possessive here] i'th'Heliconian Well;/Which I may not, my pride doth but aspire,/To read what others write, and then admire" (Bradstreet 157). However, the poem does not end at these lines. Inspired by the powerful presence of a woman capable of silencing learned doctors, as Elizabeth does earlier in the poem, Bradstreet sharply turns away from the humility of the previous lines to question the slanderous attacks on womankind generally: "Now say, have women worth, or have they none?/Or had they some, but with our Queen ist gone?/Nay Masculines, you have thus tax'd us long,/But she though dead, will vindicate our wrong" (Bradstreet 157). Elizabeth, for Bradstreet, allows for this questioning of early modern gender ideology, while representing a lost feminine authority still capable of validating womankind. And, it is the self-conscious recognition of her royal forbear that allows Bradstreet to create a vindicated space from which to write. The nostalgia in Bradstreet's elegy, thus, is twofold. Her re-creation of an elegiac Elizabethan poetic world redraws the lineage of English poetry and history to include the doubly displaced New England female author. The purer era that Bradstreet hearkens back to in her elegy to Elizabeth, first of all, was one of political peace and halcyon days: "Was ever people better rul'd than hers?/Was ever Land more happy, freed from stirs?" (Bradstreet 156). At the same time, her lament on the death of Elizabeth associates the political purity of this era explicitly with the gender of its female monarch and a now lost time of feminine authority and power. So, in the final lines of Bradstreet's elegy, the wistful longing

for this lost political happiness and feminine command become indistin-
guishable from each other:

> But happy *England*, which had such a Queen,
> O happy, happy, had those dayes still been,
> But happinesse, lies in a higher sphere,
> Then wonder not, *Eliza* moves not here. (Bradstreet 157)

The nostalgia in these lines envisions a happier past that, through her
association with it, provides Bradstreet with an authorizing spirit for her
poetry. However, at the same time, the lament intimates that this authorization will never be permanent nor complete, that her poetic identity
will be forged not through shared values and comfortable didacticism, but
rather through struggle, longing and discontinuity.

*   *   *

Beyond the nostalgia common to exilic authors, Bradstreet, and other
New England writers both before and after her, took up the attire of the
simple outsider, that rhetorically constructed, detached yet engaged, com-
mentator on affairs. Bradstreet, for example, in her first two poems, "To
her most Honoured Father *Thomas Dudley*" and the "Prologue," deploys
a series of adjectives that describes herself as "simple," her voice as
"mean," "lowly" and "humble," and her verse as "ragged" and "rudely
penned" (Bradstreet 5–7). In fact, Bradstreet's propensity to express her
humility and simplicity is perhaps her most habitual move in *The Tenth
Muse*. The constant disavowal of poetic sophistication by Bradstreet is a
complex rhetorical strategy that plays along several different registers and
cannot be dismissed simply as "formulae . . . which writers were obliged to
include in their works."[78] Certainly, such humility *was* a poetic set
piece employed by numerous Renaissance authors, a tradition that
Bradstreet understood and into which she wrote. But from Bradstreet's
position, as a woman and as a colonial subject, this formula takes on an
entirely different set of connotations. As Ivy Schweitzer has argued,
Bradstreet's constant self-deprecation acknowledges the male poetic
discourses within which she writes while also alluding to her exclusion
from the authority of that discourse.[79] However, the title page, which
advertises the colonial origins of Bradstreet's poetry, and the opening
series of dedicatory poems, also attune the reader to the distance from
which Bradstreet writes. The rustic persona, the simplicity that Bradstreet
projects, thus becomes part of what identifies her poems as coming from a
simpler, supposedly less sophisticated, peripheral community. Bradstreet

imagined *The Tenth Muse* in just such a manner in a later verse, "The Author to her Book," where she again treats her work self-deprecatingly and looks to make it more fashionable: "In better dress to trim thee was my mind,/But nought save home-spun Cloth, i'th'house I find" (Bradstreet 178).

While reading the title page and the dedicatory verses that accompanied *The Tenth Muse*, one cannot shake the feeling that Bradstreet's poems were presented as somewhat of a curiosity, a surprising literary endeavor from an even more surprising source, a colonial woman.[80] Bradstreet's rhetorical humility seems to play into this presentation. Yet her claims to humility also impart an air of simplicity, reinforced by her position as a distant author, that differentiates and thus empowers her poems. After all, simplicity has more than one connotation, and while delineating an unrefined pastoral crudeness, it also implies an honesty and straightfor-wardness not found in the more sophisticated. This second connotation, at least, is what stood as the rhetorical ballast for arguments that propounded the "plain style." Tellingly, throughout *The Tenth Muse* there persists a disjunction between Bradstreet's apologies for her simplic-ity and her ambitious poetic efforts. As she promises to stand aside and allow more accomplished poets to speak, she just as consistently ignores these promises. Most prominently, at the open of the "Prologue," Bradstreet admits that "To sing of Wars, of Captaines, and of Kings,/Of Cities founded, Common-wealths begun,/For my mean Pen, are too superior things" (Bradstreet 6). Yet she proceeds with a lengthy, didactic poem, entitled "On the Four Monarchies of the World," that takes up the bulk of the volume and also includes a sharp commentary on the current state of affairs in England circa 1642, "A Dialogue between Old *England* and New." This disjunction signals that we should not take Bradstreet's humility at face value, but also recognize it as a poetic pose, one that differentiates her poetry and allows her to transform her "crudeness" into a plain-speaking simplicity. In the Proem to her elegy upon Elizabeth's death, she self-deprecatingly imagines a throng of poets attempting to praise Elizabeth in which her voice is heard noticeably, "bleating . . . before thy Royal Herse" (Bradstreet 155). The image is self-mocking and abases the poet before the great subject of her elegy, yet it also allows her voice to stand out among the crowd, the distinct sound of a "loyall Braine," whose "rudeness is no wrong,/Though I resound thy greatnesse 'mongst the throng." Self-deprecation as a poetic mode in the seventeenth century helped to deflect the taint of print from a prac-tice, the writing of poetry, which was generally still viewed as the leisurely pastime of the gentry and nobility, not the work of professional writers. In Bradstreet's volume, John Woodbridge evinces this anxiety over the publication of her poems in the prefatory material, where he assures the reader that Bradstreet had no inclination to put these poems into print and that, further, they were "but the fruit of a few houres, curtailed from her sleep, and other refreshments" (Bradstreet 546). Bradstreet's self-deprecation plays into this protective amateurism, and helps to delineate her verse as the leisurely scribblings of a country wife, not the refined professional work of the city poet. Of course, as we have seen, her poetic ambition stretched far beyond "scribbling," thus redirecting her humility as a sidelong criticism at those other, more professional poets.

As numerous critics have noted recently, Bradstreet's humble, rustic persona was strongly driven by the anxieties and contradictions that were inherent in a woman poet taking on the mostly male-dominated traditions of lyric poetry.[81] Yet it also was one of the more prominent appropriations of this persona by authors from New England and should be understood as part of such a trend. Numerous colonial writers projected a similar image of themselves to the metropolitan print public, differentiating themselves from the sophists in England who commonly published. Their attraction to this persona in part resulted from an attempt to deflect the nervousness of publishing from a distance in the rapidly changing world of mid-century England and the London print market. In taking on this role, the authors from New England turned their distance from the homeland into a polemical advantage, a strategy that places a rhetorical commonplace, that of the plain-speaking, honest writer, into sharp and rather real relief.

Perhaps the author most attuned to the rhetorical advantages of the rustic author from New England was Nathaniel Ward. As I have noted, Ward cribbed his cobbler from the Marprelate tradition, an earlier series of Puritan satires which developed this printed character in contradistinction to the corrupt sophisticates loitering at court. Ward essentially kidnaps Marprelate and relocates him to Massachusetts, thus implying that true Puritan simplicity has crossed the Atlantic. Much like Bradstreet, in the title and throughout the satire Ward presents himself as a "simple" subject of England plainly elaborating the ills of the land, as can only be seen from the New England perspective. The tone of Ward's satire is rustic and crude throughout, and his readers would have recognized his language as a strange amalgam of Marprelatian neologisms and puns, familiar country images, and New World exoticism. While such phrases as "pumpkin-blasted," "Nor-west passage," and the numerous references to the New England colony remind the reader of the text's colonial origins, the more frequent pastoral figures attach the colonial cobbler to the English countryside as well. Ward's cobbler, thus, is at once exotic and familiar, an English countryside dweller who lives in the New World. Ward's purposefully exotic vocabulary, moreover, reminds us that these writers, when they drew occasionally on the rustic vocabulary and geographic sensibilities only available to them on the other side of the Atlantic, both incorporated the displacements of exile into their rhetorical stance while reminding their readers of the distant, shadowy world of the New England colony.

The rhetorical advantages to which Ward employs such a position can be seen most prominently in his extended, bold rhetorical questioning of Charles I, where he uses his status as a humble outsider to attack the king and his counselors, or as Ward fashions them, the king's "Ear-guard." By situating himself in such a manner, Ward writes from the safer position of the plain-speaking cobbler looking out for the best interests of king and country while sharply criticizing Charles for his "sinfull marriage," the "luxury of your Court and Country, your connivance with the Irish butcheries, your forgetfull breaches upon the Parliament, your compliance with Popish Doegs" (Ward 58–9). Despite these vehement attacks, or rather because of them, Ward styles himself as the king's ideal subject, someone providing the utmost service to the king and "whose heart hath beene long carbonadoed, *des veniam verbo*, in flames of affection towards you" (Ward 59–60). Much like his resituating of the Elizabethan Marprelate tradition to Agawam, Massachusetts, Ward moves English duty and faithfulness away from the court, where proximity to the king had previously represented favor, to the distant, and thus honest, New England subject. It is precisely because of his distance from the king and his corruption that Ward can perform the duties of the ideal Englishman as an objective critic. In *The Simple Cobler*, Ward thus deflects the anxiety of publishing such a topical work with his pose as the cobbler, while also purporting that his position from New England allowed him a special perspective on his homeland's ills.

Along with Ward's creation of this rustic Marprelate, other Puritan authors also asserted an alternative ideology attendant upon their migration to the New World. This ideology portrayed the Great Migration not as an attempt at radical innovation, but rather as an effort to flee from the changes and corruptions of their homeland. In the numerous texts defending the migration to and political structure of Massachusetts, colonial authors emphasized that the settlers had maintained, in their community, the exact religious and civil ordinances of God. For example, writing in defense of the General Court's actions in the Antinomian controversy, Thomas Weld notes that the colony is blessed to have preserved all of the ordinances of God "in the native purity and simplicity, without any dressings or paintings of humane invention."[82] John Cotton constructed a similar notion of community when he drew up an unused draft of the laws of the colony, arguing that the word of God was completely sufficient for civil and ecclesiastical law.[83] Both Cotton and Weld insist that the Bay Colony has implemented the laws of God, embodied in the language of the Scriptures, untainted. In so constructing their polity, Weld and Cotton drew upon a rhetoric that had been developed on the eve of the Puritans' departure from England. The farewell sermons make it clear that maintaining God's ordinances in their purity is attendant upon their migration from England.[84] The fact that this ideology was first formulated by the New England migrants at the moment of their departure signals that its claims helped to justify and make sense of their decision to leave behind their homeland and the Puritan cause within the Church of England.

As much as the projection of simplicity and rusticity by early colonial writers arises out of and reinforces this ideology, so too, relatedly, does the New England authors' characterization of their writing as free from ornament and ostentation. The compilers of the Bay Psalm Book's translations of the songs of David make a gesture to simplicity and purity in their Preface, where they eschew "barbarisms" for a "rather plaine translation" and pointedly remark that they have "attended Conscience rather than Elegance."[85] In his examination of ecclesiastical doctrine, Thomas Hooker sounds a similar note, presenting his text as coming "forth in such a homely dresse and course habit, the Reader must be desired to consider, It comes *out of the wilderness*, where curiosity is not studied."[86] These authors professed a purity of language that called upon the commonplaces of "the plain style" whose attraction to their predominately Puritan readers is obvious. Read in light of the construction of New England's pure theocracy, further, this plain style, much like the objectiveness of the rustic, becomes reliant on the migration of these writers to New England. Just as they were forced to remove themselves from England in order to preserve the purity of God's ordinances, so, once they left, they preserved a purity of language not seen currently in the metropolis. Notably, Bradstreet, in charting her lineage back to Sidney in the halcyon days of Elizabeth, does so while praising Sidney as the "brave Refiner of our *Brittish* Tongue" (150).

The first generation of New England Puritans never abandoned their Englishness wholesale, and indeed continued to express the belief that England remained God's chosen country. However, the attraction of this Englishness, ultimately, was in its ability to create a coherent sense of identity in the face of displacement by delineating their own community as the "saving remnants" of the English nation. Thus, in many of their writings for the transatlantic print market, early New England authors construed their colony as the true followers of God's will for England. In *The Day-breaking if Not the Sun-rising of the Gospel with the Indians*, John Wilson reports an exchange in which the natives asked him whether the English ever were as ignorant as the Indians were. Wilson replies that there are two types of English: "those that are just as wicked as the Indians now, and those that were wicked but learned the way of God."[87] The boundaries that Wilson draws here between the reformed English and the unreformed allow him to ignore any geographic niceties. There is little doubt where the Massachusetts colonists stand in this redrawn England; in an earlier missionary tract, Wilson claims that all the other English colonies call upon New England to "help them preach the Lord."[88] Thomas Shepard also makes the Bay Colony's position explicit in his own missionary report, as he also uses the native population to criticize those back in England and praise those in New England: "Let these poor Indians stand up incentives to us, as the Apostles set up the Gentiles a provocation to the Jews: who knows but God gave life to *New England* to quicken *Old*."[89]

Shepard and Wilson both hold up the example of the New England colonies as a reformed ideal that England should look to imitate, a practice that Ward follows in *The Simple Cobler* when he redraws the boundaries of the English nation to include the colonies at its center. Numerous other writers sought to educate an English reading public with the example of New England during the 1640s. Part of this inclination arose from the feeling that the upheavals of the Antinomian controversy in the previous decade had taught the Massachusetts authorities useful lessons about religious and civil strife from which England could learn. But the didactic aims of these colonial writers also derived from a more pervasive ideology that construed the Massachusetts colonies as more English than England.[90] Indeed, many of the rhetorical and discursive tendencies that I have elaborated above arise out of and feed into this ideology. The New England Puritans were especially drawn to this notion of their community as the "saving remnants" because it served both to justify and to impose a retrospective order upon their departure from

England. Often, for exiles, the disruptions that the experience involves shade readily over into the bold, performative assertion of coherent identity. The memories of the departed homeland, that is, are transported and made concrete through the rhetorical purification of the exiled community.

That the transportation of memories, of language, and of English ways necessarily involved a purification, from the exiles' perspective, is made clear through the consistent move to intolerance by many of these writers, especially intolerance of alternative linguistic signification. Nathaniel Ward's reorientation of loyalty, honesty and simplicity across the Atlantic sharpens the sense of calling that English Puritanism, as a whole, encourages. Yet it is impossible to ignore in Ward's satire that its most immediately striking, and indeed dominant, feature is its monolithic intolerance, both for what he considers heretical religious opinions and, seemingly illogically, for the foreign fashions of English women. In the first half of his satire, Ward repeatedly assails the adherents for religious toleration, sounding this single note over and over again along different registers, even at times admitting the over-strenuous prosecution of his theme. The following passage is characteristic: "If the state of *England* shall either willingly Tolerate, or weakly connive at such Courses, the Church of that Kingdome will sooner become a Devils dancing-Schoole, then Gods Temple: The Civill State a Beare-garden, then an Exchange: The whole realm a Pais base then an *England*" (Ward 11). Punning on the French for Low Countries and denouncing their liberal attitude towards heterodox opinions, Ward advocates a higher road for England, above toleration, which seemed a very real threat in the middle of the 1640s with the growing power of the more radical elements in the New Model Army. Moreover, the demonstrative that Ward uses to identify "that Kingdome" subtly distances the speaker from his homeland, reminding us that elsewhere Ward defends the interventionist practices of the Massachusetts General Court in matters of religious dissent.

In the above passage, Ward holds out hope for the preservation of a true reformation of religion in England, a hope that he elsewhere repeatedly associates with the removal of any dangerous opinions to beyond the borders of the English religion and state, as he imagines them. He calls upon men to live within the "pale of Truth" rather than in the "purlieus, where they are sure to be hunted ever and anon" (Ward 7). Satan works upon the "frontiers of error" and desires nothing more than to spread his religion along these frontiers. How religions of differing opinions could coexist under the same state is "beyond the Artic" of Ward's comprehension. Ward's use of these geographic tropes evinces a particularly colonial turn to his attacks on toleration. That these metaphors are enlisted in the service of excluding heretical opinions reminds us that, in Ward's imagination, the Bay Colony did not exist outside of, but rather at the center of, the purified English nation. The geographic character of Ward's language, further, allows us to see that his redrawing of the boundaries of the English Puritan community remains reliant upon keeping heresy out of that community. Throughout his tirade against toleration of religions, he argues that any type of mixture in religion is inherently unstable and dangerous to religion and the state. Thus, he implores young men to avoid "errorists" since they have a leprosy that is contagious and easily spread. Similarly, Ward avers that "the least Error, if grown sturdy and pressed, shall set open the Spittle-doore of all the squint-ey'd, wry-necked, and brazen faced Errors that are or ever were of that litter" (Ward 22).

While this disdain, even fear of mixtures, is partly attributable to the rhetoric of Puritanism, the argument has shifted in its journey across the Atlantic. Prior to their migration, the Puritans viewed themselves as the little leaven that would leaven the entire Church of England's membership to reformation.[91] However, by the time of the Cambridge Synod of New England in 1646, a meeting, it should be noted, meant specifically to explain their religion's opinions to the homeland, the elders, much like Ward, repeatedly warn against heterodoxy. They return to the metaphor of the leavened bread, however now calling heresy the little leaven that could potentially leaven, and thus corrupt, the whole lump of Church members.[92] Ward himself uses the leaven metaphor exactly as the Cambridge Synod had in his later work, *Discolliminium*, published in 1650.[93] The emphasis is on keeping others out, rather than on reforming those in England. Notably, one of the most significant innovations of the New England independent churches was to require an account of a conversion experience from each potential member, an attempt to guarantee their worthiness as a chosen "saint."

The pervasive intolerance of many of the New England elders and magistrates lent itself to a particularly closed and uniform notion of the migratory community. Many of the colonial leaders went to specific lengths to perpetuate the perception that the Bay Colony was consistently unified in religious and civil matters. John Winthrop's *Journal* provides the best insight into this tendency to project unity upon the Massachusetts community. After each account of a dispute or argument between factions or individuals, Winthrop, almost instinctively it seems, calls for a resolution or asserts himself that all differences have been reconciled.[94] Similarly, Thomas Hooker, who, despite his claims for unity, led a group of settlers to Hartford out of dissatisfaction in Boston, repeatedly assures his readers in *The Survey of the Summe of Church-Discipline* that the doctrines in his treatise represented a "joint concurrence of the most of the Elders in New-England."[95] Hooker's assurances hint that much of this talk of unity, and the intolerance that accompanied it, resulted from the settlers' desire to present an indivisible front to their English readers.[96] By presenting themselves so, the colonists answered the printed attacks that depicted the colony as populated by "Colluvies of wild Opinionists, swarmed into a remote wilderness to finde elbow-roome for our Phanatick Doctrines" (Ward 6).[97]

The shift to intolerance can also be attributed to the fact that the migrants no longer had the immediate desire or ability to continue the reformation in England. The first generation of settlers did retain an interest and engagement with the godly back in their homeland, and, as Perry Miller argued long ago, viewed their own efforts as a spur and example for their brethren in England.[98] But their immediate concern would have been more local because of their isolation. As a result, the Bay Colony settlers, while holding a transatlantic community of the godly firmly in their mind, would also have turned their attention inward. The settlements' isolation goes some way towards explaining their intolerance in that they no longer necessarily had to interact or accept oppositional factions. For many of these oppositional factions, in fact, it was easier to remove themselves to a more remote locale rather than attempt to remain unhappily in close proximity to those whose opinions differed from theirs. Certainly we should also consider the impact of the colonial encounter with indigenous peoples, which would have spurred the colonists to formulate a unified communal ideology in the face of the natives' difference. For example, Winthrop construes the geographical space of New England as a "vacuum domicilium" that the settlers have filled, justifying the colonists' theft of the natives' land, while also figuring the New World community as a plenist whole that has filled this vacuum.[99]

But the settlers' isolation and their contact with the Indians only goes some way towards explaining the vociferous, in the case of Ward at least, and rather pervasive intolerance. Another, and indeed crucial, factor in the New England settlers' intolerance would have been the migratory experience itself. The increased intolerance of the New England Puritans can be seen, first of all, as an attempt to place a retroactive coherence on their migration to the New World, in a sense a kind of justification for leaving home, both for themselves and for an English audience that they had left behind. This seems to be the thrust, in part at least, of Edward Johnson's typologically infused narrative *Wonder-working Providence* (London, 1654), one of the foundational texts of the Puritan Great Migration myth. In this text, Johnson formulates the settlement of the Bay Colony as the calling by Christ directly of a unified chosen community of saints "to goe to a desert Wildernesse, thousands of leagues by the Sea."[100] Because of the nature of this divinely inspired endeavor, Johnson cautions against "conceited Opinion which, spread by wolves rotten teeth, will fester like gangrene."[101] The intolerance is necessary, according to Johnson, due to the nature of the Puritan migration. We might reverse Johnson's logic, however, and argue that his intolerance, and the attendant view of the Puritan community it entails, justifies and shapes his notion of the migration itself. By insisting on the purity of the exiled community in the New World, Johnson is able to make sense of and order the disorderly and disruptive nature of the migration. We may recall that the Bay Colony's rhetoric of purity and simplicity appeared prominently on the eve of their departure in sermons that were printed to explain the reasons of their departure from England.

Further, the fact that these concerns over impurity and infection persisted registers the unsettled nature of migration and the pressures it places on self-definition and communal identity. From Calvin forward, Puritan ideology inculcated a sense of unsettledness and permanent crisis to its followers, an unsettledness, as Walzer has noted, that proved particularly attractive to the Marian Puritans seventy years ago. God was always on the verge of departing from an individual or from an entire community. However, what was unique about New England Puritanism was its marked shift away from the pilgrimage of the individual to the purity of its institutions and the community.[102] John Winthrop's seminal departure sermon, *A Modell of Christian Charity*, brings this sense of unsettledness into sharp focus as Winthrop worries over the possibility of divine desertion for the entire New England endeavor: "The eies of all people are uppon us. Soe that if wee shall deale falsely with our God in this worke wee haue undertaken, and soe cause him to withdrawe his present help from us, wee shall be made a story and a by-word through the world."[103] The new sense of communal unsettledness and purpose that we can see in Winthrop's sermon arose from the disruption of institutions and group identity that migration enacted. Because the migrants left behind the familiar materials, institutions and hierarchies of neighborhood, parish and manor, they became increasingly concerned with the nature of these as they were reformulated and transformed in the New World. Intolerance and the insistence upon a unified populace enforced a rigid and well-defined sense of both purpose and identity to the early colony.

This insistence by the New England authorities also belied the coextant sense of freedom and novelty that comes with exile as well. That is, the intolerance of the early New England colonies developed as the author-itative alternative to the revolutionary freedoms that exile also enabled. Perhaps the most famous, and controversial, episode of heresy and intol-erance in the early history of New England was the Antinomian contro-versy of 1636–7. This controversy forcefully illustrates the persistence of a desire to maintain stability and of a nervousness over the constant emer-gence of heterodox opinions within the colony. But, most importantly for our examination of the discursive character of exilic texts, Anne Hutchinson's persecution and trial reveals that Massachusetts authorities found Hutchinson's attitude towards language and semantics to be her most pernicious error. As Patricia Caldwell has insightfully detailed, the Antinomian controversy represented a "monumental crisis of language," since Hutchinson exhibited a profound distrust of the ability of human words to communicate spiritual reality adequately.[104] Throughout the trial, Hutchinson insisted that her words could not relate her experiences with God, nor could human words interpret the divinely inspired words of the Bible. As a result, the authorities reacted swiftly and harshly to what they perceived as a "fatal rupture in communal continuation," a contin-uation based upon the notion that communal consensus on Scriptural and spiritual meaning was absolutely necessary to the peace and spiritual well-being of their colony. Thus, Hutchinson's trial and subsequent excommunication indicates that the magistrates and elders' insistence on absolute purity was grounded in an insistence on the absolute purity of interpretive practices.

The magistrates' deep concern for Hutchinson's ambiguities goes some way towards explaining the bizarre puns and neologisms that populate Ward's *The Simple Cobler*. At first glance, Ward's language seems to be the nervous energy of a peripheral writer addressing a metropolitan and sup-posedly more sophisticated audience. His adoption of the Marprelate voice, which had returned to popularity in Civil War London, and his over-enthusiastic praise for Marchamont Nedham, the prolific Parliamentary pamphleteer, both support this interpretation (Ward 66). Yet Ward's tone and his ability to sustain such vitriolic attacks for several pages point to no such hesitancy or nervousness. It seems more appropriate to view Ward's incessant puns and seemingly gratuitous neologisms as an attempt to over-invest his writing with meaning, as the signs of a writer striving not to miss a single opportunity to reinforce his theme at every turn, to overwhelm the reader with his presence. The most colorful and ridiculous sentence of *The Simple Cobler* serves as an excellent example: "If the whole conclave of Hell could so compromise exadverse and diametricall contradictions, as to compolitize such a multimonstrous maufrey of heteroclytes and quicquidlibets quietly; I trust I may say with all humble reverence, they can do no more than the Senate of Heaven" (Ward 27). Ward here is honed in on emphasizing that any sort of toleration of religions, any sort of contamination by heretical opinions, would permanently prevent the state from peace. The neologisms and alliteration run furiously through the first clause of this sentence, as he describes the hellish attempts to gather diverse heretics peacefully. At every turn, Ward's language refocuses attention to itself and in turn to the unnatural mixture that it describes. Thus, "exadverse"'s Latinate prefixes move in diametrical directions, and "quicquidlibets" is a nonsensical pun that means, literally, whatever you want it to. It should be noted, as well, that as the sentence turns to address the Senate of heaven, the extravagant language disappears and the cadence slows to a steady pace.

In a sense, Ward has covered the distance between Ipswich and London by attempting to fill his prose with meaning. In several places in *The Simple Cobler*, Ward insists that he writes in all seriousness, and more specifically, with a constant eye towards his meaning and his audience. We should not be surprised then that, in his satiric errata at the end of the book, he makes no apologies and, in fact, insists that changing any one word in his work would "seame-rend all." This insistence on coherence allows for no interpretation except the numerous ones the prose has already anticipated. Whatever his different metropolitan readers can think of, Ward has already written it into the text. We can see in the tendency of his prose to refocus attention upon itself and on its glosses of its own meaning, Ward attempting to anticipate and respond to all readers, to fill all the text's interpretive spaces. We can also see Ward striving to rewrite or overwrite, much like the New England authorities in their persecution of Anne Hutchinson, the dismantling of semantic fixity that comes with the communal disruptions of displacement.

CHAPTER 2

Exile and the semantic education of
Thomas Hobbes's Leviathan

After the restoration, and back in the favor of Charles II, Thomas Hobbes dedicated his optical treatise *Seven Philosophical Problems* (1661) to the king, his former mathematics student and fellow exile. In the closing periods of this dedication, Hobbes apologetically reflects on the reception of his political work, particularly *Leviathan*:

There is therefore no ground for so great a calumny in my writing. There is no sign of it in my life; and for my religion, when I was at the point of death at St. Germain's, the Bishop of Durham can bear witness of it, if he be asked. Therefore I most humbly beseech your sacred Majesty not to believe so ill of me upon reports, that proceed often, and may do so now, from the displeasure which commonly ariseth from difference in opinion; nor to think the worse of me, if snatching up all the weapons to fight against your enemies, I lighted upon one that had a double edge.[1]

Hobbes, first of all, reminds the king that he also was in exile once, citing his particular troubles in France in the late 1640s, and using it as a sign of his supposed continuous loyalty to the Anglican and royalist cause. The final clause is delicately calibrated, wistful yet poised, apologetic yet uncompromising. The metaphor implicitly evokes the desperate and scattered existence of exile, while also admitting the diverse ways in which the works of royalist exiles could be used during the early 1650s. It should be remembered that Hobbes saw his magnum opus under the rather different light of the Cromwellian Protectorate in 1656, when in the final section of *Six Lessons for the Savilian Professors of Mathematics*, he immodestly claimed that *Leviathan* "hath framed the minds of a thousand gentlemen to a conscientious obedience to present government."[2] If *Leviathan* was a double-edged sword, then its author seems to have sharpened both sides at various, appropriate times.

Hobbes's image of the double-edged sword can serve as a useful guiding metaphor in an analysis of his writing during the royalist exile. First of all, it attunes us to the vagaries of living away from a homeland with its subdued desperation and its evocation of haphazard action. Not only did dislocation to the Continent confuse and disrupt attempts to restore the Stuarts to power, as Hobbes's metaphor implies;[3] it also forced a removal from many of the material, religious, and social structures that the royalists used to order their lives. The impact of this removal cannot be underestimated when determining the relationship between exile and the imaginative works of those royalists that fled to the Continent. The image of the "double-edged" sword, second of all, seems particularly appropriate given the various manifestations that these texts accepted after publication. Hobbes's apology, and the actual reception of *Leviathan* upon its publication in 1651, remind us that the London print market during these years was extremely polemical and volatile. With the lapse in the Licensing Act in 1642, the onset of a very publicly waged martial and print war, and the advent of the weekly newsbook, an unprecedented amount of printed materials, particularly about current events, was available to the reader in and around the environs of the metropolis. Thus, Hobbes's apology to the restored monarch reminds us that the exiled royalists largely lived outside the circulation of these materials. The text from the royalist exile passed back into this quickening print community, one from which its author, often idling away on the Continent, must surely have felt a sharp separation. The text thus crossed not only geographic but political and ideological boundaries, leaving itself vulnerable to, and perhaps even encouraging, antagonistic, inquisitive or subversive readings.[4]

The suggestion that the exilic text left itself open to these types of readings may seem an obvious point to belabor, and true for all early modern English texts that passed into print, especially at this time.[5] Yet I make it to counteract the initial instinct to read all works written from exile as about and for the exile community exclusively. Much excellent work has recently been done on the politics of literature during the Interregnum. However, critics have often been too quick to read the literature of the defeated royalists as one-sided political allegory or defiance.[6] These important studies have reclaimed the mid-century from literary oblivion and thus have begun to show the often hazy influence of the experiences of war, Protectorate and restoration on the development of English literature in the seventeenth century, as well as the role that literature played in the formative events of these years. Unfortunately, while these critics have often been sensitive to the complex and shifting politics of the Interregnum (David Norbrook and Thomas Corns especially), too frequently most analyses have reduced the texts they study, and the political moments into which they were written, to either/or propositions. The overriding effect of much of this recent work is a picture of the London book market split intractably along ideological lines, with royalists writing only for royalist ears and eyes, and Parliamentarians only for Parliamentarian ears and eyes.[7] However, the tendency to limit texts, and by implication their readers, to one political or ideological interpretation does not accurately represent the record of their production and consumption and leaves far too many questions unanswered about the ways in which these texts were apprehended during this period.

Let me just use two examples to illustrate the complexities of the politics of the mid-century book trade, complexities of which authors would undoubtedly have been conscious. Recently, Hobbes's works in the early 1650s have been construed as part of a republican political offensive around the time of the Engagement Controversy and the institution of the Commonwealth.[8] For example, David Norbrook notes that Hobbes's works were being extracted and used polemically by government newsbooks, and that *Leviathan*'s impatience with monarchist discourse must have appealed to many republicans.[9] According to Norbrook, Hobbes's works gave republican arguments a new rhetorical edge. However, the politics of Hobbes's publications at this historical moment seem far more complex, especially when we consider the boom in the publishing of Hobbes's works in 1650–1, most of which have Dedicatory Epistles signed by the author from Europe, and some of which came from ostensibly royalist publishers such as Richard Royston.[10] In fact, the 1651 translation of *De Cive* contained a laudatory preface from the royalist Charles Cotton. By enlisting Hobbes in the republican cause at this moment, we elide the significant presence of a prominent exiled writer in the middle of the growing "republican" literary and political tradition. The fascinating quickening of the literature of civic theory and philosophy during the Engagement Controversy was the product of diverse voices, often from both sides of the Channel.

A more illuminating, yet much more complex, example of literary politics at this historical moment involves Payne Fisher's *Irenodia Gratulatoria*, a Latin panegyric written for Cromwell in 1652. Fisher's poem is a bewildering document for those who wish to trace the politics of mid-century texts and readers. Fisher had to a certain extent a distinctly royalist pedigree: he had reacted unfavorably to the regicide and his 1650 Latin poem *Marston Moor* contained commendatory verses from the royalist Edmund Benlowes and a commendatory citation of the *Eikon Basilike*. Yet the 1652 panegyric, despite its clearly un-republican

Augustan tendencies (the English translation's title was *Veni, Vidi, Vici*), contains praise for Milton's *First Defense* and, even more radically, Lilburne's Leveller tracts. Further, *Irenodia Gratulatoria* was advertised in Marchamont Nedham's *Mercurius Politicus*, a newsbook espousing strongly republican views at the time, and which praised Milton's *First Defense* in the same issue in which the advertisement for Fisher's poem appears.[11] The advertisement in *Politicus* reminds us, however, that despite all its republican leanings, Nedham's newsbook felt no qualms about advertising what various critics have and would characterize as "royalist" works: Davenant's *Gondibert*, Hobbes's *Human Nature*, Cowley's *Poems*, and numerous romances and plays printed by the supposedly "royalist" publisher Humphrey Moseley. Moseley also seemed to be involved in the production of Fisher's panegyric, as he entered the poem in The Stationers' Register on 4 July 1652, with John Holden. Perhaps most tellingly, if a London wholesaler walked into Holden's shop at the sign of the Blue Anchor in the New Exchange in 1652, he or she could have leafed through the *Irenodia Gratulatoria* or picked up Davenant, Hobbes, Cowley's *The Guardian* (a play, as the title page notes, performed for Prince Charles in 1641 at Cambridge), or an English translation of Descartes's *Discourse on Method*.[12]

A full account of the production and potential field of consumption for *Irenodia Gratulatoria* serves as a sobering, and at first distressing, reminder of the difficulties of labeling any text. Yet I do not detail these bibliographical "niceties" out of a purely revisionist impulse to deny the existence of ideological difference in, or the efficacy of political labels for, the printed text. Rather, this complex account vividly illustrates the competitive and diverse space that these texts inhabited alongside other pieces of what we would carelessly call "literature," as well as pamphlets, sermons, newsbooks and philosophy. Thomas Corns has noted that while a broad survey of the Thomason Tracts will reveal a print market divided deeply along "clearly demarcated ideological lines," this characterization does not take into account the "discrimination, nuances and elusiveness present in much of the better writing of the period."[13] Surely, numerous pamphlets display their ideological or political colors radically and clearly to the reader. Yet Corns may be applying his disciplinary prejudices too readily in his attachment of "elusiveness" to "the better writing of the period." While I do not argue with Corns's privileging of the "better writing" in his study (I shall do the same), we should recall that these writings jostled and competed for attention with a much more numerous selection of pamphlets, ballads, broadsides, and even ephemeral manuscript publications.[14] The marketplace of print and manuscript in the 1640s and '50s was more crowded than ever, and, as Nedham's advertisements for Davenant and Cowley or the "royalist" Moseley's printing of Anthony Ascham's argument for engagement with the Commonwealth tell us, less obviously demarcated than we would like.

Further, as Carlo Ginzberg and Michel de Certeau's work has shown, readers often ignore *our* notions of what and how they should be reading.[15] The dedication of the Beaumont and Fletcher folio in 1647 to the Parliamentarian Earl of Pembroke, or the inclusion of two or three commendatory poems from consistent supporters of the Parliamentary cause in Lovelace's classic cavalier collection of poems, *Lucasta*, indicates that appreciation of poetry and drama can certainly not be limited to those sympathetic to the Stuart cause. Just because a work was produced by a "royalist" does not mean it was only read by "royalists," or even in a royalist manner. Indeed, by labeling Cowley's Pindaric Odes "royalist," as some recent critics have, they close off the rich possibilities of antagonistic, parodic, subversive, or merely inquisitive readings of these complex poems.[16] In general, most authors directing their work towards London print publication would have understood the potential for a wider and much more diverse set of responses. The large number of texts written mainly to answer and attack another text alone indicates the extent of antagonistic reading in this period. In the mid-century English print market, authors could not have been unresponsive to the ideological complexities of their potential audiences as they sought to position their text within the mass of pamphlets, sermons, newsbooks, poetry and drama. Thus, reading Cowley's Pindarics as royalist allegory tends to occlude how they were read by a contemporary audience and occlude how Cowley might have anticipated just such an audience in the poems.

To some extent, the exilic text printed in London, then, should also be seen as an event that reaches out to, engages with (and the pun is intended here), those who remained in England. As we shall see, for some royalist exiles such as Edward Hyde, the future Lord Chancellor, a text published in London even constituted a betrayal of the royalist cause. In part, these feelings of betrayal illustrate the tenuousness of the legitimacy of the royalist cause after the regicide and Engagement Oath controversy; however, they also, through their vehemence, allow that these print events lie somewhere between the royalist enclaves on the Continent and the Parliamentarian-controlled metropolis. When we recognize the texts of the royalist exile as transitional, as "in-between," we can move beyond searching for allegorical references to the royalist cause and begin to detail what it meant to write with the knowledge of a broad, but geographically, and often politically and ideologically, distant audience in mind. Such an approach to royalist exile literature, it should be emphasized, does not minimize or downplay the profound psychological and political upheaval that the experience of displacement entailed for the adherents to the defeated Stuart cause. As I have noted, the act of writing back to the homeland was conjunctive, one that filled the "interstices between the literary activity of two homes, one lost, one not yet familiar."[17] In these texts, we can see the exile develop a new relationship with his or her native country, a relationship predicated upon the specific displacements engendered by the royalist flight to the Continent: this flight's origins in the political upheaval of a previously ordered society, its resultant concerns over obedience and control, both political and linguistic, and its encouragement of Parliamentarian representation of the royalists as Continental interlopers in English affairs.

*   *   *

Before turning to Hobbes and *Leviathan*, I would like to detail the various pressures that the royalist dislocation placed on the exiles' negotiation with the homeland – the pressures dislocation placed on their ability to claim a coherent political and communal identity, as well as to construct an authoritative space from which to write. By 1650, eight years of conflict, defeat, exile and regicide had left their mark on the royalists. The followers of the deposed king and exiled queen faced a complex set of problems in formulating a clear sense of English identity. Migration entails a wholesale loss of many, if not all, of the continuous structures within which individuals are able to define and identify themselves.[18] Most immediately, the royalist exiles lived without many of the material objects that surrounded them in their homeland and provided a sense of continuity and familiarity, a sense of identity to them. The royalist exiles in Europe often displayed a keen appetite for Continental fashions and materials, an appetite cultivated by the cosmopolitan tastes of late Caroline court culture.[19] Often, the exiles' correspondents in England requested particular French items; acquaintances of Ralph Verney and his family variously asked for the "latest fashionable gown" from Paris or combs from Dieppes.[20] Yet these exiles still missed familiar English materials. Thus, Ralph Verney requests some of the "old sack" from his wife when she returns to England, even though, as he explains, the French wine tastes well enough.[21] On a more personal level, John Evelyn inventoried all of his "moveables" when he left for France; and, in an act that strikingly illuminates the unsettledness that the exiles must have felt, often rewrote his will before he traveled.[22] Without their familiar English wine, or, at times, even most of their personal, non-heritable property, the royalists on the Continent would have felt unmoored from familiar material surroundings. This material uprootedness contributed to a more metaphysical sense of displacement. Even Henrietta Maria, largely surrounded by familiar friends and family, lamented, "I need the air of England."[23]

Perhaps more elementarily, the royalists lived amidst other cultures on the Continent, a fact of existence that consistently reminded them at once of their "foreignness" and their distance from England and English culture. Beyond the absence of familiar materials, many exiles had considerable difficulty adapting to French and Dutch culture. Evelyn details a rather humorous but potentially dangerous encounter, in which he and his traveling companions are attacked by a mob in the French countryside for encroaching upon the grounds of a private garden.[24] These more innocuous cultural misunderstandings belie the serious quarrels and differences that the royalists had with a Continental, and, more perniciously to some exiles, Catholic, country. Ralph Verney complains about the dishonesty and affectation of the French, lamenting that he can persuade no English or Protestant servants to wait on his family in France, and railing at one point against French "civility:" "should I live ten thousand yeares among these pratlinge people, I thanke God I have not soe much courtship, nor soe little honesty, as to learne this flattering quality."[25] Verney also worries over the influence French culture and education will have upon his children, writing to his wife that Rouen is a terrible place for their boys since there are "noe Protestant masters alowed to keepe a schole here."[26] The potentially tainting influence of Catholicism, an influence whose tangible effects could be seen in the increasing Catholicism of Henrietta Maria's circle, proved a consistent concern for many royalist exiles. These concerns reached even to the highest levels of the royalist community when, after Henrietta Maria barred all non-Catholics from her presence, Charles, residing at the Hague, demanded that his mother hand over the Duke of Gloucester, whom he and Hyde felt was being unduly influenced by Henrietta Maria's Catholic coterie. Further, while Charles and James enjoyed a familiarity with French court culture, and French style and habits more generally, as well as the privileges of royalty, even they had their troubles. During the Fronde, the brothers were harassed and ridiculed out of Paris by an incensed public, incited by pamphlet and gossip accounts of their ill-conceived attempts to mediate the dispute between Mazarin and the Prince de Conde's faction of Frondeurs. Many of the pamphlets emphasized the dangers of allowing the "English," traditional enemies of France, close to a young King Louis XIV.[27]

These cultural clashes, given a specific point by the daily material reminders of their dislocation, contributed to the exiles' sense of uprootedness, their sense of distance that was marked by the moment of their departure from a once peaceful and ordered homeland. In their letters and diaries, the exiles conceived of themselves as "sojourners" or "banished" from their homeland, left to wander the Continent until some unknown future political victory, or capitulation, just as Hobbes's primitive man wanders the earth in perpetual war with others. Ralph Verney perhaps most poignantly articulates the mental state of many of the exiles when he expresses a vague desire to wander further from home, perhaps to Italy or Turkey, and compares his spiritual condition to the Arabian desert.[28] Verney's sense of aimlessness and despair exhibits the difficulties of formulating a clear feeling of identity and "home" while faced with the ruptures of exile. That many of these exiles, including Verney, kept journals and diaries of their experiences is evidence of their attempts to order and process the fractured daily existence that comprised their lives. In writing these diaries, the exiles were consistently reminded of their status as foreign "sojourners" as they reflected and wrote in their native language. Their private language remained an indelible reminder of their banishment and tenuous status as "English."

Yet, beyond the immediate foreignness of the exiles' language to the French or Dutch, the English language as the royalists had known it and desired it was also increasingly distant from what was spoken and written in and around London. This distance was given specific point by the royalists' political defeat and marginalization. After all, how does one define "honour" after the collapse of the royalist cause, and the subsequent rush to compound or flee to the Continent? How does one, more generally, define masculine virtue without any of the traditional sources of this virtue; hospitality, management of the estate, or martial valor? How does one define "loyalty" or "obedience" or "lawful" after the execution of King Charles I and the implementation of a required Engagement Oath? We can see the complex answers to these questions in the struggles of the royalists on the Continent. Wounded honor in part drove the rampant duels (and ridiculous posturing) between the rival factions of Sir George Digby and Prince Rupert in France after the royalist defeats of 1644–5.[29] Lack of a household and the typical strictures of masculine duty could have led to the excessive debauchery of Charles Stuart and his followers. And various exiles struggled to decide between, and to justify, going into further debt with their persistent Continental creditors to stay with their king, or else returning to England to Engage lawfully with the enemy. How does one, finally, define "England" or "Englishness" while a significant group of English men and women lived on the Continent, obeying foreign laws, sometimes fighting for foreign forces, and speaking and reading the English language in foreign lands?

Cromwell and his followers, with the confidence that comes to those in power and the control of the press, construed Charles Stuart and his "fraternity" (a recurring, condescending appellation) as representatives of Scotland. Throughout the letters of Cromwell's secretary of state, John Thurloe, Cromwell's supporters refer to Charles as the King of Scots or the Scotch King – this after Charles had taken the Scottish Oath in 1650, and led a combined army to defeat at the battle of Worcester.[30] Thus, according to one of Thurloe's Continental informants, the exiled Englishmen at the Hague succeeded in arousing hatred for "the English more and more" by denouncing the Parliament. England and the English often become synonymous with the politics of Parliament and its supporters in these letters. The Parliamentary/Protectorate newsbook *Mercurius Politicus*, as well as other pro-Parliamentarian pamphlets, took up the King's political association with the Scots and used it to brilliant polemical advantage, fulfilling the worst fears of those of Charles's advisors opposed to the Scottish invasion.[31] In *The Case of the Commonwealth Stated* (1650), Marchamont Nedham's call for reasoned obedience to the *de facto* power in England, Nedham continuously characterizes the king's supporters as foreigners and Scotland as "that country which sticks like a scab upon the fair body of this fortunate island."[32] If Charles Stuart were to return, England would be visited by "foreign desperadoes" who would garner all of the new king's favors to the detriment of the English people.[33] By naming Charles the King of Scots, Parliamentarian polemicists denied Charles and his exiles their English identities while simultaneously arousing anti-Scottish sentiment against the king. They also strove to clarify such confused terms as "loyalty," "obedience" and "England" after the execution of Charles I through this disassociation. Yet, despite the rhetorical force of associating Charles Stuart's political identity with the national identity of him and his followers, even Parliamentary supporters had difficulty sustaining their denial of the exiles' Englishness. Thurloe and his correspondents occasionally lapsed in their identification of Charles with Scotland. Often, they refer to the "English court" in Europe in relation to Charles and his followers. Henrietta Maria is vaguely referred to as "the Queen that was of England" both in these letters and Nedham's newsbook.[34]

The ideological and political marginalization of Charles Stuart and his followers was enabled and exacerbated by the exiles' distance from the London print metropolis. To return to a statement from the introduction, a twentieth-century German exile once described this distance: "German for me has become a foreign language of which I happen to know all the words."[35] This exile's sense that a once native language has become foreign points up the difficulties the exile has identifying with the homeland left behind. In the case of the royalist exiles, a separation from the English language as it was spoken at the center of the English-speaking world, London, would have highlighted their marginal status as a community of English political exiles. The realities of their marginal linguistic status were correlated with their marginal political status, their separation from a metropolitan language attached to their political defeat and exile.

While the realities of their exclusion from a specifically English-speaking community centered in London might have been little different from those of a provincial inhabitant, the royalist exiles, importantly, perceived of themselves as outside this particularly English circuit, one uniquely centered in the metropolis of London. Of course, most immediately, they lived surrounded by foreign languages, constantly reminded of their status as English-speaking "sojourners" in a foreign land. Even though many of the Stuarts' followers knew, and were comfortable reading and writing, French, many complained of their difficulties speaking and comprehending the language.[36] But beyond the immediate disjunction of language difference, the royalist exiles also saw themselves as separate from the "vernacular print community" centered in metropolitan London. The English book trade of the seventeenth century was remarkably and uniquely centralized due to the Stationers' Company's unprecedented 1557 charter, which limited all printing to members of the Company, and all printing in English, outside of Oxford and Cambridge, to London. Thus, books were almost exclusively produced in, and emanated from, the metropolis. While the lapsing of the 1642 Licensing Act loosened the Stationers' hold on the book trade slightly, for the royalist author and reader the mechanisms of English book production and consumption remained primarily in the distant environs of London.[37] Further, while the lines between vernacular print communities had yet to be sharply and decisively drawn, the years between

1620 and 1640 marked a broad recession in the European book trade that led to a significant increase in the trade in domestic book markets.[38] With this recession, and the disruptive impact of the Thirty Years' War, English traders had notably ceased attending the Frankfurt Book Fair. If we are to envision the "life-cycle" for early modern books in terms of Robert Darnton's "communications circuit," then the exiles, importantly, were excluded from this circuit as they had experienced it in England.[39] The unprecedented boom in pamphlet and polemic publishing after 1642, and the attendant onset of a nascent public sphere based in the metropolitan print market, would have only exacerbated the royalists' sense of exclusion and marginality.

This exclusion would have meant, first of all, an increased forfeiture of authorial control over the particulars of publication. While variable in general in the seventeenth century, the author's control over print production was necessarily lessened by the geographic realities of exile. Hobbes can serve as a useful example here. His letters to Samuel Sorbiere, who was overseeing the publication of the 1647 *De Cive* printed by the Elzevir house in Amsterdam, illuminate the difficulties that the exiled author faced. In these letters, Hobbes consistently worries over his inability to assist the compositor in the setting and proofreading of his text due to his distance from the printshop.[40] When Elzevir finally completed the first issue, he sent Hobbes his copies through the Parisian bookseller Pierre Le Petit, after Hobbes never received the copy that Sorbiere had sent him.[41] Unfortunately, at the last moment, Sorbiere and Elzevir had decided to insert a portrait of Hobbes with the inscription "Thom. Hobbes Nobilis Anglus Ser. Principi Walliae a studiis praep."[42] The inscription came as a complete surprise to Hobbes and was the object of some consternation. Hobbes, who at the time had been tutoring the young Charles in mathematics, expressed his extreme displeasure at the inclusion of the ambiguous inscription, complaining that: "those who are at present power in England are assiduously searching for and seizing upon any pretexts on which to stir up popular ill feeling against the royal family."[43] After receiving Hobbes's letter, Sorbiere instructed Elzevir to remove the inscription. This episode indicates the important ways in which the disruption of communication between author and publisher can affect the reception of a work. As readers identified Hobbes as the tutor to Prince Charles, the son of the embattled King of England, they invariably associated Hobbes's theories with those of the English royal family. Through the inscription, Hobbes's text, in part, becomes the Stuarts'. In this case, the exiled author's lack of control over publication, while not an entirely uncommon situation in early modern texts, allowed more space in which the meaning of a text may dangerously wander.

We can also see the royalists' perception that they lived on the edges of the English-speaking world in the apologetic prefaces and dedications to royalist texts printed in English and published on the Continent during the exile. In the preface to a Catholic pamphlet printed in Louvain in 1647 that consoled Catholics back in England, the writer apologizes for the errata: "And surely considering a strange tongue, put into the mouth of a Presse, a little stammering may be tolerated, specially, when the *Errata's* you will finde here, are of a much more dispensable kind, then those we finde in your Country *Presses*."[44] The apology excuses the printer's errors by comparing them to the much more pernicious doctrinal errors that the Catholic reader would find coming from London. However, similar apologies appear in other English works printed on the Continent throughout the century and point up the barriers that language raised in the printshop. In the preface to *The Flaming Heart*, another Catholic work dedicated to Henrietta Maria, the author excuses the printing: "the rather, because it was performed, both in a strange Countrie, and by strangers."[45] Samuel Brown, the only "royalist" printer operating a fully-fledged printing house on the Continent, produced less than high quality work, often ephemeral in quality. Regardless of how these texts actually differed from their English counterparts, the caveats that many of them expressed in their prefaces encouraged a perception of their difference and contingency, brought on by virtue of the circumstances of production. Further, controls over what could be printed, specifically in France, limited the types of English texts that the exiles could get from Paris booksellers. The 1630s and '40s marked a consolidation of licensing power in the Imprimerie Royale and its overseer, the publisher Sebastian Cramoisy.[46] Unsurprisingly, then, the list of English-language texts printed in Paris between 1640 and 1660 contains very few non-Catholic works. While the Parisian press could perhaps serve the needs of Henrietta Maria and her immediate circle, the majority of Anglican exiles would find little directed specifically at them. Even something as topical and supposedly sacred as the *Eikon Basilike* could take on an entirely different form on the other side of the Channel. The French printer the Sieur de Marsys altered the King's Book to make it "free of Huguenot errors" and added a new death speech for Charles I.[47] It is telling that the only book of English poetry printed in Paris during the exile was Richard Crashaw's *Carmen Deo Nostro* in 1652, which, perhaps to clear any suspicion of

Protestantism, came with a description of the printer, Pierre Targa, on the title page: "printer to the Arch-bishop of Paris."

We can see the royalists' perception of their marginal place in the English print community also in their perennial complaints that they had no news of occurrences back in the homeland. The exiles lived outside of the standard distribution networks, the shippers and booksellers, that spread books from the printshops of London through the capital, and, slowly and haltingly in the seventeenth century, throughout the English countryside.[48] While the book trade, with its network of agents and systems of exchange, was generally amenable to long-distance trade, the infrastructure for wholesale distribution of English books on the Continent was not fully in place by the mid-seventeenth century.[49] This is not to say that the exiles on the Continent were wholly unable to obtain books printed in England. Yet their reception of recently printed English books remained contingent and uncertain. The exiles' lack of, and constant requests for, news from England in their letters show the difficulties they had obtaining printed materials.[50] If, according to Benedict Anderson, the advent of periodical newsbooks enabled readers to imagine themselves partaking in a simultaneous communal "mass ceremony," then it was a ceremony in which the exiled royalists did not participate with other English men and women.[51] Indeed, while at Oxford earlier in the decade, Lady Ann Fanshawe discovered the pleasures of this ceremony: "to that day had never in my mouth, 'What news,' I begun to think there was more in inquiring into buseness of publick affaires than I though off."[52] She and other exiled royalists must surely have felt their isolation from current English events keenly. Lady Fanshawe's involvement in the consumption of news serves as a useful reminder of the extent to which the majority of these political exiles had participated in the vigorous market in English books until their flight. While the royalists might have gotten news at the same rate as a distant provincial reader, their letters and diaries show that they perceived of themselves as cut off from news of their homeland.

The exiles not only had trouble receiving printed news from England; most also were without the numerous books they had gathered in their private libraries. While earlier Catholic exiles, settled in Louvain in the 1570s, had success transporting and maintaining large libraries, most royalists did not.[53] Evidence from diaries and letters suggests the exiles' difficulties in transporting large collections of books across the channel. John Evelyn notes the arrival of some requested books from England with relief, implying the irregularity of such shipments: "I this day received safe, diverse books & other things I had sent for out of England."[54] Later, after his return to England, Evelyn arranged for the purchase of a portion of Bishop Cosin's library when he returned to England, "the Deane intending to sell his library remaining in England."[55] Parliament had sequestered Cosin's library from Peterhouse in 1644 and the Bishop left for France without his books.[56] The absence of their libraries involved more than just the absence of books for the exiles. It also entailed the disruption of the aristocratic and scholarly reading practices that were organized around these libraries. While for Hobbes and others Mersenne's scientific community in some ways helped to mitigate the loss of these libraries, this community remained specialized and, due to Mersenne's death in 1648, temporary in its character. Undoubtedly, Continental intellectualism influenced the trajectory of the royalist exiles' thoughts, as evidenced perhaps in the French-epicurean tinge to many of the Cavendish circle's theories.[57] But equally influential, and more immediate, was the English exiles' absence from the traditional reading practices that the physical presence of their own libraries enabled. If we are to imagine a set of English humanist reading practices, with their emphasis on actively selecting and glossing multiple texts at one time, these would surely have proven difficult to exiled royalists without the majority of their, or their patrons', books.[58]

The royalists' perception of their distance from the London print metropolis and from daily interchanges in English became related to their status as political exiles in the pamphlets and sermons published for the exiled community on the Continent. In these pamphlets, the exiles attempted to redraw their marginal status vis-à-vis their departed homeland, arguing for the legitimacy of their proper use of the English language, and thus their political legitimacy as the "true," faithful remnants of the English nation. For example, the pamphlets printed by Samuel Brown at the Hague often expressed a political distance from the English language as used in London. *Traytors Deciphered*, printed in 1650, argued that the name of the English "Parliament" was "a false guide to mislead the people" into thinking that it represents them.[59] Similarly, the same pamphlet consistently characterizes the language as currently spoken in England as a misuse of true language. George Wishart's *The History of the King's Majesties Affairs in Scotland* claims to present the "clear and naked truth" in an attempt to persuade Charles to join with the Scots. Wishart emphasizes that he will not involve "the truth in obscure, doubtfull, or ambiguous termes."[60] He then proceeds to define Charles's "kingdom" by excluding those presently in power in England, explaining instead that his loyal subjects in Scotland and on the Continent are Charles's "country." These pamphlets consistently move to distinguish between those that speak English in the name of Parliament and those that speak plainly, without malicious intent, i.e. the supporters of the royal family. The move seems characteristic of exiled communities who frequently represent themselves as the "saving remnants" of the nation, its only true representatives. Brown's pamphlets fell back on the distasteful politics of those in power, not only for obvious polemical purposes, but also to repaint the exiles' distance from the living language with the sharp lines of partisan ideology. The comfortable familiarity of political rhetoric, in many ways, conceals the potential for loss of authenticity and control over the language, seen, for example, in the unconscious adoption of the Parliamentary moniker "the King of Scots" by many royalist letter writers. Away from the printing presses and book stalls of London, these exilic pamphlets recast their separation from the English print community as a political sign of their true Englishness. Identifying "us" and "them" becomes much easier when one must distinguish between "royalist" and "Parliamentarian" and not "English" and "English."

Yet the pressures of displacement on the royalists' self-identification as English proved more persistent and not so easily dispelled by the comforts of political ideology. A more nebulous, not so easily simplified, community of readers emerges in *A Fountain of Royal Tears*, a pamphlet supposedly printed in Paris shortly after the regicide.[61] The imprint presents the work as written in exile. Yet the title page also invites not only the exiles to pray with their sovereign, but "all those that yet Retain a spark of Religion to *God*, or Loyalty to their *Prince*."[62] The pamphlet casts a wide net with the first person pronoun throughout, lamenting to God that "we are justly plagued for our manifold sins and infirmities," and that "we...have despised thee; and dishonor'd, nay Murdered him thou commandest us to honor."[63] These laments seem to construct an audience that includes English men and women on both sides of the channel. The inclusiveness of the first-person pronoun, its invitation to those "that yet Retain a spark of Religion," perhaps seeks to capitalize on the upsurge in sympathy after the regicide and the *Eikon Basilike*. It also takes up royalist arguments, after Pride's Purge, that the current governing body in England does not represent the people at all, merely the interests of a few, "Factious and Rebellious men," "those that call themselves The Commons Assembled in Parliament."[64]

However, the indirect accusation of the italics on the title page also lurks in these pronouns as they strive to include English men and women on both sides of the Channel. The strain proves too much in the second prayer, where the first person slips into the third unexpectedly:

Let the bloud of Christ shed in his members appease thy justly incensed anger, against us for our sins: O Lord, behold how they have not only destroyed their King who was the lively Image of thy Sacred Majesty on Earth, but yet rest so unreasonable, and unsatisfied, that they content not themselves with the destruction of him and his loyal Subjects.

After a long litany of "their sins" the pamphlet finishes the period: "forgive we beseech thee the crying sins of this Nation, the chief of which as Perjury, Murder, Sacriledge, and contempt of thy holy Word and Commandments."[65] The slip into the third person betrays a byproduct of the prayers' inclusiveness: the pleasures of the reader who can mentally acknowledge that the "we" does not include you. The possibility that English men and women on the Continent and in England could perhaps both take part in this pleasure demonstrates the potential for a wide-ranging, sympathetic audience. Nevertheless, the pamphlet still falters at the moment that it seeks to define "this Nation." The audience that it seeks cannot coincide with the English nation, a homeland with which the exiles felt compelled, yet were hesitant, to identify.

*   *   *

Thomas Hobbes was one of the first supporters of the king to flee, perhaps rightfully fearing persecution for the circulation of the pro-royalist *Elements of Law*, his earliest attempt at moral and civic philosophy. He left London in 1640, soon after Charles I dissolved the Short Parliament in May. Shortly after arriving in Paris, Hobbes completed the 1642 edition of *De Cive*, then returned to work on the first section of his grand philosophical system *De Corpore* (*De Cive* was originally conceived as the last of three volumes). However, in response to the request of his friend Samuel Sorbiere, he revisited *De Cive*, preparing it for wider European publication with the Amsterdam firm of Louis Elzevir in 1647. After completing this volume, he felt compelled by the reports of further royalist defeats to respond to the providential claims of the Parliamentarian forces, since "such Crimes and Sufferings I/will not impute to the Diety."[66] Delayed by service as Prince Charles's mathematics tutor and a severe sickness in 1647–8, Hobbes did not complete this little "trifle," his "Politique in English," as Hobbes described it to Robert Payne, until 1651. So, for Hobbes, the negotiation between exile and home took place primarily in *Leviathan*, an effort that Hobbes specifically directed to an English audience, translating, sharpening, and elaborating upon, many of the theories he had already developed.

Leviathan engages with the English homeland, and thus the experience of exile, primarily through its construction of a political community dependent upon semantic control. Hobbes's ideal commonwealth is only possible through the sovereign power's absolute authority over the meanings of words. In emphasizing semantic control in his construction of the commonwealth, Hobbes displays a characteristic exilic nervousness over the capacity of words to mean directly as a result of the loss of authenticity that comes with exile.[67] Hobbes himself had linked linguistic and political disorder inextricably even in his earliest theories. This connection would have been sharpened by the specifically political orientation of the royalist exile. Of course, the royalist community on the Continent was an exile defined broadly by political allegiance, an allegiance that forced the exiles to the margins of power during the Interregnum. Yet they also lived on the margins of the vernacular community, centered in the metropolis of London. Their definitions of words, such as "England," "loyalty" or "obedience," thus became attached to their politically marginal position. Because Hobbes wrote from without the metropolitan-dominated political and print world, he could not, and would not, simply make a common call for semantic control. Instead, he envisioned his own unique political community, an imaginary space didactic in its agenda in whose closed system Hobbes operated as his own sovereign, thus eliding the contingencies of exile. In *Leviathan*, Hobbes not only responded to the conditions of displacement; he consumed them, developed crucial theories because of them, attempted to order them. In the tightly reasoned political structure that is *Leviathan*, Hobbes did not seek to imitate or reflect the experience of exile for representational purposes; he sought to give it structure, to reconstitute the experience itself. The ideal polity that Hobbes details in *Leviathan* attempts to reconstruct a lost ideal while also creating an entirely new one for the reader. Hobbes's treatise, like many works from exile, is at once reactionary and radical, idiosyncratic and didactic.

As I have noted, Hobbes had been particularly attuned and sensitive to the potential for political and linguistic disorder from the start of his life. After the restoration, in his *Verse Vita*, Hobbes would unforgettably link his birth, which occurred under the shadow of the impending invasion of the Armada, with the birth of anxiety and the ill times that he felt plagued him throughout his life:

> Th'ill Times, and Ills born with me, I bemoan:
> For Fame had rumour'd, that a Fleet at Sea,
> Wou'd cause our Nations Catastrophe;
> And hereupon it was my Mother Dear
> Did bring forth Twins at once, both Me, and Fear.
> For this, My Countries Foes I e'r did hate,
> With calm Peace and my Muse associate.[68]

These lines show a man who had organized his life through a fear of violence and disorder, a fear that often specifically manifests itself in his philosophical writing in his attempts to control language. In fact, in his civic philosophy, language played a critical role in ensuring a well-ordered state. Lindsay Kaplan's work on slander has shown that the Tudor and early Stuart courts, as well as legal theorists, became increasingly concerned with the "capacity of discordant words to disrupt the peace or jeopardize the stability of the realm."[69] Hobbes displays this growing attention to the potentially disruptive power of words even in his first major printed work, the translation of Thucydides's *Eight Bookes of the Peloponnesian Warre* (1629). There, Hobbes sought to curtail the reading and interpretation of classical texts. At this early stage in his career, Hobbes already demonstrated a deep concern for right reading and the importance of common interpretive practices. The multitude does not have the semantic tools necessary to read these potentially dangerous texts correctly and thus should be kept from them.

Eleven years later, when he began to formulate his grand philosophical system in the manuscript *The Elements of Law*, Hobbes emphasized the centrality of the proper use of words to both his own endeavors as a political *scientist*, and to the building of a peaceful commonwealth. In *The Elements*, after outlining his sensationalist basis for the human thought process, Hobbes discusses the origins of language: "A NAME or APPELATION therefore is the voice of man, arbitrarily imposed, for a mark to bring to his mind some conception concerning the thing on which it is imposed."[70] For Hobbes, language is what allows us as rational beings to remember the causes, and thus the effects, of certain actions. Through our implementation of names, we can reason from conceptions caused by sensation to true propositions, and finally, to general principles, by joining these propositions with "right reason." According to Hobbes, we use "right reason" when we "reasoneth from principles that are found indubitable by experience, all deceptions of sense and equivocation of words avoided" (*EL* 22). It is this process which Hobbes delineates as "Science," the "knowledge of the truth of propositions, and how things are called" (*EL* 24). Hobbes's definition of "science," a process he clearly believes he has followed in formulating his civic and moral philosophy, exemplifies his novel blend of rationalism and empiricism. From names, we, as human beings with reason, can deduce verifiable principles. Yet we can verify these principles only by testing them against our experiences. Further, the scientist must derive the definitions with which he or she begins the deductive process from "the experience men have of the proper use of names in language" (*EL* 24).

However, Hobbes argues that few, if any, teachers of political and moral philosophy have used this method. He viewed himself as one of the first men to attempt to approach political theory from a scientific standpoint. In an unpublished manuscript from 1646, Hobbes, with characteristic immodesty, observed: "I shall deserve the Reputation of having beene ye first to lay the grounds of two Sciences, this of Optiques, ye most curious, and yt other of naturall Justice."[71] Before Hobbes's own efforts towards a civil *science*, scholastic and humanist philosophers had relied upon their own interests or the authority of the past for their definitions. These *dogmaticii*, whom he opposes to the *mathematicii* (men who proceed from sound definitions and with right reason):

Name things not according to their true and generally agreed-upon names; but call right and wrong, good and bad, according to their passions, or according to the authorities of such as they admire, as Aristotle, Cicero, Seneca and others of like authority, who have given the names of right and wrong, as their passions have dictated. (*EL* 177)

By denying classical authority as a source for truth, Hobbes continues his sustained criticism of humanist philosophers, a criticism that extends to his distrust of elocution and the abuse of words for rhetorical purposes.[72] In general, universities and books, through these teachers, have led men away from deriving language from experience, thereby unmooring words from their true meaning. Significantly, Hobbes places much of his attack on the dogmatics in his chapter that deals with "The Causes of Rebellion" (*EL*, Part II, ch. 8) to illustrate the pernicious effects that their abuses of language have on the state. These teachers have led subjects away from the "true meaning" of important words, thus encouraging misunderstanding of the sovereign-subject relationship, disobedience, and eventually rebellion and the dissolution of the commonwealth. Except for "discontent," each of the other causes of rebellion that Hobbes cites in this chapter stems from an equivocation "maintained in the books of the dogmatics" (*EL* 171). Thus, for example, subjects believe that the sovereign is obliged to his own laws because "men ordinarily understand not aright, what is meant by this word law, confounding law and covenant, as if they signified the same thing" (*EL* 172). Similarly, theories of mixed government, anathema to Hobbes, have arisen "from want of understanding of what is meant by this word *body politic*" (*EL* 173). For Hobbes, proper definitions, freed from the abuses of humanist scholars and common misusages, are crucial to a well-ordered state.

Quentin Skinner's work on Hobbes has thoroughly discredited characterizations of the philosopher as the isolated "*bete-noire*" of the seventeenth century.[73] In a pair of articles in the 1960s, Skinner examined the complex ways in which *The Elements*, in print for the first time in 1650, and *Leviathan* participated in the debates surrounding the *de facto* power of the Commonwealth.[74] Ever since Skinner's work, political historians and philosophers have shunned the tradition of setting Hobbes's work completely "outside the main stream of English political thought in his time."[75] Indeed, throughout his career, Hobbes himself cites the events of the English Civil War as important motivation towards the development of his political philosophy. He completed the last part of his projected three-part philosophical system first, since, as he explained in his preface to the 1647 edition of *De Cive*: "it happened that my country, some years before the civil war broke out, was already seething with questions of the right of Government and of the due obedience of citizens."[76] This explanation of the genesis of *De Cive* echoes his claim, in the 1656 *Considerations Upon the Reputation, Loyalty, Manners and Religion of Thomas Hobbes*, that *The Elements* was the first treatise that ventured forth in the king's defense.[77] We have also already seen that Hobbes viewed his *Leviathan* as a response, in part, to the providential claims of a victorious Parliament.

In Hobbes's concern for language specifically in *The Elements*, he constructs a detailed response to many of the political questions raised by the personal rule and the brewing constitutional crises of 1640. Throughout his manuscript, Hobbes presents his own definitions of numerous keywords of the English crisis, such as "conscience," "honour" and "citizen." Hobbes believed that if English men and women came to a proper understanding of these words they would also have a proper understanding of the subject's relationship to the sovereign. The "conscience" of the subject cannot differ from that of the sovereign in public affairs since the subject has deposited all of his or her "conscience" and judgment in the sovereign already. Thus, any claims of resistance based upon the danger of violating a higher "conscience" cannot be justified. "Honour," according to Hobbes, is simply "the acknowledgment of power": "to honour a man (inwardly in the mind) is to conceive or acknowledge, that that man hath the odds or excess of power above him" (*EL* 34–5). By basing "honour" on power, Hobbes demystifies any nostalgic notions of old English honor. As Richard McCoy has argued, this principle of an older honor was upheld by many aristocrats in the 1620s and '30s and served as ideological support for an incipient "aristocratic constitutionalism" in which noble subjects held rights to office and the king's ear.[78] Hobbes rejects any arguments for the existence of this "honour," thereby responding to the nobility, who in 1640 called for a more equal relationship between king and subject based upon inherited freedom and aristocratic principle. Ten years later in *Leviathan*, Hobbes would clarify the polemical point to his redefinition of honor, stating categorically that "of Civill Honour, the Fountain is in the person of the Common-wealth, and dependeth on the Will of the Soveraigne, and is therefore temporary."[79] As we will see, Hobbes consistently works in *Leviathan* to close down even further any potential equivocations of keywords; yet as early as *The Elements*, he has identified misuse of language as the primary source for disobedience to the sovereign and is working to regain control of important political terms for Charles I amidst the political debates of 1640. Even the title to Hobbes's 1642 treatise, *De Cive*, is polemical: readers, weaned upon the humanist virtues of the *vir civilis*, were most likely shocked to find that Hobbes makes virtually no distinction between the roles of "citizen" and "subject."[80] The sole virtue necessary for both is obedience.

Hobbes returned to his civic philosophy eight years later when composing *Leviathan* for an English audience. Eight years of war, defeat and exile had left its mark. When one contemplates the effects of exile on Thomas Hobbes's moral and political philosophy, we envision him writing that famous clause, "And the life of man, solitary, poore, nasty, brutish, and short," while in a strange land far from the familiar and the familial. During much of the time that Hobbes spent writing *Leviathan*, the royalist exiles sat in Paris beset on all sides by the angry mobs of the Fronde, unable to receive any news from their homeland. The destitute nature of the English exile community during the uncertain months of the Fronde and their own king's captivity and execution seems, in part, to have driven Hobbes's vision of the state of nature.[81] Indeed, the notion that we remain property-less, essentially homeless, and in constant fear while in the state of nature, stands as an intriguing corollary to the state of exile. Hobbes would later describe his exile, after losing favor with Charles's retinue in 1651, in terms that remind us of a person's state before the institution of civil society: "[I] stood amazed, like a poor Exile,/Encompassed with Terrour all the while."[82] Certainly, the contingencies of the royalists' livelihood in France and the upheavals that had suddenly seemed to have erupted everywhere the exiles went gave a substantial rhetorical point to the more radical vision of the state of nature that we find in *Leviathan.*

Accordingly, Hobbes's account of the state of nature has been his most prominent legacy according to many of his readers.[83] These heuristic readings of Hobbes's masterwork that focus on his ominous picture of the state of nature, to the exclusion of Hobbes's firm insistence on a rational formation of the civil state, call attention to the pervasive cynicism that lingers in *Leviathan.* In *The Revolution of the Saints*, Michael Walzer has compellingly argued that exiles, jettisoned from the affective and local constraints of the dynastic social structure, came to posit individual interest over dynastic interest, and thus began to imagine a politics of resistance and revolution. The political and moral philosophy of Calvin proved particularly attractive to the French Huguenots and English Marian exiles who adopted his notion of a "community of saints" and, as a result, pushed for revolutionary changes. While Hobbes could never be mistaken for a prophet of this revolution, Walzer's outline of a Puritan conception of civic government, driven by the experience of exile, finds numerous corollaries in the philosophy of Hobbes. Most fundamentally, much like the Puritans, for whom the Calvinist world view proved immensely influential, Hobbes's civic government does not form naturally (man is by nature *not* a political animal), but artificially.[84] The natural world does not encourage political order; rather, order must be imposed upon it. As Walzer notes, much of the Puritan attraction to a worldview that was inordinately aware of life's dangers derived from the originary experience of the Marian exiles. The pessimism and fear in Calvinist political ideology, and its resultant emphasis on obedience, spoke directly to the unsettling nature of the Puritan experience with its absence of traditional communal structures such as the family and the neighborhood.

Leviathan signals its profound distance from Calvinism in its Introduction, where Hobbes emphasizes that civil government, while imitative of God's creation, is made through human means, not divine.

However, a similar sense of alienation and distrust broods over the work and particularly over Hobbes's expanded account of the state of nature. Even the commonwealth stands tenuously together, seemingly always on the verge of dissolution.[85] In his chapter on the "Rights of Sovereigns by Institution," Hobbes details these "rights" at times negatively, arguing that without them citizens would remain in a state of perpetual war. The threat of civic dissolution remains throughout much of *Leviathan*, and Hobbes's arguments frequently devolve almost instinctively to this point. It should be emphasized that the depravity of humans has been consistently overstated in accounts of Hobbes's theories, spurred by frequent reference to his most famous clause; importantly, his civil state can only occur because the majority of humans have a basic, rational desire for peace. Yet the persistence of misconceptions regarding *Leviathan*'s description of human nature tells us unequivocally where much of the rhetorical and imaginative force lies in Hobbes's writing. That Hobbes should have expanded this vision of a dispersed, constantly warring humanity while experiencing the execution of the head of his ideal state, the loss of many of the familiar material and institutional structures left behind or lost in England, and the reality of living in a variously welcoming foreign land, illustrates the powerful psychological impact of exile.

However, beyond the overt impact that exile might have had on the rhetorical power of Hobbes's vision of the state of nature, exile also underlies the more endemic nervousness over the fixity of political community and language, and Hobbes's decidedly authoritarian reaction to this nervousness. As I have detailed above, he had already shown a concern for the political dissolutions that linguistic upheaval could engender in *The Elements of Law*. But his attempt to construct a political community through semantic control receives considerably more attention in *Leviathan* as he struggled with the exigencies of displacement and the act of publishing from the margins.[86] His worries over releasing *Leviathan* to the public can be seen from the opening dedication, where Hobbes presents his treatise much more hesitantly than he did *The Elements*. *The Elements* was a manuscript publication, and as such, at least in the initial exchange, maintained the air of a coterie piece, intended for a closed and more specific community of readers. Hobbes dedicated the work to the Earl of Newcastle, William Cavendish, his sometime scientific collaborator, frequent correspondent, and the cousin of his patron, the Earl of Devonshire. According to the dedication, the treatise arose out of "private discourse" between Hobbes and Newcastle, "which by your command, I have here put into method" (*EL* 19).

Further, Hobbes dedicates his treatise to Newcastle, a member of the Privy Council and the "governor to the Prince His Highness," so that it might insinuate itself with "those whom the matter it containeth most concerneth" (*EL* 20). While it is unclear whether *The Elements* ever insinuated itself into Charles I or Prince Charles's hands, the confidence expressed by Hobbes in his dedication illustrates the assured, and patronized, position from which he published his manuscript.

By the time he had written the dedication to *Leviathan* Hobbes had spent approximately ten years in exile and had begun to consider a return to England.[87] *Leviathan*'s political sympathies have occasioned much debate ever since Clarendon imputed that a desire to return home was one of the primary reasons Hobbes published his work.[88] If we are to believe Hyde, it would be strange indeed that Hobbes personally presented a vellum copy of his treatise to Charles Stuart, and, further, summoned the ghost of a departed royalist soldier as the ideal citizen in his dedication. On the other hand, how else are we to read the "Review and Conclusion," in which Hobbes laments "that the Civill warres have not yet sufficiently taught men, in what point of time it is, that a Subject becomes obliged to his Conqueror" (*L* 484)? The swift change in mind perhaps evidenced in the "Review and Conclusion" smacks of opportunism, as Hyde later suspected.[89] Yet the entire work seems to point to an author with one foot in France, and the other in England, hoping for hospitality from both, daring to expect it from neither. Hobbes writes from the interstices between home and exile, his work at home, and he in France. Indeed, Hobbes potentially even believed, according to his own system, that he wrote his *Leviathan* outside of civil society, since no civil authority protected him in exile after his fall from favor in Charles's entourage.

Whatever Hobbes's actual political motives for publication, the dedication to Francis Godolphin, a man whom Hobbes had never met, but from whom he still awaited the payment of a legacy, presents Hobbes as an author utterly unsure of the reception of his work. Gone is the express command of the dedicatee to publish. Instead, Hobbes hints at the possibility that the dedication is unwanted: "I know not how the world will receive it, nor how it may reflect on those that shall seem to favor it" (*L* 3). The auxiliary "seem" here leaves Godolphin free of any active involvement in the treatise, a potential taint from which Hobbes openly releases his dedicatee later in the address: "If notwithstanding this, you find my labor generally decryed, you may be pleased to excuse your selfe" (*L* 3). His work, instead of insinuating itself to those in power, expects a negative reception, a fact betrayed by his repeated concerns over its potentially damaging effects on Godolphin. While Hobbes certainly works within the conventions of the hesitant, humble dedicatory epistle, the extent of his anxiety over the reception of *Leviathan* throws into sharp relief the absence of a patron and the marginal and transitional status of his treatise's publication.

Hobbes's anxiety over the reception of *Leviathan* was certainly not unique for royalists publishing in England at this time. As Annabel Patterson and Lois Potter have shown, royalist concerns over censorship and the "psychological need" for secrecy drove them to invent new and adapt old forms in publications during the Interregnum.[90] But Patterson and Potter both tend to assume too readily that readers of these texts fall into two easily identifiable categories: the royalist partisan and the Parliamentarian censor. The publication of an exilic work back in England, as I have suggested, inevitably crossed political boundaries and allegiances by entering into the London print market. After all, supporters of the king were not the only ones to read romances or poetry, nor were they the only ones to read Hobbes. If the exiles lived outside of the vernacular community organized around the London print market, then publication in that market necessitated, to some degree, a reentry into that community, with all of its political implications. Importantly, Hobbes, Davenant, and Cowley all involved themselves actively in the London publication of their works, and all either had just returned or were about to return to England. The publication in London by exiles disrupted the reductive political divisions of "us" and "them" that pamphlets such as *Traytors Deciphered* strove to keep. Clarendon's criticism of Hobbes reenacts the reactionary, "you are either with us or against us" logic in *Traytors Deciphered*, as does his similar later criticism of Cowley's *Poems*. That Clarendon remembered such stories also reminds us of the immediacy of the crisis royalist exiles faced in 1650 after the execution of Charles I. More and more, compounding presented itself as a "reasonable" option, a fact Nedham and other *de facto* theorists seized upon in their pamphlets. Thus, Hobbes's apologetic dedicatory epistle displays nervousness, not only over the invasive eyes of the censor, but also over the disapproving eyes of his fellow exiles. His dedication to Godolphin sounds a common theme in various English publications of the exiles after 1649: "For in a way beset with those that contend, on one side for too great Liberty, and on the other side for too much Authority, 'tis hard to passe between the points of both unwounded" (*L* 3). While, to us, it may seem surprising that Hobbes would expect readers to censure his liberality, his statement displays an understanding of the balancing act between sedition and capitulation that publication by an English exile entailed in 1651.

The balancing act, or as he envisions it, the gantlet he runs, gives rise to a newly individualistic ethos in *Leviathan*. Quentin Skinner has thoroughly detailed Hobbes's return to *oratio* in *Leviathan* as a means to convince his readers of his philosophy. In *The Elements*, Hobbes confidently denounced rhetoric, judging that right reason, clearly expressed, would convince all readers who merely "bring attention" (*EL* 2). Yet by the time he wrote *Leviathan*, Hobbes, in Skinner's phrase, "had almost entirely lost his confidence" in the power of reason alone to persuade.[91] We can attribute much of this loss to Hobbes's doubts over his audience, exacerbated by the particularly delicate political circumstances of regicide and Engagement in 1650 and the precariousness of the exiles' political identity brought about by these circumstances. Out of this position arises a belief that most will not accept his doctrine, even though, in his eyes, he has based it upon the solid foundation of right reason. In the "Review and Conclusion" Hobbes echoes the confidence, although in a more subdued tone, that he expressed in *The Elements*: "he that shall read it with a purpose only to be informed, shall be informed" (*L* 489). However, other readers will not read for such purposes because they have "already engaged themselves to the maintaining of contrary opinions":

For in such cases, it is naturall for men, at one and the same time, both to proceed in reading, and to lose their attention, in the search of objections to that they had read before: Of which, in a time wherein the interests of men are changed . . . there cannot choose but be very many. (*L* 489)

With his eye on the volatile political circumstances of late 1650 and a potential return to England, Hobbes repeats the doubts expressed in the epistle to Godolphin, presenting himself as a lonely, independent thinker in a sea of faction.

Skinner identifies Hobbes's self-presentation as a fair-minded independent thinker as a rhetorical pose, but it is one complexly informed by his philosophic and semantic theories. I have argued that Hobbes's pose betrays his worries as a royalist exile writing in 1650–1 into the London print market. The dedicatory epistle and the "Review and Conclusion" show an author who has positioned himself between two politically defined reading communities, a position necessitated by the implications of publication while in exile. However, the hesitations that appear in the dedicatory epistle and the rhetorical pose of the isolated thinker unmistakably disappear entirely from the rest of the text. Indeed, as many critics have complained from the seventeenth century to the twentieth, Hobbes presents his own definitions, his own theories, as objective, the common experience of all humans.[92] In *The Elements*, as we have seen, Hobbes attempted to base an objective, reasoned language upon the observation of experience and the proper use of names. Yet the process of deriving the "true meaning" of words in the earlier treatise remains unsubstantially realized. He chastises those who look to custom and common usage for the "true meaning" of words. However, he also implores all civil philosophers and teachers to base their propositions upon the "true and generally agreed-upon" names for right and wrong, good and bad. In fact, most men and women, generally, cannot arrive at the "true meaning" of words, since "there is scarce any word that is not made equivocal by divers contextures of speech, or by diversity of pronunciation and gesture" (*EL* 37). Hobbes even allows that a speaker that "intendeth not to deceive, alloweth the private interpretation of his speech to him whom it is addressed" (*EL* 77). While the assumption lingers in *The Elements* that he has presented the "true meanings" of words, implied by Hobbes's characterization of his own treatise as science, he never forces this assumption upon the reader openly and still maintains that ambiguities occur in almost all cases.

In *Leviathan*, on the other hand, Hobbes's own writing answers the questions that arise out of his theories of how language means. As Geoffrey Hill warns, in his characteristically dense prose: "[The] return upon the 'intrinsecal' from the non-inherent is one of several epitomes of stylistic method that may be perilously abstracted from the texture of his work."[93] Indeed, Hobbes's style and rhetorical moves remind the reader again and again that his own definitions and right reason constitute true meaning. While in *The Elements* Hobbes strove to derive a theory for objective language, in *Leviathan* Hobbes enacts this theory. For example, in *The Elements* Hobbes notes that universal names such as "man" are indefinite "because we limit them not ourselves, but leave them to be applied by the hearer" (*EL* 36). In the corresponding section in *Leviathan*, Hobbes does not mention specifically the indefiniteness of universals, and at the end of his explanation of these words, continues to another point: "But here wee must take notice, that by a Name is not always understood, as in Grammar, one onely Word . . . For all these words, *Hee that in his actions observeth the Lawes of his Country*, make but one Name, equivalent to this one word, *Just*" (*L* 26). Throughout *Leviathan*, Hobbes makes similar rhetorical moves, closing down the meaning of particular words or phrases, and in the process constantly arguing for the objectivity of his own epistemology. Thus, phrases such as "it is evident," or else the normative force of the past participle, supercedes descriptive argument. The opening to the third part, "Of a Christian Common-Wealth," is characteristic:

> I have derived the Rights of Soveraigne Power, and the duty of Subjects hitherto, from the Principles of Nature onely; such as Experience has found true, or Consent (concerning the use of words) has made so; that is to say, from the nature of Men, known to us by Experience, and from Definitions (of such words as are Essential to all Politicall reasoning) universally agreed on. (*L* 255)

We can see here the extent to which Hobbes strives to construct his own audience in such passages, assuming a common experience, a common consent, a common agreement on the meaning of words. The rhetorical force of much of Hobbes's philosophy lies in this call to common experience.

When we look at the way in which the intrinsic inheres in Hobbes's definitions we can begin to see specifically how the exilic experience informed Hobbes's work. Kevin Dunn has situated Hobbes at the threshold of the Age of Reason, arguing that *Leviathan* relies upon the "common sense" of the audience for its authority.[94] This may perhaps explain the tentativeness of the epistle to Godolphin and the "Review and Conclusion," where Hobbes seems to hold little hope of any such sense in his audience. If this is the case, however, the same tentativeness illustrates the imagined and rhetorical nature of this audience. In a sense, the rhetoric that Hobbes employs in *Leviathan*, with its overt appeals to the "common" experience of the audience, ignores the tentativeness of the prefatory material. Hobbes constructs his own audience through his rhetoric, one that stands in for the potentially unsympathetic Parliamentary or royalist partisan. If the displacements of exile forced the royalist exiles to the margins of political and linguistic power, Hobbes's rhetorical closure of the semantic possibilities of language attempted to counteract the force of these displacements.

Hobbes begins his construction of his own experiential language most famously in the "Introduction" where he refigures the old metaphor of the body politic in mechanistic terms. The innovative nature of his vision of the artificial body of the commonwealth is followed by his instructions on how men might understand one another. At this point, Hobbes cites the familiar Socratic adage, "*Nosce teipsum*," as a useful guide.

Interestingly, he translates this phrase inaccurately as "read thyself." Thus, the reader is alerted to the idiosyncratic presence of the author from the start of the treatise. Hobbes shifts the common meanings of the body politic metaphor and a classical saying in an effort to teach the reader their correct meanings. The Socratic maxim "was not meant, as it is now used, to countenance, either the barbarous state of men in power, towards their inferiors; or to encourage men of low degree, to a sawcie behaviour towards their better; But to teach us" that all humans have similar passions (*L* 10). Hobbes's correction of the possible misinterpretations of this adage illustrates the potential effects of misconstruing meaning, as well as the didactic role that he envisioned for his text in the state. As in *The Elements*, Hobbes argues in *Leviathan* that abuses of language are the primary force in the dissolution of the state. In the well-ordered state, the sovereign or his appointed servants become the arbiters of meaning. Otherwise, we would remain in a state of nature, on the most basic level unable to differentiate between *meum* and *teum*. Only through submission to the authority of the sovereign can we form a civil society, since language, and thus property, would remain a site of constant contest without it. Hobbes's civil society remains together only as far as the sovereign and his ministers close down the processes of how words mean.

Unsurprisingly, Hobbes saw the role of the writer, as appointed by the sovereign, as a teacher of the people. In Chapter XXX, "the OFFICE of the Soveraign Representative," Hobbes outlines the duties of the sovereign to his people. According to Hobbes, the sovereign must teach the people the principles of justice, since in doing so he protects both the people and himself from rebellion. This teaching must occur in the Universities, where, at present, the youth learn contradictory opinions that lead to confusion and rebellion. At this point Hobbes interjects for the reader, "is it you will undertake to teach the Universities?" To which he answers: "it is not fit, nor needful for me to say either I, or No: for any man that sees what I am doing, may easily perceive what I think" (*L* 237). Hobbes, indirectly through the reader, thus writes himself into his discussion on the correct instruction of subjects. In doing so, he attempts to reposition himself as a writer into the correctly ordered civil state. The civil philosopher, and in his contemporary exchange with Davenant, the poet as well, serves as a minister of the sovereign, instructing the people in the true meanings of words, and thus ensuring a peaceful political community.

Ultimately, *Leviathan* serves as a guidebook on "how to read" correctly. Hobbes's imagined readers learn the correct uses of language from the author, learn to "read" by understanding the meanings of words as they are laid out in Hobbes's text. The reader is taught "common sense," and the "common" senses, of words. His text is not coercive in the sense that we *must* agree with it; indeed, as rational human beings we are free to disagree, as he states in his introduction: "yet, when I shall have set down my own reading orderly, and perspicuously, the pains left another, will be onely to consider, if he finds not the same in himself" (*L* 11). However, if we do not become a part of Hobbes's imagined audience, do not accept the assumed commonalities of this audience, then Hobbes firmly believed that we would also be renouncing any possibility of membership in a well-ordered political community. Ultimately, for Hobbes, the construction of a community of readers who all maintained the same interpretive practices went hand-in-hand with the construction of a well-ordered political state. In *Leviathan* he takes over these interpretive practices, the processes by which language means for his readers, and in doing so seeks to reconstitute a reading and political community that had been irreparably damaged by the upheavals of defeat and exile.

CHAPTER 3

The expulsion from Paradise:
Milton, epic and the restoration exiles

The King thought not fit to communicate the hopes he had, but left all men to cast about for themselves, "till they were awakened and confounded by such a prodigious act of Providence as [God] hath scarce vouchsafed to any nation, since he led his own chosen people through the Red Sea." (Edward Hyde, *The History of the Rebellion*[1])

But I trust I shall have spoken perswasion to abundance of sensible and ingenuous men: to som perhaps whom God may raise of these stones to become children of reviving libertie; and may reclaim, though they seem now chusing them a captain back for *Egypt*, to bethink themselves a little, and consider whether they are rushing. (Milton, *The Readie and Easie Way*[2])

As much as 1660 marked a restoration, a miraculous return from the long Egyptian captivity for Edward Hyde, his master, the soon-to-be Charles II, and the exiled adherents to the royalist cause, it also marked a return to the long Israelite exile under the Stuarts and their ministers for the faithful supporters of the Good Old Cause. Indeed, the figure of the English people as the Israelites wandering their forty years in the desert nicely represents the divergent fortunes of the royalists and republicans in this moment of transition and uncertainty. In a very real sense, the Israelites of Clarendon and Milton's common allusion passed each other as ships in the night, somewhere in the English Channel, some taking Charles and his followers to their triumphant return, others sneaking the regicides and those intransigently opposed to Monck's settlement over to the Continent and the safety of the Low Countries and Swiss cantons.[3] While the ends to which this allusion is used by each writer point in clearly antithetical ideological directions, its repetition does remind us that after 1660 displacement and exile had been or were the common fates of English men and women on both sides of the ideological divide. In this chapter I would like to cross that divide as I move from the closed political theories of Thomas Hobbes, to the expansive, yet in many ways equally restrictive, world of Milton's writings circa 1660–7. It is in

87

these writings that we can see the effects of the experience of exile on one of the more prominent revolutionary authors after the restoration as he contemplated England's return to Egypt. In both *The Readie and Easie Way* and, more fully, in *Paradise Lost*, Milton works to resituate himself within the print world of London while attempting to comprehend the defeat of the revolutionary cause and his sequestration. Just as in the other pamphlets and diaries of the defeated revolutionaries, which I detail here alongside *The Readie and Easie Way*, Milton seeks to counteract the specific exigencies of political and religious displacement and his marginalization as a writer through the formulation of new modes of speaking as well as transformations of old.

Based upon their biblical allusions, one thing that both Clarendon and Milton, and indeed all commentators, did seem to agree upon was that Charles II did not effect the change that brought about his return. For Clarendon and for many other royalists, the restoration occurred through the miraculous and unforeseen intervention of a God who sought to return order and peace to his chosen nation.[4] Much like the wondrous victories of the godly Parliamentary armies in the 1640s, and the "Protestant winds" that wafted William III fortuitously to England's rescue in 1688, most supporters of the restoration could only see the hand of God in all this change as Charles was invited back without the need for bloodshed or foreign intervention.[5] The providential vocabulary used by Clarendon, Richard Baxter and others, of course, served as a powerful rhetorical technique to legitimate the return of a king who could not claim *de facto* authority over a nation, and who did little, if anything, to cause his own return to power. As recent work has emphasized, the restoration was far from a foregone conclusion after the fall of Richard Cromwell and the Protectorate, nor was it perhaps as welcomed in all quarters of the country as has been assumed.[6] The language of providential deliverance strengthened the shaky claims to legitimacy of the restoration court by, in part, evoking divine-right theory and its insistence that God preferred monarchic government to all others.

Milton and his political kin saw godly favor tending towards a different form of government, that of the Sanhedrin for example, and thus saw little of providential *deliverance* in the restoration. Rather, just as Milton's elegiac, almost certainly knowingly futile, plea to his countrymen in *The Readie and Easie Way* places blame upon the shortsightedness and fickleness of the multitude, supporters of the "Good Old Cause" in 1660 interpreted the return of Charles II as a sign of God's displeasure and punishment for the political and religious shortcomings of the English people. At various junctures in his memoirs written from Vevey, Edmund Ludlow calls upon the same language as Milton, designating Monck and his party as those "for makeing them a captaine to lead them into Egypt."[7] Ludlow's evocation of the Israelites' vacillation and faltering in the desert helps to formulate an account that understands the events of 1660 as divine retribution for the nation's sins. Since "without [God's] providence not a sparrow falls to the ground, much less the blood of any of his pretious saints," God "seemes to take the rod into his owne hand to correct them for their disobedience and unsuitable returns to all those eminent appearances of his amongst them; Charles Steward and his party not contributing the least to their restitution."[8] Similarly, Algernon Sidney, also writing from exile on the Continent, in *Court Maxims* dismisses those who would favor monarchy because of the success of Charles II's return, emphasizing instead that the commonwealth defeated itself as "God suffered divisions to arise amongst us for the punishment of our sins, and *so we came to be betrayed.*"[9]

As Sidney's argument suggests, those who attributed the restoration to divine anger denied that Charles's return reflected any heavenly verdict upon the virtue of kingly rule. They instead used a similar providential rhetoric that previously had helped to explain and validate the Parliamentary victories of the 1640s, the execution of the king and the institution of the Commonwealth in 1649. Just as God had granted England profound favor in helping the nation to accomplish what Milton in the *Defensio Secunda* hyperbolically characterized as "the most heroic and exemplary achievements since the foundation of the world," he had also singled out his chosen nation for punishment and shame at their failure to follow the reformation through to its conclusion.[10] The restoration fulfilled all of the republicans' fears while demonstrating, for them, that the nation had abandoned the reformation willed by God and begun by the civil wars and Parliamentary rule. Further, their insistence that divine anger spurred the restoration implied that a similar act of God could cause the collapse of monarchy and the return to republican or godly government at any moment. Indeed, the popularity of the numerous dissenting and radical pamphlets that described natural disasters, prodigies and God's active displeasure with England can be seen to arise partly out of their readers' continued belief that God still oversaw his chosen nation and will soon deliver it from the rule of Charles II. Many defeated and exiled revolutionaries continued to hope, at least in the time shortly after the restoration, that the English nation's apostasy would be short-lived. For example, while struggling to come to terms with the suffering of Major Thomas Harrison and the other imprisoned regicides, Edmund Ludlow asserts: "Yea, it will bee but a very little while before the indignation of the Lord shall cease, and his anger in the destruction of his enemyes."[11] A posthumous treatise of Sir Henry Vane addresses itself to the persecuted, "in this day of Israel's Captivity, but approaching Redemption (which hastens fast)."[12] Ludlow and Vane's hopes remind us that, for many of the defeated, religious and political deliverance remained enmeshed even after 1660, as much as late-century Whig republications wished to separate them.[13] By asserting a providential account of the restoration these exiles and prisoners reinforced their faith in a godly intervention in English politics that could occur immediately and without warning.

Ludlow and Vane's faith in the eventual deliverance of the English nation, which in Ludlow never faded completely, would have seemed less like denial in the early 1660s after the rapid and confusing events of 1659–60 and the continued unrest of portions of the nation. Exiles almost immediately hope for and expect a return in an attempt to replace the upheavals of the present with a faith in the future. They rarely view their removal from the homeland as an irreversible step but rather a temporary withdrawal. On the eve of his departure in 1660, Ludlow, while maintaining faith in God's eventual intervention, also "supposed within three or fower monthes the heate and rage would be over, when I might have an opportunity to retorne againe."[14] (Ludlow was to return only briefly in 1688, and was banished shortly thereafter for his anti-monarchic campaigning.) Ludlow's over-optimistic hope for his speedy return echoes the words of numerous twentieth-century exiles who never expected to spend much time away from their homeland. Charles Simic remembers as a child disliking the home-style dinners with fellow Yugoslav exiles since "The talk made it difficult to enjoy the cuisine. Exiles usually imagine that theirs is a temporary situation. It was just a matter of days before communism collapsed and their homes and their lives would be restored to them just as they were."[15] While Simic, as a child, was more interested in the pleasures and novelties of New York City, his older compatriots, much like Ludlow and Vane, continued to yearn for a swift return and a transformation of their memories into the reality of their homeland. We might also recall, although in a different context, Satan and Beelzebub's assurance that they cannot remain in Hell for long in the opening moments of *Paradise Lost*.

It is useful, for a moment, to consider Milton's *The Readie and Easie Way* from a similar context of departure, dislocation and expected return.

The Readie and Easie Way has always seemed to me a thoroughly depressing and troubling piece of political writing for its expediency, its desperation and its vehement righteousness. By the time that Milton was writing the Preface to the first edition and preparing the greatly expanded second edition of this appeal to the people of England, Monck had seized control of London and had ordered the return of the excluded members to Parliament. This decision virtually assured the return of the king, as Monck and Milton surely knew (at least fundamentally). Many known supporters of the Rump Parliament had already gone into hiding, including James Harrington, the erstwhile organizer of the Rota Club and fellow hopeful republican. Increasingly, Milton himself had come under fierce attack from ever-bolder royalist and Presbyterian pamphleteers; the first edition of *The Readie and Easie Way* had been broadly derided in March 1660 after its release, while one of the pamphlets imagined Milton on his way to Tyburn, elaborating on what already would have been a strong possibility in Milton's mind as he continued to publish in his own name while others sunk into anonymity.[16] Milton viewed the second edition of *The Readie and Easie Way*, the publication of which he financed largely himself, as the "last words of our expiring libertie" (*CPW* VII: 463); at the start of the tract he pleads that "before so long a Lent of Servitude, they may permitt us a little Shroving-time first, wherin to speak freely, and take our leaves of Libertie" (*CPW* VII: 409). While we should be careful not to assume immediately that Milton's conviction that "the way propounded is plane, easie, and open before us" (*CPW* VII: 445) looked obviously unrealistic to him and his readers, we should also be careful not to depict Milton as so blindly out of touch with the realities before him and his nation in April 1660.[17] The proximity in this, his last plea to the wayward nation, of Milton's lament for the passing of the English republic to his assured reliance on the reason of his audience to choose the correct path points to the increasing gap between his rhetoric and the louder and louder calls for the return of Charles Stuart. Just as Ludlow and Vane continued to expect their imminent return to a repentant nation, Milton's reasoned pleas reveal an unwillingness to let go of his hopes for and memories of the wonderful advancement of the godly reformation he had envisioned so often throughout his revolutionary writings. On the eve of his departure from the public sphere, and from liberty (in a very real and even physical sense), Milton continued to envision his easy return to the short-lived days of the English republic.

That Milton even decided to publish this tract on the eve of Charles's return, and at his own expense, illustrates the sharp sense of loss that

Milton and others experienced at this time, as well as the lingering memories of the heroic push for liberty that England had undertaken yet had now abandoned. With its vehement and intransigent sense of right, even in the face of imminent defeat, it also hints that the defeated revolutionaries, after 1660, would never entirely jettison their hopes for political salvation. Many of these revolutionaries unswervingly emphasized the suffering of the faithful in the wilderness of this world after the restoration. However, as much as this renunciation of immediate worldly fulfillment eventually helped to promulgate a longer view of providential history than the millenarianism espoused in the 1650s and the hopes for an immediate return expressed shortly after the restoration, it also kept these hopes firmly at the center of that history. In the revolutionaries' version of history, the reign of Charles II could never be legitimate, merely an apostasy to which God would eventually put an end. The representation of the suffering and persecution of God's people, so prevalent in the writings of many nonconformists, thus was implicitly tied to claims to the illegitimacy of Charles II, and, as such, was political. Most dissenters still expected their sufferings to be rewarded not only in the life to come, but also through the fruition of their religious and political hopes on earth.[18]

Historical work in the past twenty years has gone a long way to refuting the old orthodoxy that the finality of the restoration utterly shattered the defeated revolutionaries and their ideologies.[19] Richard Greaves, particularly, has detailed a significant amount of radical activity in the 1660s, evidenced in the stockpiling of weapons, a resilient and prolific radical press, correspondences with the English exiles and Dutch governments, and persistent rumors of large-scale uprisings.[20] Of course, not all exiles and dissenters advocated the decisive political action for which Algernon Sidney and other exiles pushed in the early years of the restoration.[21] Sidney himself grew extremely impatient with what he saw to be the unwarranted inaction of Ludlow and several other exiled regicides during the Anglo-Dutch war. For this reason, Blair Worden has noted that Ludlow in his manuscript memoir increasingly stresses the virtues of patience and suffering, contrasting him with those who preached an imminent return to England and power.[22] However, we should not mistake Ludlow's refusal to assist Sidney in 1664–5, which had more to do with his distrust of the Dutch than any newfound apathy towards English politics, or his insistence upon patience and suffering quietly, for a withdrawal from the world of politics. While in Vevey, Ludlow continued to read English newsbooks from London avidly, seeking shipping contacts through Paris and Lyon, and thus keeping abreast of the current political

climate through these and letters from his wife and friends such as
Slingsby Bethel. Although Ludlow advocated waiting passively for a
divine sign that it was time to act, recognizing such a sign entailed
remaining actively engaged with the political events back in the
homeland.

While Greaves's work alerts us to the continued political activity of the
defeated, recent literary criticism concerning the revolutionaries and
nonconformists, apart from a few exceptions, has emphasized the withdrawal of these writers away from the broader public sphere. In the most
substantial recent work on the literature of nonconformity, N.H. Keeble
constructs a picture that, while arguing for the significance of the literary
achievements of nonconformists, depicts these writers retiring from
public life to write works that are firmly concerned with interiority and
subjectivity.[23] Similarly, Blair Worden, in his thoughtful analysis of the
influence of Milton's republicanism upon *Paradise Lost*, comes to the
conclusion that the poem enacts a withdrawal from his former republicanism and politics and addresses itself to a purely dissenting, religious
audience.[24] Yet Ludlow's avid interest in the political occurrences of his
distant homeland reminds us that the decision to wait and suffer did not
necessitate a wholehearted turn to religious experience and away from
politics and the homeland. Indeed, accounts of the spiritual withdrawal of
radicals and dissenters after 1660 cannot adequately explain Ludlow's
habitual interest in obtaining news from England, nor, entirely, the decision by the exiles to write for the metropolitan print audience in and
around London. As Worden, perhaps distinguishing between Milton and
other revolutionaries, has posited, *A Voyce From the Watchtower* was not
merely a commemoration of the Good Old Cause, but also seems to have
been part of a "coordinated literary campaign against the government," a
campaign in which the exiles Ludlow, Sidney, Slingsby Bethel and Henry
Neville all had a part.[25] We might think that the publication of *Paradise
Lost*, also coming on the heels of the Dutch fleet's razing of English ships
in the Medway and the plague and Fire of London, had an eye towards
this campaign as well. Further, beyond any specific contemporary
motives, publication represented a way to communicate with a wide
range of people, indeed perhaps even the entire nation, when silenced
by physical, political or religious displacement. In *The Militant Christian*,
Steven Coven, a nonconformist Presbyterian minister living in England,
notes that: "This book may Travel where the Author cannot . . .; It may
have its Liberty, when he is Bonds; it may speak when his mouth is stopt;
it may dwell in *England*, when he is Banished."[26] Authors like Coven,

while aware of and attentive to a closed audience of exiles or banished dissenters, also anticipated that their texts would cross over back into the London print market, and thus would travel "where the Author cannot."

In detailing the sustained engagement of the defeated revolutionaries with public events, I do not wish to dismiss or deny the reality of a revised spirituality that concentrated more on suffering and less on radical political action; it is impossible to ignore Ludlow's conviction, for example, that "the strength of the Lord's people sometymes consists in quietness and confidence."[27] Rather, I want to emphasize that this spirituality existed along with, and indeed as we have seen, in part assumed, an ongoing interest in the public affairs of a homeland that had gone astray. For the exiled and sequestered revolutionaries removed from the English "nation" by the government, these two seemingly disparate desires reflected and reinforced their status as both of and not of their homeland, their status as exiles. As much as these men and women distanced themselves, and were distanced by the government, from participation in the political and mainstream cultural life of the English nation, they maintained a strong sense of their identity as Englishmen and women. As exiles, their experience and writing are characterized by the same in-betweenness we have already seen that seeks to redress and comprehend the sense of distance and marginalization that exile entails. The contemplation of the loss of a world that these radicals and dissenters knew until Charles's return leads to the nostalgia and commemoration, as well as the turn to inward spirituality, that various critics have detailed in the restoration works of Milton and Ludlow, for example. However, we should also recognize that the texts of the defeated revolutionaries, such as Ludlow's memoirs or the *Speeches and Prayers* of the executed regicides, while commemorating the lost revolutionary cause, also participated in a polemical justification of that cause in order to undermine the legitimacy of Charles II's government.[28]

The direction of much of this polemic and its attendant formulation of some form of communal identity lay in the depiction of the persecuted revolutionaries and dissenters as the pure remnant of England's godly reformation. Before them, the Marian and New England exiles had created in their writings a communal identity that centered on the suffering and persecution of the godly, resituating the genealogies of purity and Englishness to the margins. We can see the same reorientation in the works of the regicide exiles and prisoners. In Owen Lloyd's visionary pamphlet, *The Panther-Prophesie*, the allegory represents, alongside the

religious majority in England, a church "in this Corner" which prays for
the return of the Son and his revenge upon the rest of the country.[29] For
George Sikes, in *The Life and Death of Sir Henry Vane* (1662), God's true
Church has been worshipping outside of the "synagogues," "in the
mourning persecuted wilderness-condition, out of which she is shortly
to appear and speak for her self." Sikes, later quoting Vane, argues that
"the true Church indeed, the very living, real, spiritual members of
Christ's Body, have been for many hundred years a dispersed, captivated
people, under all worldly powers, civil or Ecclesiastical."[30] Sikes's picture
of the true Church builds upon a Puritan historiographical tradition that
had arisen out of the exile during Mary's reign, and had been elaborated
in the 1640s by revolutionary writers such as Milton, who argued that the
Catholic Church had become corrupted shortly after the departure of the
Apostles.[31] However, whereas Milton had used this history to differentiate
between the reformations enacted during the sixteenth century and those
beginning to be brought about in the years of Parliamentary rule, Sikes
saw the suffering of the godly as the norm in this world, since "the natural
man of the Saint is persecuted into a desolate wilderness condition."[32] In
representing the natural condition of the godly on this earth as desolate
and hunted, Sikes builds a doctrine that transforms and justifies the very
wreckage of the experience of defeat and persecution, the marginalization
and sharp sense of loss, into a sign of godliness. Similarly, in his jeremiad
addressed to England, Daniel Baker argues that the godly can only be
found "within thy Bowels," and the voice of wisdom only in "unwhole-
some *Prisons*, *Holes* and *Dungeons* and *Caves* of the earth."[33]

In continuing to justify the revolutionary cause, these texts exhibit a
deep nationalism that arises out of the uncertainties engendered by the
banishment from one's homeland and the dismissal of the exile's structures of thought and ways of speaking as illegitimate. In engaging with the
homeland they had left behind, the exiles did not renounce their own
Englishness, but rather sought to rewrite Englishness in their own image.
While the restoration exiles sharply differentiated themselves from the
mainstream, metropolitan culture of London through their depictions
of the true church as persecuted and exiled in the wilderness, they also
continued to evince a strong sense of their own Englishness, certainly
intensified by the loss of the homeland they had known. It is this nationalism that seems to be missing from recent accounts of the literature of the
exiles and persecuted in the restoration. That Ludlow and many of the
other exiles hesitated at plotting with the Dutch during the Second Dutch
War arose as much out of their reluctance to fight against their native

country during a foreign war as out of their distrust of the Stadtholder for the betrayal of the regicides John Okey, John Barkstead and Miles Corbet in 1662.[34] Similarly, when the Dutch sailed up the Medway in 1667, the exiles and radicals did not consider this an opportunity to attempt a revolt in the confusion, but rather seized the occasion to ridicule Charles's government for its corruption and attacked its effeminacy and ungodliness as the cause for this embarrassment to the English nation.

The defeated revolutionaries' attempts to chastise Charles and the rest of the nation were not uncommon throughout the 1660s and often gathered their rhetorical strength from the writers' positioning themselves as prophetic visionaries. The jeremiad was a particularly common form and can be seen in texts ranging from Daniel Baker's classic expostulation, *Yet One More Warning to Thee O England*, to George Sikes's remarkably wide-ranging attacks in his biography of Henry Vane, to Milton's condemnation of the reformative shortcomings of the English people in his "Digression" to *The History of Britain*. Ludlow also constructed a similar rhetorical position when he titled his unpublished manuscript, *A Voyce From the Watchtower*, a phrase that anticipates a specific relationship with its audience in which Ludlow speaks prophetically from a distant confinement. Ludlow's title has its analogue in the numerous printed pamphlets that advertised their genesis, often on the title page, in the bowels of various prisons. Many of the authors who wrote in the prophetic tradition drew upon this tradition's tendency to depict God's messengers and churches as pilgrims or strangers forced to wander the wilderness of this world. Thus, in an epistle before Vane's *Two Treatises*, the anonymous author praises Vane, whom Sikes called a "constant wanderer" for the Lord, as a minister to a scattered flock driven into the wilderness.[35] Vane becomes a messenger who embodies the Puritan emphasis on constantly searching and wandering for God's truth, an emphasis that spoke directly to the experience of exile and persecution.

In constructing a more sharply drawn political persona, the defeated revolutionaries could also call upon the rhetoric of Tacitean republicanism, which saw a revival in the works of Sidney and Ludlow, for example. Sidney, who would later become the hero of the "country party" in the eighteenth century, speaks for the republican cause in *Court Maxims* through the character of Eunomius, a "Commonwealths-man," who, since now "engaged in none of our affairs," can, for the courtier Philalethes, "explain some things that very much perplex [him]."[36] This simple outsider, in the Tacitean tradition, is contrasted with the base corruption of Philalethes and the court.[37] Similarly, Ludlow consistently attacks in republican terms those involved in the return of the king, noting that Monck and others were driven not by a desire to do the public good but by private interest. Sidney and Ludlow employed the language of Tacitean republicanism not independent of but alongside the language of dissent and jeremiad. Thus, for example, Ludlow looks to an apocalyptic deliverance from the apostates who turned their back on reformation to bring back Charles II: "By the furnace of affliction he intends to purify and purdge the one, but to reject and cast off the other, who aymed rather at greatness than goodness, and at their owne more then the publique interest."[38]

Ludlow's republican and prophetic voice from the watchtower attempts to transform the marginalization that he and other restoration exiles experienced into authorization, while anticipating a politically, religious or geographically distant audience by subsuming that distance into the rhetorical structures of the text. At times, the exiled writers betrayed their separation from the immediacies of their homeland, for example in Sidney's *Court Maxims*, where Sidney's courtier, Philalethes, becomes more of a caricature of stock royalist political philosophies than a legitimate voice for those philosophies. Yet the energy of these texts is not in their necessarily broad condemnatory portraits of metropolitan fashion or politics, but rather in the prophetic and oppositional, yet still engaged, voice that the writers adopt. The powerful discourse of the jeremiad only becomes so through its combination of a profound anger at, yet deep concern for, the homeland; and only derives its visionary rhetoric through a sharp revision of and distance from the public events and occurrences of that homeland. The power and authority of the jeremiad or Tacitean chastisement would not exist without the assumption of a distant home that the author has lost (or a homeland that had lost its way), yet for which he or she still cares.

Like many on the losing side of the political upheavals of the seventeenth century, the defeated revolutionaries had to deal not only with their physical banishment and marginalization but also with the marginalization of their politics and language. Those writing from exile had to reverse the dominant interpretation of events to reflect their now oppositional perspective. It is this hostility to the dominant discourses that largely drove Hobbes's authoritarian linguistic relativism in *Leviathan*. The restoration exiles and dissenters also lamented the ignorance of those who determined the meaning of the English language. George Sikes evinces a Hobbesian linguistic relativism in remarking upon spiritual language, noting that "words too, are but the types, letters, shadows, resemblances, rhetorical figures and significant expressions of spiritual, heavenly, new-creation things."[39] By insisting upon the disjunction between human language and spiritual reality, Sikes authorizes his own systematic, and often political, reversal of terms. Vane, a "true Prophet and Subject is handled as a Traitor," while "All this that is so Terrible to the Inhabitants of the Earth is good news to those that are in the Wilderness."[40] Much as Hobbes's semantic authoritarianism consistently reverses meanings to teach the reader where the commonwealth has gone wrong, Sikes's theoretical undermining of a linguistic determinism exposes the manipulation of rhetoric by those in power while asserting his own now marginalized meaning as true correspondence. Sikes, in some ways like Hobbes, has a firmly Calvinist outlook;[41] he denies the human ability to ascertain spiritual truth through reason, arguing for the sway of the spiritual powers of the saint over the rational powers of humans and noting that "all the weapons, wisdom, righteousness of man are not the spirit or weapons of God."[42] Sikes's denial of the powers of human reason helps him to comprehend the failure of even those who seemed the most saintly to complete the spiritual reformation they had begun in England. The enforced banishment of the godly after this failure, and the subsequent deformation of language, thus are understood by, and in part drive, Sikes's insistence upon the inherent corruption in man's natural being.

However, not all of the defeated revolutionaries subscribed to the rigid Calvinism found in Sikes's life of Vane, even after the defeat of the cause. In fact, Milton, Henry Neville and Algernon Sidney derived their faith in a republican form of government from their conviction that the English people, schooled in civic virtue, could develop the ideal form of government. As a result, the defeat of the Good Old Cause, and Parliament's overwhelming vote to bring back the Stuarts, would surely have dealt their faith in the people's reason a severe blow. To be sure, from the early years of the Civil War, English republicans combined calls for a government that represented the people's interest with an uneasy distrust of the English people themselves.[43] Even with the distinction that most republicans such as Milton and Marchamont Nedham made between the multitude and the political nation, republicans emphasized as early as the 1640s the necessity of educating the English people in civic virtue. The didacticism that we have come to expect in exilic texts thus had already figured strongly in republican theories from the time the Commonwealth was in power. The wavering of the Presbyterian party in 1647–8 and the generally negative public response to the execution did nothing to assuage the republicans' fears of an unlearned public, and prompted, in Milton's *Eikonoklastes*, a vituperative attack on the ignorant readers of the King's Book. Rump apologists found themselves arguing, with Hobbes, that when the people could not ascertain their own interest, a minority could enforce this interest upon them – a position somewhat chilling for the modern reader, looking back through the lens of twentieth-century totalitarian justifications. Yet, as much as a distrust of the people remained a part of English republicanism during the Civil War, when Cromwell declared the people unfit to elect its own leaders and began to abrogate power to himself, many of these same theorists felt betrayed, believing that Cromwell had subverted the public interest. After the Protectorate fell, republicans such as Harrington, Vane and Milton had high hopes that the nation would get the reformation correct this time.

These hopes, of course, went unrealized as the people chose their captain back for Egypt and most who publicly and strongly advocated a return to Parliamentary rule were imprisoned, left the country, or retired into their own interior exiles to contemplate their defeat and the English people's choices. Yet, from this marginal position, many of these writers continued to exhort and cajole the reading public and continued to rely on a rhetoric based upon a faith in the readers' ability to comprehend, through reason, what is in the public interest. However, at the same time, they engaged in an attack on the nation's choices, on the English people's lack of foresight and inability to interpret correctly, much like Sikes and Hobbes. For example, in *Mene Tekel* Roger Jones begins his argument for a Parliamentary commonwealth that follows the public interest by asserting that he will treat all points from "Scripture and Right Reason, with what brevity and perspicuity this weighty and knotty Subject, and the capacity of Common Readers will allow."[44] Yet, in the middle of justifying the reasonableness of the people's right to choose a magistrate fit for their governance, Jones breaks off to speak in the voice of Jeremiah, lamenting "What a pilot and Mariners the multitude have chose, woful experience hath now taught them. O *England*, why sleepest thou? 'tis high time to awake!"[45] To a certain extent, Jones's treatise operates because of this disjunction between an argument justified from reason and the people's failure to follow it. It attempts to convince through chastisement and surprise. To a certain extent then, reason is one of the terms under reexamination in *Mene Tekel*; Jones attempts to appropriate a rhetoric representing the middle ground, thereby providing an authoritative, plain-speaking weight to his minority position. However, while providing additional leverage to the rhetorical construction of the exile as the practical outsider, this disjunction also points up the contradictions in republican theories and the difficulties of writing for a wide-ranging audience from a marginalized position.

Jones's republican-tinged condemnation of tyranny was printed in 1663, three years into the Israelite exile of the defeated revolutionaries; yet we can identify a similarly contradictory rhetorical posture in Milton's *The Readie and Easie Way*, a text, as I have suggested, that can be usefully read as written on the eve of Milton's "departure" from the public sphere into his "interior exile." Indeed, Milton's final Interregnum prose tract, because of its specific rhetorical qualities, has the seeds of the fully developed poetics of exile in *Paradise Lost*, and thus can serve as a useful entry point into a reading of the theodicy that took Milton five or six more years to develop fully. *The Readie and Easie Way* remains an enigmatic piece, with its combination of high rhetorical flourishes that sharply chastise the English nation and simple prosody that pragmatically describes the reasonableness of Milton's compromised proposals.[46] The unevenness of Milton's tone in *The Readie and Easie Way* can be explained to some extent by the exigencies of writing as events moved swiftly around Milton. In the time between its first composition and Milton's extended revision of the piece, Monck had taken control of the city, the excluded members, most of whom advocated the return of kingship, had been allowed back and the Solemn League and Covenant had been revived. Yet, however desperate the expedients that Milton proposed in his tract were, his seemingly unguarded assurance of his proposals' agreeableness stands out noticeably in this time of declining fortunes. For example, Milton states somewhat too blandly, particularly in March–April 1660: "I doubt not but all ingenuous and knowing men will easily agree with me, that a free Commonwealth without single person or house of lords, is by far the best government" (*CPW* VII: 429). This seems to me more than "urgent optimism" to use William Riley Parker's words; rather, the emphasis in the sentence falls on "all ingenuous and knowing men," as Milton identifies these characteristics in an ever-decreasing minority while chastising the multitude.[47]

In Milton's insistence on the easiness of the way we can see his firm belief in the ability of human reason to ascertain the right course, a belief that had come through so strongly in *Areopagitica* fourteen years earlier, begin to shade over into jeremiadic chastisement. The transformation of the republican discourse of reason into jeremiad parallels the transformation of Milton's rhetorical position from defender of the decisions of Parliament to prophet exhorting the nation to stop its current course.

In *The Readie and Easie Way*, then, Milton holds on to a reasoned rhetorical stance as the course of events, and the language of public opinion and popular interest, turned away from him and towards Charles II and his supporters. Just as in Jones's *Mene Tekel*, the adherence to this language of reasoned proposal draws attention to itself as an idiosyncratic adherence to a cause and language now out of favor with the majority. Milton's last prose tract, that is, should be seen more as willful defiance than as urgent optimism. However, the fully realized jeremiadic portions of the tract, with their profound sense of betrayal at the loss of a divine opportunity, emphasize that Milton's call for reasoned proceeding is also a nostalgic longing for the English nation of *Areopagitica*. *The Readie and Easie Way* exhibits a significant doubt over the reason of the English people at this moment, particularly in its insistence on a large-scale educational program for the entire nation.[48] More disturbing is Milton's argument purported in defense of civil and religious liberty that "more just it is doubtless, if it com to force, that a less number compell a greater to retain, which can be no wrong to them, thir liberty" (*CPW* VII: 455). In these moments, we can see the extent to which Milton's faith in the intrinsic value of human reason has been shaken by the events of the 1650s and the departure of the English nation from Milton's reasoned path to civic peace. While, to be sure, Milton's faith in the English people as a whole had always been far from complete, *The Readie and Easie Way*'s nostalgic reliance and idiosyncratic insistence on a reasoned rhetoric, while the text exhorts and cajoles a wayward nation, illuminate its author's mindset at the moment of his departure from the scene.

Milton's last prose writing for eleven years is a "willful act of the imagination" similar to the exilic imaginings of other defeated revolutionaries in 1660 and afterward. In its continued engagement with and attendant desire for the eventual deliverance of the English nation and its assumption of a prophetic, warning voice, *The Readie and Easie Way* takes up a position within the crowded print market of the restoration and does so through its defiant resistance to the status quo, just as the various jeremiads of the defeated revolutionaries would. Further, its reorientation of the rhetoric of the middle ground illustrates its adherence to an increasingly nostalgic mode of speaking and its distinctive use of language, just as Sikes would rely on a systematic reversal of terms to underscore the unjust abuse of the godly. Over the next five years, Milton would continue to explore his novel place as an author, as well as the efficacy of human reason, while contemplating the defeat of the Good Old Cause, his sequestration in the house on Jewin Street and his banishment from the public sphere and a publicly authorized voice.

* * *

According to the not always reliable Edward Phillips, by the time Milton had completed the second edition of *The Readie and Easie Way* in March 1660, he had already begun work on *Paradise Lost*, the poem that would occupy the next several years of his writing life. Perhaps by the early months of 1660 he had completed the early books that take place in Hell, and we might note that devils already seem to inhabit, indeed quite explicitly, the world of *The Readie and Easie Way*. In his chastisement of the "royaliz'd presbyterians," Milton warns prophetically that the "common enemies" of the Presbyterians and the faithful supporters of a commonwealth have already begun to appear in "the diabolical fore-running libells, the faces, the gestures, that now appeer foremost and briskest in all public places; as the harbingers of those that are in expectation to raign over us." The Presbyterians should heed these "insultings of our newly animated common enemies crept lately out of thir holes, thir hell, I might say, by the language of thir infernal pamphlets, the spue of every drunkard, every ribald" (*CPW* VII: 452). The language recalls several passages in Milton's epic, most directly his description of Belial's reign over those

> . . . luxurious Cities, where the noyse
> Of riot ascends above the loftiest Towrs,
> And injury and outrage: And when Night
> Darkens the Streets, then wander forth the Sons
> Of *Belial*, flown with insolence and wine. (I: 498–502)[49]

The description of the sons of Belial here is the first sustained "intrusion" that we might readily identify as resulting from Milton's circumstances after, or on the eve of, the restoration (the word "restore" in line 5 teasingly alerts the reader early on to the potential contemporary signification of the poem). The description of riotous and drunken excess in "luxurious Cities" transforms the metaphor of *The Readie and Easie Way* into allusion, an allusion that would surely not have been lost on the contemporary reader in 1667 as the court came under increasing criticism for its lasciviousness and revelry.

Yet, the allusion, for all of its political clarity and applicability, stands out in these early books exactly because it points so directly at restoration excess associated with the return of the Stuart court. This is not to say that

Paradise Lost does not have moments of political "recognition," that *Paradise Lost* remains entirely above its restoration milieu. After all, contemporary republican and monarchic discourses abound both in hell and heaven and infuse the poem with much of its meaning and power. Further, Milton, at various points, seems purposefully to digress or allude to contemporary concerns. The long digression on the Paradise of Fools as Milton follows Satan's traverse of the heavenly spheres in Book III almost gratuitously attacks Catholic ritual, and thus, perhaps, the religious trappings of Charles's court. Similarly, Laura Lunger Knoppers has shown how the poem advocates the domestic, internal joys of Paradise in order to criticize the lavish and political shows of celebration that accompanied the restoration.[50] However, for a writer so earnestly and actively involved in the politics of the Civil War and Interregnum and so likely antagonistic to the present regime, the poem seems intensely shy about its engagement with contemporary events. It is this seemingly un-Miltonic failure of engagement with the civic that has led Milton scholars to explain the poem's reticence as an effect of censorship or of a decision to withdraw from worldly politics.[51]

Instead of attributing *Paradise Lost*'s reticence to confront contemporary affairs to a fear of censorship or relating it to a more general reflection of authorial psychology, I would like, for a moment, to consider this reticence as part of the poem's negotiation with its reader, as one of the poem's and the author's most profound modes of self-presentation. Milton's poem has always sat uneasily within its restoration context, despite recent and usefully corrective efforts to identify the specific areas in which *Paradise Lost* responds to and shapes immediately contemporary discourses.[52] In fact, the authorial pronouncements in the poem encourage this removal of the poem from its time of publication. Undoubtedly, the poem does substantially engage with restoration readers in various ways; yet we might also understand the very aloofness of the poem as a method of engagement. Beyond the aversion to direct political commentary, Milton, at specific junctures in the poem, presents himself and his creative efforts as sequestered from the public world in which he so recently had participated. Most famously, in the epic invocation that opens Book VII, Milton asks the reader to envision him composing the poem:

> . . . though fall'n on evil dayes,
> On evil dayes though fall'n, and evil tongues;
> In darkness, and with dangers compast round,
> And solitude; (VII: 25–7)

This passage has typically been cited as an evocation of the difficulties he faced as an enthusiastic republican and former supporter of the Commonwealth and Protectorate. What has just as often been missed is the deliberateness, indeed exaggeration, of this evocation.[53] The enjambed chiasmus that emphasizes the poet's dejected condition, along with the final trailing "And solitude," artfully set Milton off from a public world that has turned its back on the poet. Throughout his career, Milton had depicted his every utterance as a theatrical, public event, from the authorially intrusive ending to his elegy for Edward King, to the fit of passion that opens *Areopagitica*, to the national pride that animates the autobiographical details of the *Pro Defensio*. In *Paradise Lost*, Milton encourages his readers to imagine a blind, solitary poet, working on his grand epic, divinely inspired nightly by his heavenly muse. The image of the isolated epic poet, along with a general refusal to "lower" the poem to partisan contest, the direct appropriation and refiguring of classical epic models, and the assertion, in Book IX, that the poem came as a culmination of a lifelong, yet delayed, ambition, becomes part of the poem's sustained effort at elevation.[54]

The reach for sublimity that the poem enacts in the various invocations and elsewhere can be understood as one strategy, one of the more identifiable strategies, through which *Paradise Lost* attempts to negotiate an often complex relationship with its restoration readers. Milton's construction of the lofty, prophetic voice, while answering to his political and social marginalization after 1660, also sought to appeal to a broad range of readers estranged by the court's worldliness and embrace of epicurean pleasures. The poetic stance Milton takes in the poem was reinforced by the print presentation of the text itself. Without a dedicatory epistle, preface to the reader, or any other markers on the title page, the first edition seems purposefully to eschew any connections with other aristocratic agendas or vested interests, and thus distances itself from the "taint" of courtly influence.[55] By the time *Paradise Lost* was published in 1667, broad criticism of the court's lasciviousness and failed foreign policies had expanded well beyond the more radical elements of the English reading public. To many readers, Milton's poem, its affecting of sublimity and removal, along with its spiritual decorum, must have seemed a welcome relief from the insistent debauchery of the court and the noise of heroic theater. As Nicholas von Maltzahn has detailed, many of the epic's first readers, including supporters of monarchy, were particularly impressed by the authority and sublimity of Milton's grand poem.[56] While at the time of the poem's composition, circa 1659–65, Milton could not have foreseen the specific events that would govern these readers' reactions, he did continue to associate a broad increase in private interest and corruption with the return of monarchy. His decision to formulate a prophetic, distanced poetic voice placed him in opposition to patronized poets while appealing to a range of readers through a calculated sublimity and a broadly epic ambition.

The issue of audience has remained at the center of studies of and arguments over Milton's poem, especially since Stanley Fish's seminal work on the ways that *Paradise Lost* shapes the reader's experience. Milton's envisioning of an audience "fit . . . though few" in Book VII, perhaps the most cited line in the poem and a frequent starting point for readings, invariably concentrates readers on the aggressively didactic nature of the epic and its appeal to a limited audience. For example, Sharon Achinstein argues that the dangers of censorship forced Milton into writing an allegory that sought out and attracted a dedicated audience, while cajoling and training this audience throughout the poem.[57] While Achinstein rightly emphasizes the extent to which the poem exerts an intrusive pressure upon its readers, her depiction of allegory as a mode in which the reader willingly submits to the whims of the author enables her to overstate the exclusionary capacity of *Paradise Lost*. It would be dangerous to assume, that is, that Milton anticipated only fit readers would read his poem, that the process of selection would occur before its purchase. In fact, the poem seems to have sold fairly well, going through a print run of around 1,400 in five to seven years.[58] Much of the scant evidence we have of early readings of the poem come, generally, from royalist sympathizers (John Evelyn, John Dryden) or Presbyterians (Robert Beale, John Hobart), readers invariably excluded from twentieth-century critics' construction of Milton's "fit" audience. While these readers might acknowledge Milton's turbulent politics, guiltily they admitted his genius. As Robert Beale wrote to his friend John Evelyn: "You will Joyne with mee to whisper in a smile, that he writes so good verse, that tis a pity he ever wrote in prose."[59] When we recognize these readers, the tone of Milton's "fit audience find though few" becomes perhaps as much congratulatory, or challengingly inviting, as admonitory; the image of the poet in solitude far from the "barbarous dissonance/Of *Bacchus* and his revelers" as much inviting a range of readers to participate in this sublime cultural distance than excluding them from this participation.

Indeed, while much has been made of Milton's vision of a small audience of the godly who would read his poem, few scholars have explored the underlying tension that lies at the heart of this line's (and the entire poem's) formulation of *Paradise Lost*'s readers – a tension that we have already seen in *The Readie and Easie Way* and that can usefully be traced to the failure of the Good Old Cause. From the early 1640s, Milton had maintained a firm faith that all Christians, through the efficacy of human reason, and with the assistance of divine grace, could read and understand Scripture. Milton refused to relinquish this faith in his fellow citizens, at least in theory, even as he increasingly saw the need for the few to rule over the many. Thus, even as he chastised his fellow Englishmen for foolishly abandoning the cause in *The Readie and Easie Way* and called for a permanent Council of State to control the polity, he insisted that his audience need merely follow the dictates of common sense in order to complete the political and spiritual reformation that Milton so desperately desired. We might remember that in *Leviathan* Hobbes similarly appealed confidently to the common experiences and sense of his audience, while holding out little hope that his work would be received favorably by readers of any political persuasion.[60] In *Paradise Lost*, Milton's famous line about his audience succinctly indicates the inherent tensions in Milton's poem between the vision of a learned "fit" readership, studying and resolving the difficulties of the epic through their own reason, and a consistent belief that "vulgar readers" will understand little of Milton's theodicy. These exact same tensions reappear when the poem attempts to adjudicate theologically between free will and grace. Milton's famous line on his audience hovers between a particularly Miltonic elitism that becomes more pronounced at those moments in which the country turned away from him, and an equally Miltonic desire that all humans should exercise their reason in the service of truth.

An awareness of the potential for a wide-ranging audience and of Milton's ambivalence over his poem's reception can begin to shed some light on his experience as an "interior exile" in the months immediately prior to, and the years after, the restoration. I have been arguing that *Paradise Lost* anticipated and in specific ways directed itself to a broad range of contemporary readers. In this anticipation and direction, Milton remained acutely aware of his marginal position shortly before and during the restoration. Part of the distance and marginalization that Milton experienced would have included a sharp sense of the loss of a world that he had known until recently. The poem shows an author negotiating the distance from the London reading public, a displacement that came with the defeat of the cause for which he fought wholeheartedly, the abandonment of this cause by the majority of the English nation and his removal from a position of overt political or cultural authority.

Milton's deliberate construction of a prophetic, solitary voice at various junctures in the poem not only reflects his position as an interior exile, as numerous commentators have noted; it also, much like the construction of similar voices by regicide exiles such as Edmund Ludlow, transforms the marginalization that comes with this position into authorization as the poet calls upon a tradition of Christian persecution and exile to arm and authorize his own writing for and against a wide-ranging, potentially hostile, audience. We might see then specifically in *Paradise Lost*'s engagement with its various English readers a record of the effects of the complete loss of a political, social and cultural way of life, as well as the effects of the denial to Milton of a confident public voice. The effects of this "interior exile" on Milton manifest themselves most clearly in the generic, theological and epistemological concerns of the epic as Milton attempted to find and define a place for his poem that answered to a psychological and political distance from many of his readers, and as he ruminated upon the sharp loss and displacement he felt upon the restoration of Charles II. Further, the poem's insistent worries over and innovative attempts to override its semantic shortcomings arise, as we shall see, out of a reaction to the removal from the discourses of authority that accompanied Milton's interior exile.

What needs to be emphasized here is that Milton's confident, prophetic persona, as well as the poem's gestures towards comprehensiveness and linguistic certainty that a majority of the poem's readers have recognized, arise out of and never fully dispel the profound upheavals that the experience of exile entails; that is, the elision of exile is never fully successful. Recent criticism has begun to revaluate the long-standing perception that Milton was a poet of absolute confidence and certainty and *Paradise Lost* the poetic culmination of these attitudes. Beginning with John Rumrich, and guided by the cantankerous but brilliant spirit of William Empson, a series of critics, including Victoria Silver, Jeffrey Shoulson, and most directly and recently Peter Herman, have argued that Milton rather remains deeply contradictory, uneasy and uncertain in his representations and assertions.[61] My analysis of *Paradise Lost* as written from "interior exile" further elucidates the fundamental incertitude that lies at the heart of Milton's epic, while beginning to explain the authorial psychology behind the "feeling" of absolute coherence that so many readers have taken away from the epic. Much like Hobbes's *Leviathan*, *Paradise Lost* places authority and sharp uncertainty side-by-side, never succeeding in resolving the tension between these two modes of writing. While importantly directing us to the uncertainties

rife throughout Milton's epic, the recent revaluation has not fully
accounted for Milton's decision to write an epic, an epic that often
represents itself as a compendium of human learning, at this precise
moment of defeat. My reading of *Paradise Lost* attempts to show how
Milton's poem, much like other exilic texts, negotiates often unevenly
between uncertainty and self-assertion, between marginalization and
authority, between the provisional and the eternal.

That Milton chose to write an epic, surely the triumphant genre of
empire and conquest since the ascendance of the Virgilian model, might
puzzle at first. While Milton might have imagined his *Pro Defensio* as the
apex of Parliamentarian nationalism in the 1650s, it finally took the failure
of the Good Old Cause and the return of monarchy for Milton to write
his poem "doctrinal to a nation." The turn to poetry, and specifically to
epic, cannot be attributed simply to a decrease in Milton's public duties.
The epic ambition of the poem, at least in part, can be seen as an
oppositional stance at a time when those in power were widely excoriated
for epicurean apathy and indolence, and when those writing for the powerful, such as Dryden, were translating such grand heroic forms into the
new and "debased" media of heroic drama, tragicomedy and satire. But
Milton drew upon a different epic tradition, one that dates back to
Lucan's *Pharsalia*. These epics, especially Lucan's, enabled the formation
of an oppositional voice, even a republican poetics of sublimity, that
responded to the imperial and authoritarian discourses of those in
power.[62] *Paradise Lost* might also be placed, albeit a tad uncomfortably,
within a more recent tradition of English epics of exile that included, in
the 1650s alone, the incomplete poems *Gondibert* by William Davenant
and the *Davideis* by Abraham Cowley, as well as the translation of the
Luciads by Richard Fanshawe, and, later in the century, Dryden's translation of the *Aeneid*. While Milton leaves us little evidence of an indebtedness, beyond a few structural and generic echoes, to his exiled
predecessors, he would surely have been aware of their efforts to bring
the epic to the English language, and perhaps found, if not inspiration,
then a sympathetic understanding for their ambitions after defeat.

Indeed, the English epic in the seventeenth century is a thoroughly
exilic phenomenon, a fact that has inexplicably received little remark.
Richard Helgerson, one of the few to notice this congruence, has
suggested that exile enabled these authors to free themselves from the
strictures of the patronage system, and thus enabled them to conceive
grand, heroic poems of opposition.[63] However, Helgerson's explanation
brings too modern a sensibility to bear upon early modern writing,

most obviously when he assumes that poetry written in proximity to the monarch "seemed inevitably to decline towards mendacious flattery and triviality."[64] Instead, I would argue, exile did not enable; rather it spurred these writers to seek a generic form that was simultaneously authoritative and nationalist as they positioned themselves in relation to their readers. As we have seen, part of the appeal of the epic voice to Milton and his readers was its sublime resonance. At a time when the exigencies of banishment or sequestration prevented Milton, and other exiles, from the assumption of rhetorical authority or commonality, epic provided him with a classical resonance. A stance that elevated him over the need for contemporary approval, this privileged, sublime voice also spoke, and in the vernacular, from the pinnacle of poetic achievement. As David Quint has argued, the epic form after Virgil became inextricably tied to national history and ambitions, the epic poet a spokesman for national destiny or identity (whether defeated or not).[65] That the exiled writer would have sought poetic expression in such a patently nationalist genre highlights, just as the regicides' reluctance to side with the Dutch in the 1660s did, one of the more noticeable markers of the experience of exile: a continued, often exaggerated, sense of national identity. Epic would appeal to an exiled author largely because of its mode of national engagement as the exile continued to view his or her own political or religious community as the saving remnants of the nation. In a sense, the epic serves as a generic recasting of English identity by the exiled poet, an attempt to appropriate its authority as the pinnacle of English poetic and cultural achievement and make it speak the political, religious, even ideological, language of the exile.

Milton surely understood, probably even relished if his long-held ambitions are to be believed, the audacity of his project at precisely this moment of uncertainty and disappointment. The poem does not shrink from this audacity at its opening, where Milton's narrator boldly proclaims his ambition:

> I thence
> Invoke thy aid to my adventurous Song,
> That with no middle flight intends to soar
> Above th'*Aonian* Mount, while it pursues
> Things unattempted yet in Prose or Rhime. (I: 12–16)

From the start of the poem the reader is made aware of its sublimity, that he or she is in the presence of a book deserving reverence in its reading and re-reading. Yet, at the same time that Milton evokes the portentousness of his overarching achievement, he also implicates, with the word "adventurous," his ambition in the much baser desires of Satan and fallen humankind. As has been noted, throughout the poem, Milton consistently associates the colonial word-group based around adventure with Satanic and fallen desire in the poem.[66] Yet, while his association of adventuring and exploration with inordinate desires may broadly impugn the imperial designs of European powers, here we see Milton demonstrating that he is fully aware of the satanic potential of his aspiring to theodicy even as he seeks to dispel this potential by calling upon the Holy Spirit for inspiration. Indeed, William Riggs has argued extensively that *Paradise Lost* seems to draw parallels between Milton's narrator and Satan at all relevant moments, "that Milton saw the potential in his own circumstances as aspiring singer of divine epic the consequences of Satan's 'ambitious aim.'" Riggs eventually falls back to the comfortable interpretation that Milton imagines these similarities so fully in order to distinguish and contrast his audacious aspirations from Satan's own desiring after divinity through a sustained contemplation of ambition tainted by overweening pride.[67] However, because of the very obviousness and persistence of the parallels between the narrator and Satan, the poem never seems to diffuse these anxieties fully despite Milton's recognition of his heavenly muse. Instead, the Satanic echoes cumulatively cast serious and insistent doubts over the poet's efforts at theodicy.

The connection between his grand poetic aims and sinful or satanic appetite briefly suggested in the opening invocation receives fuller treatment in Milton's second call to his muse in Book III, where Milton's poetic flight from Hell deliberately follows Satan's journey through Chaos. In this opening to Book III (lines 1–55), Milton plays between images of "dark" and "light" to parallel his "dark descent" into Hell in Books I and II with his own blindness and isolation, and the light of Heaven with an inward, divinely inspired, poetic creativity and exceptional vision. The "Audacious" (II: 931) voyage of Satan continues to echo in this passage in Milton's flight with "bolder wing" (13) as well as in his hesitant query "May I express thee unblamed?" (3) which worries over the sanctity of his poetic act. The prominent juxtaposition of the "utter" and "middle darkness" (16) of Hell and Chaos with Milton's own physical ailments and isolation from "the chearful wayes of men" (46) has a particularly human pathos that reminds us of the specific difficulties of his epic endeavor while eventually distancing the narrator from all of us who cannot see "things invisible to mortal sight" (55). Milton lingers here upon the darkness and frailty of the fallen condition and his own

dangerous descent into that darkness, epitomized by Hell, while eventually attempting to diffuse this complex of images in the celestial light of
his divine muse. Ultimately, the divine light does not blind the reader to
the very human lament in lines 22–50. Overall, the passage admits to the
potential for blasphemy, emphasized by the darkness from which Milton
writes, and places him poignantly within our fallen, earthly sphere. It also
removes the poet precisely because of this darkness from our world; he is
at once human yet separate and his specific worries over his epic ambitions admit to the mixed blessings of such a position.[68]

Milton's privileged yet uncertain position here has an analogue in the
exchanges between Adam and Raphael in Books VII and VIII, where
Adam, privileged himself with the presence of a divine messenger, presses
his heavenly guest for more information about the mysterious workings of
the cosmos. These exchanges express a deep ambivalence, typical in the
poem, over the human thirst for knowledge. After Raphael relates the fall
of Satan and his crew, Adam, recovering from the shock of this story, is
"Led on, yet sinless, with desire to know" (VII: 61). The qualification
absolves Adam from any wrongdoing while it simultaneously assumes the
potential for sinfulness in such a desire. This desire for knowledge seems
to proceed naturally in Adam, "as one whose drouth/Yet scarce allay'd still
eyes the current streame,/Whose liquid murmur heard new thirst excites"
(66–8). Perhaps Milton alludes here to Eve's own "vain desire" shortly
after she awakes from her birth, hears a "murmuring sound" (IV: 453) and
becomes enraptured by her own reflection in a lake, an allusion that
associates Adam's desire with the vain self-infatuation of Eve. The adverbs
"yet" and "still" in the lines point up that Adam's thirst is potentially
unquenchable, and clearly in need of control as Raphael later moralizes:
"But Knowledge is as food, and needs no less/Her Temperance over
Appetite" (126–7). Later in Book VIII, Raphael tells Adam that we
"ought/Rather admire" the heavens (VIII: 74–5) and admonishes him
to "serve and feare" God, to "be lowlie wise" and to "Dream not of
other Worlds" (168–75). Just as his epic ambition could shade over into
devilish pride, the search for knowledge must be sharply circumscribed, a
path to worship, not an end in itself.

But Milton was far from an orthodox Calvinist Puritan; his Arminian
leanings, and that doctrine's emphasis on free will over predestination,
made him privilege the human search for truth. It is this search for spiritual and earthly truth that guides the creation of his pedagogical program
in *Of Education*, as well as the monumental task he sets himself in *De
Doctrina Christiana*, where he states firmly, in reference to his decision to

undertake the construction of his theological system, that "in religion as in other things, I discerned, God offers all his rewards not to those who are thoughtless and credulous, but to those who labor constantly and seek tirelessly after truth" (*CPW* VI: 120). Earlier in *Areopigatica*, Milton had forcefully argued that knowledge, of any sort, cannot corrupt the virtuous individual, and, further, that the dissemination of erroneous doctrine "known, read, and collated, are of main service & assistance toward the speedy attainment of what is truest" (*CPW* II: 513). At least in Book VIII, the discrepancy between Raphael's admonitions and Milton's firm belief in the efficacious spiritual search for knowledge expressed elsewhere may be attributed to the specifically scientific, and not spiritual, information Adam seeks. This seems to be Adam's understanding of the dangers of knowledge when he qualifies his questioning in Book VII by clarifying his purpose: "not to explore the secrets ask/Of his Eternal Empire, but the more/To magnifie his works, the more we know" (VII: 95–7). Yet in *Areopagitica*, Milton had lamented the censorship of Galileo and urged the English nation from the tents of Kedar, "to discover onward things more remote from our knowledge" (*CPW* II: 550). This latter phrase notably comes at a moment in which Milton specifically advocates the examination and reformation not only of spiritual doctrine, but also of "the rule of life both economical and political." The exchanges between Adam and Raphael in *Paradise Lost*, on the other hand, are remarkably equivocal regarding Adam's desires to know, even when he seems on safe spiritual ground; the moral proscription to "serve and fear" remarkably far from the militant confidence that Milton expresses in *Areopagitica* and elsewhere. Instead of rewarding those who "seek tirelessly after truth," God may in fact construct these puzzles "perhaps to move/His laughter at thir quaint Opinions wide" (VIII: 76–7).[69]

At least rhetorically, *Areopagitica* is a profoundly optimistic nationalist text. In 1644, Milton could still vividly envision, despite the Presbyterian leanings of the Parliament and its support for licensing, a nation of scholars, "sitting by their studious lamps, musing, searching, revolving new notions and idea's," moving progressively towards religious and political reformation through the open exchange of ideas (*CPW* II: 554). That Raphael admits God may have concealed some truths to laugh at our endeavors highlights that Milton's faith in the ability of the English nation to ascertain some truths had been badly shaken by the time he wrote these lines in *Paradise Lost*. Raphael's warnings express more darkly the unquenchable desire for knowledge, and hint, through the naturalized languages of thirst and hunger, that, in fact, certain answers will never be adequately discovered. To be sure, Milton's faith specifically in the progress of the English nation had taken on water previously. In 1648–9, as the Rump moved away from strictly republican forms of government, Milton bemoaned the English nation's inability to form a proper polity. In the latter years of the Protectorate, Milton grew increasingly despondent as Cromwell's government more and more took on the trappings of monarchy.[70] However, in his epic poem, the search for knowledge at times appears intrinsically dangerous and unwise, no longer merely a failure of the English nation to follow the steps that knowledge illuminates for it. The loss of faith evinced in these passages in *Paradise Lost* can be seen to arise, much like Hobbes and George Sikes's doubts over the powers of reason to overrule error, out of an attempt to comprehend the failure of their respective causes. The extent that Milton's poem contains traces of a Calvinist doubt over the efficacy of human endeavor illuminates the impact of defeat and exile upon it.

However, while Hobbes and Sikes's faltering faith in reason underlies a more radical authoritarian or Calvinist turn, Milton's poem seems to consider or dwell upon the potential for human fallibility without derogating completely human endeavor.[71] As I have noted, by the late 1640s, Milton had come to embrace his own form of Arminianism that emphasized the unmistakable ability of humans to choose freely a godly or sinful life. The poem itself seems variously assertive and ambivalent about the freedom of the human will, particularly in the insistent, if somewhat painful, divine justifications of the fall in Books III and X. Milton's God expresses the doctrinal "justification" promised in the poem in these books where he denies Calvinist predestination since

> When Will and Reason (Reason also is choice)
> Useless and vain, of freedom both despoild,
> Made passive both, had serv'd necessitie,
> Not mee. (III: 108–11)

The divine rejection of predestination here is predicated upon an active obedience from man, an active human reason that has its parallel in the militant Christian search for truth that we see imagined in *Areopagitica* and *De Doctrina*. Thus, during the course of Raphael's first admonition, as much as the angel warns Adam against pushing against the boundaries of human knowledge, he also admits that "To ask or search I blame thee not, for Heav'n/Is as a Book of God before thee set" (VIII: 66–7). In these moments, the poem doctrinally argues the necessity and efficacy of an active human reason, while admitting practically the profound and intrinsic dangers that come with this activity. And yet, as Stephen Fallon has clarified, the poem remains inconsistent in its Arminianism and its doctrinal conclusions, particularly in the critical speeches in Book III.[72] For as much as Milton's God defensively outlines human freedom in the lines above, in his very next speech he also elaborates upon a more Calvinist conception of the elect:

> Some I have chosen of peculiar grace
> Elect above the rest; so is my will:
> The rest shall hear me call, and oft be warned
> Thir sinful state, and to appease betimes
> Th'incensed Deitie, while offerd grace
> Invites (III: 183–8)

Lines 183–4 almost seem an insertion in their seemingly contradictory adherence to "peculiar grace" for the elect amidst two speeches that, at least on the surface, advocate freedom of choice. Yet, they point up the underlying ambiguities that run throughout these speeches concerning the nature of this choice, perhaps embodied most concisely in the ambiguous "saved who will" of line 173 (is the "will" here transitive or intransitive?). The overall effect of reading the two speeches by God in Book III is similar to the feeling one receives from reading *The Readie and Easie Way*. In both the politics of *The Readie and Easie Way* and the theology of *Paradise Lost* (and I should add, in the contradictory vision of the audience for *Paradise Lost*), Milton seemed increasingly attracted to the comforting vision of a chosen few, while paradoxically adhering to a firm faith in republican and Arminian right reason, a faith that at this point seems perhaps closer to nostalgia.

God does not come off well in his first appearance in the poem, and not only because of his inconsistent theology. Ever since William Empson set out to answer "neo-Christian" criticism with his sustained reading of and attack upon Milton's God, readers have noted the disturbingly authoritarian and querulous character of the divine in Book III.[73] Usefully, whereas previous critics had sought to explain away the difficulties of Milton's God, either by attributing them to a failure of creativity in the poet or comprehension in the reader, more recent work has argued that these difficulties are integral to the poem and reveal a Milton agonizing over divine justification in the moments he wrote his epic.[74] Generally, an authoritarian, unattractive God has seemed strange to many in a poem seeking to "justify the ways of God," and yet, in the context of Milton's poetic oeuvre, an authoritarian God's appearance here in the foreground of Milton's picture of heaven as the poet struggles over divine justification should perhaps come as no surprise. After all, at previous moments of crisis Milton's imagination seems instinctively to have turned to visions of a harsher divinity both for questioning and, at best, ambivalent resolution, most notably in Sonnets 7 and 19. In both sonnets, the poetic outcries (if I may call them that) originate from Milton's anxious recollection of the God of the parable of the talents, "all-judging Jove," who sits and weighs the shortcomings of those below. To some extent, the same godhead appears at the opening of Book III, ruling intractably on the sins of humankind while the Son pitifully intercedes on our behalf:

> He with his whole posterity must die,
> Die he or justice must; unless for him
> Some other able, and as willing, pay
> The rigid satisfaction, death for death. (III: 209–13)

These lines are perhaps the harshest of the epic; they are also the closest Milton comes to a poetic expression of the doctrine of atonement. The implications of blood sacrifice in these lines, and in atonement generally – a wrathful God accepting the Son as a scapegoat for the sins of human-kind – seem to have made Milton queasy throughout his religious life.[75] Beyond the Talionic logic behind atonement, Milton also seems to have balked at the potential Calvinism that an over-reliance on Christ's sacri-fice entailed. So here in Book III and in Sonnets 7 and 19, Milton remains elusive as to the extent to which divine judgment correlates to human endeavor. What I would like to emphasize, however, is the consistency with which Milton engages with what are for him the most agonizing characteristics of divine power, his absolute authority and irreversible judgment. Just as in the poem generally he engages with his most sincere doubts over the efficacy of human knowledge, doubts that are concom-itant with exile, in his vision of an authoritarian God, he seeks an artistic order to darker visions of the divine certainly encouraged by the negative political and religious judgments of 1659–60. Notably, *Paradise Lost* fore-grounds these doubts without ever resolving them beyond the poem's momentary, if persistent, assertions of justification and epic achievement.

Indeed, we might see Milton's decision to write his epic at all as predicated upon as well as driving this ambivalent expression of human endeavor. His continued theoretical and doctrinal faith in free will and reason allows him to write, even demands that he attempt, a poetic theodicy. Recent scholarship that reads Milton's presumption to theodicy as, in part, a temptation to the reader misses the persistence of this Arminianism. The poem's entire logic and metaphoric structure cannot sustain much truth-value or pathos, if, as Stanley Fish has argued, Milton merely claims to "justify the ways of God to men" as an ironic means to a didactic end.[76] Further, when we consider the reality of the wide-ranging audience of *Paradise Lost*, a reality that I have argued could not have been lost on Milton as he wrote, the poem becomes a legitimate attempt to explain God to this audience. Yet, while Milton's epic engages with and explains God to its audience, it also remains aware of its distance from the authoritative and dominant discourses of the 1660s, of, so to speak, the inherent tendency of human reason to stray. That is, the disjunctions that Milton experienced from the English nation as a whole after 1658–9 made him firmly aware that human knowledge might be marked more by regression and failure than progression and providential assurance. *Paradise Lost* at once admits and explores this potential for failure at various points; yet it simultaneously presents itself as a compendium of the very human knowledge it calls into question. Michael Seidel has noted that exiled writers tend to create sustained, fictive worlds, what Walter Benjamin has called a "fragile, precious reality," in which they can inhabit a literary space that answers to and, in some ways, fills the gaps left by exile.[77] Milton's poem, in its epic ambitions to gather all genres and fields of knowledge, in its attempts to order the encyclopedic world it has created, may be seen as an attempt at a lasting monument to the value of human reason for both an author who sorely needed reassurance and a distant audience that sorely needed guidance. Milton evokes the hazards of the search for knowledge, just as he evokes the Satanic potential of his epic ambitions, both to warn his distant readers and to dwell on these hazards in an attempt to overreach them. And yet, the experience of exile makes one aware of just how provisional our imaginative structures are. The fissures and inconsistencies in *Paradise Lost*, whether theological, narrative or epistemological, show an author exploring this provisionality while the gestures towards epic sublimity and comprehensiveness show him seeking, but never attaining, an artistic wholeness that counteracts it.

Certainly, Milton's choice of the expulsion from the Garden as his epic subject resonates in this context of doubt. The story of Adam and Eve had lingered in Milton's imagination from, it seems, at least the early 1640s. For Milton, the fall stood as the source of "all our woe" because it permanently exiled humans from the divine presence of God and the resulting natural harmony that comes from this presence. As a result, our knowledge of the divine order was irrevocably ruptured and will remain so until the Second Coming. Thus, Milton understood the task of education and the search for truth as repairing "the ruins of our first parents by regaining to know God aright" (*CPW* II: 366–7). Yet, at the same time that the fall forced this permanent rupture and loss of harmony, in Milton's famous formulation from *Areopagitica*, from the apple: "the knowledge of good and evill as two twins cleaving together leapt forth into the World" (*CPW* II: 514). Milton's theological comprehension of the fall here is remarkable in its "cleaving" of our expanded capacity to understand good and evil together. It is this firm yoking of good and evil that justifies his embrace of heterodox opinions as he explores the limits of Christian theology in *De Doctrina*. It also allows Milton to imagine the search for truth in *Paradise Lost*, and his poem generally, at once as dangerous, even satanic, yet heroic and necessary. In a sense, his continued faith in his divine poetic calling retains its firmness through this "cleaving," even as Milton lost an authoritative, public voice with which to speak. That the knowledge of good and evil should remain inevitably linked once Adam and Eve had sinned helps to explain how the English reformation lost its way, even as it delineates an oppositional, heretical space whence Milton could write after 1658–9. The poem, as a whole, is a sustained lament on the indelible loss of the exile of our first parents as well as a profound exploration of the new world order enacted by that exile.

The fall and banishment of Adam and Eve, of course, has variously been told as a tale of the fall into a corrupt language due to a lost comprehension of the divine. The story in Genesis stands, essentially, as the Judeo-Christian ur-text for all subsequent exiles, just as Adam's naming of the animals often stands as the basis for epistemological theories predicated upon objective representation and a legitimate link between word and object. In *Of Education*, Milton saw the fall as a permanent loss of a divine language. Man's fallen language can come near only to "sensible things" through which, he posits, we can come at least to a partial understanding of "God and things invisible" (*CPW* II: 368–9). In Book IX, Adam seems to enact this loss of spiritual language immediately after he eats the fruit:

> Eve, now I see thou art exact of taste,
> And elegant, of Sapience no small part
> Since to each meaning savour we apply,
> And Palate call judicious (IX: 1017–20)

In each line, a more physical meaning intrudes upon the overt sense, as Adam yokes sensational meanings to more abstract terms. The puns

Milton plays with here imply suddenly that Adam is enacting a kind of violence upon the language that intimates a deeper loss of self-control, or perhaps honesty, with the terms of discourse. Later in Book XII, Michael tells Adam "but I perceave,/Thy mortal sight to fail; objects divine/Must needs impair and wearie human sense" (XII: 9–10); the adjective "mortal" implicates the fall in the failure of Adam to discern the divine clearly and for a sustained period. The fall effected a removal from the divine presence, and an ability to ascertain and express the spiritual clearly. The disjunction between spiritual and earthly language, already a difficulty before the fall as Raphael repeatedly notes, became greater as the divine image faded from our minds. In a sense, the Tower of Babel is a second effect of the fall, a repetition of the prideful sin of Adam and Eve. In Book XII, Milton recounts the episode, portraying the arrogance of Nimrod who incurs, through his prideful tower, the wrath of a "derisive God" with "great laughter" who sows "a jangling noise of words unknown" (XII: 55). God's derision might recall his imagined laughter at our proud attempts to understand the heavens, and reminds us that here human language becomes further debased through the successive sins of pride.

The Nimrod episode in Book XII is perhaps more remarkable, however, for its emphasis on Nimrod's place as the first monarch, and his unnatural abrogation of political power and concomitant tyranny. One of Milton's early readers singled out this passage for its republican leanings, chastising the poet for his continued attraction to old principles.[78] David Norbrook has recently noted the consistency in the pamphlets written on the eve of the restoration with which Milton attacks his adversaries by associating the return of monarchy with the return of a Babelian confusion of languages. In the republican tradition, Milton argued that the courtly, private interest that would return with monarchy would result in a corrupt amalgam of interested language that lacked the linguistic discipline that came with an active and virtuous citizenry.[79] At times in *The Readie and Easie Way*, his concerns over monarchic language manifested themselves in a Hobbesian authoritarianism in which the few control the many in the interest of general liberty. The similarity to Hobbes's own attempts to control semantics points up that Milton's sense of a Babelian confusion of privately interested language may not merely reflect his republican leanings, but more essentially is a reaction to the loss of linguistic authority that the possibility of defeat and political banishment entailed. In fact, the upheavals and exiles of the seventeenth century continuously ruptured the English language as the new political authority transformed the meanings of words such as "loyalty" and "obedience" while removing other words from the acceptable lexicons of power. The extent to which these terms, and the English language generally, was contested throughout the century made political or religious banishment a banishment from a confidence that the exiles' version of the language could operate definitively.

We can see this lost linguistic confidence throughout *Paradise Lost*, both in an overt nervousness over its own semantics, as well as in the insistent accumulations of meanings that seek to convey an aura of certainty to the poem. The poem does not merely elide or ignore the loss of linguistic authority that comes with exile. Indeed, the consistently spiritual and theological subject-matter of the poem forces Milton to examine, at various turns and at great length, the difficulties of expression that arise out of the specific work that his poem attempts, as well as out of writing generally. The crux of the problem lies in Raphael's admission to Adam in Book V as he embarks upon a description of the War in Heaven, and the poem is anything but clear at this moment:

> High matter thou injoinest me, O prime of men,
> Sad task and hard, for how shall I relate
> To human sense th'invisible exploits
> Of warring Spirits. . . . .
> . . . . and what surmounts the reach
> Of human sense, I shall delineate so,
> By lik'ning spiritual to corporal forms,
> As may express them best, though what if earth
> Be but the shadow of Heav'n, and things therein
> Each to other like, more than on earth is thought? (V: 563–77)[80]

Various critics have focused on the first four lines of this passage, David Loewenstein most recently, to emphasize the profound disjunction between heavenly and earthly epistemologies in Milton's mind. According to these critics, this disjunction explains the difficult politics of the exchanges in Heaven and Hell.[81] By having God and his minions speak seemingly in monarchic language, Milton didactically aims to illuminate the unbridgeable distance between heavenly and earthly politics. Ten years earlier, Milton had forcefully separated the two realms in the *Defensio* in response to the analogy between heaven and earth that lies behind Salmasius's divine right theory:

As to your saying it was 'patterned on the example of the one God,' who, in fact, is worthy of holding on earth power like that of God but some person who far surpasses all others and even resembles God in goodness and wisdom? The only such person, as I believe, is the son of God whose coming we look for. (*CPW* IV, pt. 1: 428)

Milton insists upon a distinction between heavenly monarchy, which is justified due to the divine nature of its king, and earthly government, where no single leader should rule, since all are of the same nature. The first part of Raphael's answer to Adam above makes Milton far from heterodox on this subject; other republican theorists of the period, including Algernon Sidney in *Court Maxims*, argued the impossibility of drawing parallels between divine and human polities.

Yet, by ignoring the closing lines of Raphael's hesitation here, Loewenstein and others have imparted an aura of semantic comfort to the poem that simply does not obtain. Just as Milton establishes the distinction between heavenly and earthly representation, he quickly calls this distinction into question, leaving the status of Raphael's, and by extension Milton's, narrative of the War in Heaven uncertain. Does Milton's poem actually come closer in its representation of the divine than Raphael at first allows? In fact, to note the poem admits and charts a disjunction between heavenly and earthly politics and their languages, as Loewenstein and various other critics have, begs the essential question that Raphael asks Adam in the passage above, and indeed, the poem constantly asks itself: how does one relate heaven, and its divine and angelic world, to human readers in an earthly language? As much as Milton might at times separate the civic worlds of the godly and the earthly, and as much as this separation might help to explain the counter-intuitive political sympathies of the poem, the poem itself can mean only through a constant allegory that relates heavenly deeds and occurrences through a human language. We can see, throughout the poem, Milton struggling with, and indeed foregrounding, the inherent difficulties of describing in detail the divine world, particularly the War in Heaven. In Books V and VI, for example, Milton seems at pains to justify his use of "days" in the heavenly chronology. The first effort somewhat weakly has Raphael parenthetically noting to Adam after evening comes to heaven and Satan retires to his northern seat, "(For wee have also our Eevning and our Morn,/Wee ours for change delectable, not need)" (V: 628–9). Later, at the opening of Book VI and a dawn in heaven, Milton at more length explains:

> There is a Cave
> Within the Mount of God, fast by his Throne,
> Where light and darkness in perpetual round

Lodge and dislodge in turns, which makes through Heav'n
Grateful vicissitude, like Day and Night (VI: 4–8)

The cave overtly serves to excuse the poet's application of human chro-
nological terms such as "Morn," "Eevning," and "Night" to demarcate
the passage of time in heaven. Yet the phrase "Grateful vicissitude" also
draws attention to the artfulness of the construction, the work that lies
behind both the divine and human creation here. The lengths to which
Milton goes here and elsewhere in his poem to justify his poetic methods
draw attention to both the supreme linguistic difficulties he faced in
writing his epic and the figurative work that he completes in attempting
to bridge these difficulties. Further, by consistently foregrounding this
work, Milton undermines the poem's own claims to certainty; a nervousness hovers over the poem's figural representations, just as it hovers over
its poetic aspirations and its faith in human knowledge.

The divine subject that Milton attempts in his epic drives much of the
nervousness that the poem displays over the semantic security of its language. However, *Paradise Lost* seems more often than not to draw attention to its own aporia, its own expressive difficulties, as a matter of
linguistic course rather than theological nicety. The epic invocations
that trail downward through the poem display this poetic nervousness
over semantics. In Book III, for example, the leading "or's" in lines 2
and 7, as well as the hesitant "May I express thee unblamed?" throw
considerable doubt upon the correctness of the invocation at the same
time that they praise and make sublime Milton's holy muse. Similarly,
at the opening to Book VII, where Milton resituates his poetic labor,
the epic naming in line 1 is immediately undercut with "by that
name/If rightly thou art call'd" (VII: 1–2). These invocations, and the
epic generally, construct a poetics of option and negation.[82] Indeed,
a glance at the concordance will reveal a detailed list of words with
negative prefixes such as "im-," "in-" and "un-" as well as the preponderance of "or," particularly in the first eight books. While these poetics
emphasize the extent to which the poem remains beyond the bounds
of human expressions, and thus the sublime and awful nature of its
subject, they also call into question the very truth-value of Milton's
poetic endeavor. The didactic exercise built into these words might be
to make the reader recognize the impossibility of attaining a final expression of truth; thus, in Book VIII, Raphael's hesitant litany of "seems" and
"or" mark his guarded exposition of the varying astronomical theories
only to instruct Adam and the reader that a final solution matters not to

the godly on earth. The "or's" and other linguistic qualifiers that litter the poem thus become a series of shrugs that are designed to train the reader that the only choice that finally matters concerns the right worship of God.

However, by concentrating on the didactic ends of the poem in these uncertain passages, we underestimate the amount of time that, and indeed the seriousness with which, the poem engages with some of the incommensurable options it presents. That is, as much as the poem is designed to teach us what we do not know, it also displays and explores the full scope of human knowledge, from botany to astronomy, from theology to history. The linguistic uncertainties inherent in the poem's poetics of negation and option, and its consistent concern over expression generally, thus should not be seen merely as a Calvinist exercise in displaying semantic incommensurability. Indeed, the "or's" in the poem, as much as presenting uncertain or unresolved options, also are accumulative; the poem itself is built largely out of this accumulation of human knowledge. Further, just as the poem attempts to encompass the full scope of human knowledge, its language pushes the boundaries of semantic capability, digging for etymologically obscure meanings at some points, deriving novel or remarkably contemporary Latinate meanings at others.

Thomas Corns has recently challenged the widespread perception of Milton's poem as a violence upon the English language, formulated most famously in T.S. Eliot's remarks upon the poem:

Every distortion of construction, the foreign idiom, the use of a word in a foreign way or with a meaning of the foreign word from which it is derived rather than the accepted meaning in English, every idiosyncrasy is a particular act of violence which Milton has been the first to commit.[83]

Corns has rightfully noted the overstatement in Eliot's criticism, an overstatement arising largely out of Eliot's own critical prejudices and agenda.[84] Corns is also correct to point out that the poem is aggressively vernacular and novel, participating in and driving the rapid transformation of English as the influx of Latin and French words continued in the late seventeenth century.[85] What we experience as linguistic obtuseness is partly, in fact, linguistic novelty. Yet Corns also tends to overstate the ease with which readers read the poem even in 1667–8. We can assume, based upon the publisher's request from Milton to add a justification of the poem's blank verse to the second issue and the content of that apology, that readers were perplexed syntactically by the lack of rhyme and considerable enjambment in the poem. In Nicholas von Maltzahn's investigation of early readers' reactions, further, we find that the initial reaction of many readers was one of unworthiness, an unworthiness that might be construed as arising out of the difficulties the poem presented to the reader.

The difficult syntactic and etymological structures, as well as the profusion of negation and options, impress upon the reader that the English language is under constant strain in this poem, particularly in the first few books. The poem seems particularly worried over semantic uncertainty, a worry that can be explained largely by Milton's experience as an interior exile. After the return of Charles II, the discourses within which and definitions of keywords with which Milton operated, be they republican, "Puritan," or anti-monarchic, were consistently delegitimated. As a result, the ways in which the English language meant for the exiled poet would have been particularly unstable. *Paradise Lost* consistently admits this instability, while, through its methods of accumulation, difficulty and novelty, attempting to construct a poetic world that counteracts it. Further, while the construction of the poem, for Milton, might have at least sporadically filled the linguistic gap created by his removal from the discourses of authority, the poem itself also negotiated this gap by anticipating a new relationship with its wide and diverse readership. As an exile, Milton had lost the authoritative space that he had held throughout the 1640s and '50s. The surface difficulties of the poem, perhaps most clearly embodied for contemporary readers in the choice of blank verse, thus place the poem and the poet in a sublime sphere just as its epic invocations do. *Paradise Lost* crosses over into the London print market from its author's interior exile by forcing its readers to recognize its difficulty and authority, while also elaborating upon the shifting and fallen semantics upon which the poem, and all writing, is based.

CHAPTER 4

Sybil's leaves: Dryden and the historiography of exile

In the closing years of the seventeenth century, a number of "Miltons" circulated through the bookstalls of London, from Jacob Tonson's ornate 1688 edition of *Paradise Lost*, complete with its own set of plates and a dedication from John Dryden, to the reprint of *Eikonoklastes* (1690), Milton's vehement, anti-monarchical attack on Charles I's *Eikon Basilike*. At the end of a century marked by conflict, the London print world seemed intent on reevaluating the work of a man who had been at the center of that conflict, and who, in its aftermath, had turned from prose polemic to epic poetry. The various afterlives of Milton in the years immediately following his death tell one of the more remarkable and complex stories of authorial revaluation in the early modern period; remarkable for the profound transformation of Milton from radical republican polemicist to the author of England's great epic poem, a transformation enacted most prominently in Tonson's lavish reprint; complex because, alongside this transformation of Milton into an English "classic," came the reprint of *Eikonoklastes*, Whig plagiarisms of this and other of Milton's political pamphlets, and, most substantially, a collected edition of Milton's *Historical and Political Works*, printed in 1699 and accompanied by John Toland's partisan *Life of Milton*. This second group of books unmistakably enlisted our deceased author as the primary spokesman for an anti-monarchic, oppositional Whig agenda.[1] While the revisions enacted upon "Milton" tell a compelling story in their own right about the public roles that author and poet entail, I would like instead to concentrate on one participant in this revaluation, John Dryden, as a means to opening up an inquiry into Dryden's own concerns with the cultural and political status of the author, concerns, after 1688, inevitably driven much like Milton's after 1660 by his banishment from the center of English political and public life.

Dryden's relationship with Milton was a complex one, shaded as it was by Dryden's appreciation for the poetic achievement of his contemporary in spite of their seemingly polarized political allegiances. Recent work has shown the various ways in which Dryden responded to Milton's heightening of the poetic and linguistic register and his sublime theodicy, from the libertine appropriation in *The State of Innocence* to the high satiric echoes in *Absalom and Achitophel*.[2] Yet in the final decade, amidst the intense rethinking of Milton's life and oeuvre that took place primarily through the 1688 *Paradise Lost*, the republications of his prose works, and the introductions and secondary materials that accompanied them, and amidst Dryden's own removal from the discourses of authority, we can clearly see Dryden renewing and expanding his relationship with Milton and his epic. While abandoning his own epic ambitions to translate classical authors, Dryden memorialized Milton's poem, most famously in his lines on *Paradise Lost* that were attached prominently to Tonson's 1688 edition: "Three Poets, in three distant *Ages* born, *Greece, Italy* and *England* did adorn."[3] The surprising elevation of Milton to unmatched classical poet detaches his former contemporary from the immediacies of recent English history and culture.[4] Instead, Milton joins a small community of great epic poets far from the political animosities and associations that the name "Milton" continued to conjure in other contexts. Dryden's lines, further, place the former Poet Laureate as a literary critic evaluating the superior literary talent of his poetic peer.

As much as Dryden participated, perhaps even in part believed, in the apotheosis of Milton into a "classical poet," we might also see Dryden, throughout his later criticism, considering *Paradise Lost* as a site of attachment, even identification, rather than distance and failure. It is evident from his detailed references to Milton in the criticism and letters of the 1690s that Dryden revisited his contemporary's poetry at great length in the final years of his life. In doing so, he often drew distinct parallels between Milton's achievement and his own efforts at classical translation. For example, in *A Discourse Concerning the Original and Progress of Satire* (1693), Dryden observes that Milton's "Thoughts are elevated, his Words Sounding, and that no man has so happily Copy'd the Manner of *Homer*; or so copiously translated his *Grecisms*, and the *Latin* Elegancies of *Virgil*" (*Works* IV: 15). In characterizing Milton's writing as translation, Dryden seems to be thinking in terms of his three-tiered definition of translation, first formulated in the *Preface* to *Ovid's Epistles*; yet, even so, it aligns Milton's poetic achievement with Dryden's sustained interest in the 1690s in classicism and the importation of Roman elegance into England through translation.[5] Five years later, in the *Dedication of the Aeneis*, Dryden would describe his completed Virgil in similar terms, boasting that he was "the first *Englishman*, perhaps, who made it his design to copy [Virgil] in his Numbers, his choice of Words, and his placing them for the sweetness of the sound" (*Works* V: 319). In Dryden's mind, both he and Milton, and Spenser before them, had succeeded in translating the elegance and stature of the Latin tongue as far as possible into the more barbaric language of modern English. More generally, Dryden envisions the two poets operating at a similarly elevated level as custodians of classical learning and literary refinement. Thus, earlier in the *Dedication*, Dryden's discussion of Milton's scales from Book IV of *Paradise Lost* takes on the air of a learned discourse with another poet rather than an antagonistic criticism of a rival.[6] As David Bywaters has argued, the literariness of these prefaces, when, for example, Dryden debated with Milton over the interpretation of the Virgilian "machines," enters Dryden into an authoritative sphere of discourse denied him by the immediate realities of his political and religious situation.[7]

However, we should be wary of the consistency of Dryden's distancing of Milton's politics, as invited by the lines on *Paradise Lost*. As the republications of Milton's Civil War polemical tracts attest, the name "Milton" still held powerful political associations in the London print world as country Whigs, particularly the Calves-Head Club and John Toland, sought to revive Milton's republican politics, his insistence on the liberties of the people in the face of tyrannic governance, in the service of anti-Williamite polemic. Dryden certainly remained far from an outright republican in the 1690s; yet we should not, indeed cannot, so readily dismiss Dryden's attraction to Milton's oppositional politics once William had solidified his power. Luke Milbourne's clear exaggeration that "Tho we own Mr. D. may be a Republican now, it's but agreeable to his Character" only makes sense because of the scattered, yet recurring, republican sympathies of Dryden's late poetry and criticism. More generally, the Jacobites created and maintained a strong and lasting political union with radical Whigs during the 1690s, a union driven by both practical necessity and common ideological antipathy towards the "corrupt" policies of the Dutch, Williamite court.[8] Dryden, in particular, praises just such an oppositional politics in the panegyric on his Whig cousin John Driden later in the decade, a poem that elucidates the personal and particular ways in which this strange alliance could be formulated. In this poem, Dryden espouses an anti-Williamite, country agenda in his examination of notions of personal and public loyalty.[9]

In one of the more politically elusive passages of the *Dedication of the Aeneis* (*Works* V: 280–1), Dryden asserts Virgil's principled republicanism while questioning the legitimacy of Augustus's claim to the throne in decidedly republican language. He then continues:

And I meddle not with others: being, for my own Opinion, of *Montaign's* Principles, that an Honest Man ought to be contented with that Form of Government, and with those Fundamental Constitutions of it, which he receiv'd from his Ancestors, and under which himself was Born: Though at the same time he confess'd freely, that if he could have chosen his Place of Birth, it shou'd have been at *Venice*: Which for many Reasons I dislike, and am better pleas'd to have been born an *English* Man. (*Works* V: 281)

The passage exhibits many of the qualities of the rest of the *Dedication* as Dryden obliquely critiques the revolutionary settlement while displaying prominently his own national pride. Yet, while we may see, in the passage, a disgruntled Jacobite upset at the corruption of the English "ancient constitution" by William's usurpation, the obliquity of Dryden's allusions to the Williamite regime takes an unmistakably republican path, just as Dryden's criticism of Augustus does immediately prior to this period. Dryden seems purposefully to occlude the nature of England's "Fundamental Constitutions," simultaneously inviting and denying the republican overtones of his nationalistic concerns.

"To My Honour'd Kinsman" tends to display a similar anti-monarchism as it seeks to praise the political conservatism and constancy of Dryden's cousin in the face of the Dutch corruption of William's court, often drawing upon traditional English republican defenses of an independent, landed gentry. Interestingly, Dryden's epistle to his cousin seems to have been one of the many moments in his final years in which Milton's epic shadowed his creative endeavors. An awareness of Milton's travails, along with his own now marginal political status, perhaps enabled Dryden to consider Milton's republican politics with newfound sympathy and understanding, particularly as he sought ideological justification for his opposition to the king of England. In his panegyric to Driden, glimpses of a pre-lapsarian Paradise flit through Dryden's depiction of Chesterton and support his digressive attack on physicians, while his praise of the bachelor Driden rests, in part, on an Adamic model from which Eve is conspicuously absent. The local concerns over regeneration and medicine are largely Dryden's own; however, it is through his consideration of his cousin as another Adam that Dryden nostalgically commemorates a conviction and faithfulness above the "slippery thrones" of revolutionary politics.[10] The associations are subtle, yet we might envision Dryden reading *Paradise Lost* as Milton's own nostalgic reflection on and statement of constancy and stability in the face of political loss and defeat. Indeed, Milton's poem seems to have been a touchstone in his attempts to justify his newfound resolution in the face of powerful opposition.[11] In contemplating his position as a prominent writer, indeed the former Laureate of England, now forced into minority political and religious status, it would have been instructive for him to turn to the Miltonic poems of the restoration.[12] Notably, it is in his defense of his Catholic conversion and ostensible religious faith, *The Hind and the Panther*, that we find Dryden operating in the Miltonic idiom with a renewed energy and interest.

* * *

In his reconsideration of his former contemporary, of Milton's constancy, convictions and even politics, Dryden forged a new relationship with the immediate English literary past. Indeed, we can see Dryden's interest in literary criticism and translations, in evaluating and recreating both classical and English literary monuments, as an effort to comprehend his own status as an author exiled from the world he knew and enjoyed, and, in conjunction, to formulate his relationship to the literary and political past. An exile's mind is inordinately concerned with the past and the future rather than the present. History becomes a crucial link to a time and space before displacement. The exile's interest in history can help him or her to rewrite the past in order to elide the physical or mental distance from a lost world while justifying the cause of this distance. The New England Puritans sought to write a history of the Church of England, featuring their Independent beliefs as the centerpiece of an English Protestantism that started with the Marian exiles. Dryden's erudite, and often arcane, discussions of classical works, his repeated gestures towards a genealogy of English authors, similarly link his marginal status to a legitimating past. Dryden, to be sure, was from the start of his career exceedingly concerned with issues of both literary and familial lineage, perhaps the first author to operate with such a highly developed sense of the "burden of the past." However, in the final decade of his life, this burden seems to press more intently upon him as he almost exclusively translates classical authors, often contributing lengthy critical prefaces that ruminate upon literature and its histories. In these prefaces and translations, Dryden works to fashion his own versions of literary history and criticism after 1688, creating a classical and English heritage that associates his poetic achievements and critical pronouncements with an aura of national validity.

The pressures of the final decade of Dryden's life, and their emanations in his criticism, drama and translations of this period, have come under increasing examination in recent years. The occasion of the tercentenary of Dryden's death in 2000 marked a relative outpouring of new criticism on England's former Poet Laureate.[13] What is particularly remarkable about this recent surge in Drydenian criticism has been the extent to which these treatments focus on the output of Dryden's final decade. Paul Hammond, extensively, and Tanya Caldwell, exclusively, investigate the translations of the last years of Dryden's life, while out of the twenty-one essays in the two commemorative volumes, eleven of them take as their primary interest the last poems and translations of Dryden's life. Part of the interest in the late Dryden, unprecedented in its implicit validation of Dryden's late work above his heroic drama or poetry of the Exclusion Crisis, might result from Dryden's removal from the authoritative and authorized roles that he held under Charles II. The Dryden of the 1690s, disappointed, sequestered and generally at odds with the ideologies of Williamite power, in many ways appeals more immediately to our modern conceptions of the artist and of the circumstances of the literary imagination. In this chapter, I would like to reconsider this removal as a removal into what we might term an "internal exile" in an attempt to comprehend more fully the preoccupations, the complex political and literary resonances, of Dryden's late period.

Indeed, a psychology of "internal exile" can usefully explain many of the rhetorical structures and habitual imaginative turns in his later poetry and prose prefaces as he increasingly turned to literary criticism and translation, to evaluations and recreations of both classical and English literary monuments. Exile entails both a sharp break in the quotidian existence of one's life and a removal from that which is most familiar and comforting; it involves dislocation, disorientation and division. As the exile is removed from familiar material, structural and familial surroundings, his or her sense of a coherent identity and continuous history is ruptured. As we have seen, the exile often attempts to create an imaginative, peaceful space, from which he or she can reflect, ruminate and write away from the pressures of dislocation. The self-conscious assuredness of the literary world provides a comfortable space within and from which these authors speak. Increasingly after 1688, Dryden found this space within the translations and critical prefaces that accompanied them. The prose criticism and the translations enabled Dryden to reformulate his literary and political relationships with the classical and English past after the Glorious Revolution in an effort to comprehend his own status as an author exiled from the center of the political and literary landscape. In particular, through his sustained engagement with Virgil in the middle years of the 1690s, Dryden sought to re-conceive and reorient his lifelong relationship with his "master." In doing so, Dryden constructed a complex and multivalent public voice in his *Dedication to the Aeneis* that surprisingly drew upon, and in part drove, the Tacitean turn in Virgilian criticism that read Virgil as a disappointed republican publicly writing for the good of Augustan Rome. In this rewriting of Virgil we can see Dryden mapping a cultural geography that answered to the complex exigencies of his experience as an author writing from a marginal position for a diverse readership. It is through an understanding of Dryden's negotiation of this distance that we can remain sensitive to the diversity and novelty of the rhetorical moves and habitual structures of thought that populate the *Dedication* and that arise out of his explorations of what it meant to write as a public author during his final decade. Importantly, Dryden's turn to translation not only allowed him access to a legitimating past, it also drew attention to his own presence as idiosyncratic mediator with this past and allowed him to inhabit and reign sovereign over these created worlds as he impressed his own self-conscious presence upon them in front of his readers' eyes. The surprising rewriting of Virgil is one example of this impression. More generally, the casual idiosyncrasy of these critical ruminations show Dryden operating eclectically with a diversity of associations as his political and personal allegiances shift at surprising turns. My use of the critical terminology of exile, then, redirects our attention away from attempting to identify a singular, consistent politics in Dryden's late work, since his allegiances remain irreducibly personal and often deliberately so, and instead towards Dryden's ruminations on and reactions to his own fate in Williamite England. Although we can see Dryden returning consistently to specific themes – the difficulties of public expression in the face of political and religious disappointment, the fragility of succession and posterity, the burden of the literary past – these themes do not constitute a consistent Jacobite poetics, but rather a complicated public psychology of expression through which Dryden asserts a willfully personal identity in an attempt to override the political and religious disruptions of the final years of his life.

Dryden's late translations and prefaces have increasingly come under scrutiny as covert, yet studied, resistance to the Revolutionary settlement and William's government. In many readings of Dryden's translations of

Juvenal and Persius, Virgil and Tacitus, the classical author and milieu serve as a cover for the author's own insertion of Jacobite principles and critiques of the present regime.[14] The work on the Jacobite allusions in Dryden's late work has been important, usefully moving us away from viewing Dryden's turn to classical translation as a retreat into the comforts of a distant literary past. Yet the Dryden we receive from much of this work is a writer who hides his true political and literary intentions behind the mask of classical authors; the modern critic, in turn, becomes the privileged decoder of an otherwise unintelligible text, the key to which is a tautological understanding of these texts through an already established set of political sympathies that are then "uncovered" in the text.[15] In many ways, this "hermeneutics of censorship" has tended to obscure the decidedly multivalent potential of Dryden's late writing by allowing critics to write off any allusive complexity as simple obfuscation, a literary "red herring" for the eye of the licensor. Usefully, recent criticism of Dryden's latest poems has gone some way to restoring the complexity of Dryden's thought in his final years to our picture of the former poet laureate. Through these efforts, we can begin to glimpse the diverse and various strategies of expression that Dryden employed, not merely to criticize covertly, but also to engage with and to comprehend the entirely new cultural and political landscapes of the 1690s.[16] My work on Dryden as an "interior exile" admits the complexity of Dryden's politics in the last decade, although its primary interest lies rather with the psychology and the self-creation that is enacted through this complexity, through what can be termed the "hide-and-seek" qualities of much of the later criticism. It is this psychology of exile that we can see driving and enabling the distinct personality and prosodic qualities of the late Dryden as the author sought a new public voice after the loss of his political and public authority.[17]

I would like to pause for a moment to consider the cultural and political distance that Dryden felt, and, more generally, my use of the critical vocabulary of exile in discussing Dryden's work of the 1690s. Dryden never left for St. Germain, nor, of course, did he ever visit his exiled monarch in France. Paul Monod, who has recently worked extensively on the Jacobite communities in St. Germain and the British Isles, dismisses Dryden as "a commercially minded Jacobite who continued to produce stage works and lucrative translations in London, but never visited St. Germain."[18] Of the commercial success of Dryden's translations there can be little doubt. Such success draws attention to the fact that the circumstances of the production of *The Works of Virgil* had very few similarities with the journeys of other exilic texts. Unlike the arduous and uncertain journey of Nathaniel Ward's *The Simple Cobler of Aggawam* from New England to London, unlike Hobbes's tentative release of *Leviathan* into a divided England, unlike even the bare, notably stark, presentation of *Paradise Lost*, Dryden's Virgil enjoyed and advertised the "patronage" of the most eminent publisher of the day, as well as a multitude of powerful political and cultural figures from both sides of the political spectrum.[19] Yet we should recall that these other texts, much like Dryden's, expected and anticipated the broad, and politically diverse, London readership. Indeed, much of the rhetorical force and innovation of each of these exilic works, from Ward's comical, overdetermined Marprelatian vocabulary, to Hobbes's idiosyncratic semantic lessons, lies in the geographically and/or ideologically distant author's reaction to the expectation of a wide-ranging metropolitan audience. Contrary to our expectations, and to much of the work that has been done on those who wrote from France or New England, the exilic text is marked not by its exclusive audience, but by a sense of "in-betweenness" as it crosses back into the English print market. In viewing exilic texts in this manner as individual, transitional events, rather than as allegories of exilic experience, I have attempted to delineate more sharply the specific construction of a rhetoric or poetics of exile in each text. My preoccupation with the movement of the exilic text, moreover, does not downplay the profound psychological and political upheavals that exile entailed, since it draws attention to the act of writing as conjunctive, one that filled "the interstices between the literary activity of two homes, one lost, one not yet familiar."[20]

In thus defining exile, I have tried to keep the specific disjunctions of each exile's experience firmly in view. Analyzing Dryden's writing in the 1690s as exile literature draws attention to the sharp sense of distance and loss that Dryden felt after 1688. Despite undoubted economic and political pressures, Dryden remained loyal to his departed king and to the Catholic religion until his death in 1700. While Dryden did distrust the intransigent policies of James and his closest advisors, he nonetheless remained steadfast to the Jacobite cause as well as persistently opposed to the revolutionary settlement and the Williamite regime. The hardships this caused him were quite immediate, even geographic, as he was forced to move, albeit a short distance, to the suburbs of Soho to avoid the double taxation laws against Catholics living in the city of London, and perhaps public harassment.[21] In the dedication of *Don Sebastian* to Philip Sidney, Dryden articulates in a moment of self-pity a detachment from city life as he thanks Leicester for remembering "a poor Inhabitant of his Suburbs," a rhetorical effort, at the very least, to delineate his marginal status (*Works* XV: 62). Moreover, as a Catholic, Dryden no longer could practice his religion in public, but joined his co-religionists in celebrating the sacraments in private. The Catholic community in England was mainly centered on the houses of country gentry, a fact that imparted a cloistered, surreptitious and detached quality to these interactions.[22] While the English Catholics of the 1690s maintained a pacifist, largely inactive political position, they continued in their private loyalty to their exiled king.[23] Their continued loyalty would have compounded their sense of distance as it prevented them from committing politically to the Williamite regime, as well as encouraging them to contemplate the plight of their fellow English sufferers in exile at St. Germain. Not only would Dryden have felt the distance from the geographic, political and religious center of England that exile entails, he also experienced the sharp sense of loss that comes with exile as well. Dryden's later poetry and prose is everywhere shot through with general laments over the poet's misfortune and the loss of economic and political security. The sense of nostalgia and misfortune that these laments evoke communicates Dryden's disappointment at the failure of James's reign, as well as at his own banishment from the political sphere, and the loss of a privileged public voice.

The explanatory power of "the experience of exile" for Dryden's late works finally comes from its ability to comprehend both distance and loss, the nostalgia of his writing during the 1690s, as well as this writing's continued engagement with his homeland. Other models, such as Marxist or Romantic notions of "alienation," or even post-structuralist theories of an "exile" from language, can help formulate an oppositional poetics that generally answers to a literature of isolation, even of communal resistance.[24] Yet, as I have noted in the "Introduction," these models do not specify clearly the displacement that comes with the particular and immediate loss of a world that the exile had known until recently. They also fail to answer to the exile's continued engagement with, and often vehement nationalism for, the homeland that still haunts their imaginations. The experience of exile, on the other hand, entails negotiating the dialectical push and pull of a lost homeland, a negotiation that often evokes both nostalgia and continued attachment. While Dryden never left his homeland, he did experience the loss of the world he had known, and a distancing from the accepted modes of political and religious discourse. As a result, his writing exhibits the same negotiations with an elusive and departed homeland as it enters the London print market, the same responses to the upheavals of exile.

∗   ∗   ∗

While developing his theories on literary periods and succession, Dryden made sure to draw attention to his own presence as mediating authority, and at many turns. The later critical prefaces especially are crowded with often obscurantist genealogies or erudite debates with dead precursors. In the *Discourse of Satire* particularly, Dryden meticulously details the various intricacies of humanist scholarship on the distant origins of satire, while taking issue with many of the finer points of this scholarship. Dryden, throughout his lengthy late period prefaces, seems to delight in adjudicating these critical controversies and in departing from the norms of previous scholarship. His sustained engagement with humanist critics such as Isaac Causabon in the *Discourse of Satire* or Rene Le Bossu and Jean Segrais in the *Dedication of the Aeneis* emphasizes the elevated sphere in which he formulates a public voice in his last decade, as Bywaters has astutely detailed. Yet it also shows Dryden operating rather actively in this elevated and somewhat arcane sphere, using his sources in various ways, revising critical commonplaces here, attacking others there, always intervening and judging in front of the reader's eyes. Indeed, the almost overbearing digressiveness of the late essays reinforces the fact that only the often obscure associations of the author confer a logical structure on the prose.[25] The casual idiosyncrasy of these late critical essays allows Dryden to inhabit a legitimating critical discourse while impressing his own unique presence upon this discourse. Dryden's critical pronouncements and prosodic structure help him to formulate a "rhetoric of distance" that substitutes the presence of the author for the assumption of a common ground with his audience, an assumption so important to Dryden's earlier rhetoric, yet in the 1690s unavailable to an intransigent Catholic and Jacobite.

Much of what surprises in the late Dryden can be attributed to this exilic desire to impose his authorial presence upon his readers as he repositioned himself in the print world after the revolutionary settlement, and, in the process, reconsidered old affections, old animosities and old commonplaces. In doing so, he also sought to fashion a conception of authorship from history that made sense of his own political and religious banishment.[26] No author consumed as much continuous attention in Dryden's later years than Virgil, whom he translated in full between the years 1693–7 after translating various fragments of his oeuvre through the 1680s. His engagement with Virgil, the classical poet of Augustan empire and more immediately of early modern monarchic power, in a decade of exile and defeat seems at first an odd and paradoxical choice. To some extent, Dryden's interest in Virgil can be explained as a nostalgic fantasy of a lost Stuart monarchy, an escape from the aimlessness of defeat.[27] Yet Dryden's *Dedication of the Aeneis* tells a different story. In this rambling, digressive dedication to the Earl of Mulgrave, Virgil consistently appears as an active, resistant presence: to the whims of the public, to the commands of Augustus, and to the dominant political trends of his day. In the process of translating and contemplating Virgil's achievement, Dryden, departing from royalist and Stuart critical commonplaces, depicted Virgil as a private republican who, with a particular political acuity, determined that writing an epic for Augustus would be most beneficial to the Roman state. By rewriting Virgil in such a way, Dryden sought to re-conceive of Virgilian authorship as a delicate, yet pragmatic, resistance, a negotiation between private ideals and public pressures. Through the *Dedication*, thus, the *Aeneid* becomes less the classic epic of empire, as Dryden's forerunners, the French theorists Ruaeus, Le Bossu and Segrais, categorized it, than an example of an author's public compromise and private steadfastness, less a sustained panegyric than a multivalent poem that, while praising Augustus, also allowed the poet's own defeated principles to emerge in places.

Despite recent critical attention that might argue otherwise, the Dryden Virgil represents a significant attempt to cross over into the diverse London print market by a marginalized author. It is not a retreat to erudition and classicism and a turn away from the public events and controversies of Williamite London. Nor is it completely a submersion or denial of his personal voice;[28] nor, entirely, a means to oblique self-expression and covert political commentary that avoids the dangers of censorship and imprisonment. These analyses miss much of the force of the translation since they remain inattentive to the various discourses within which Dryden maneuvers. Instead, I would argue that when Dryden enters into the diverse London print market, he seeks to engage the dominant modes of expression, in this case primarily political and authorial, while re-envisioning and re-orienting those modes to comprehend the political and cultural distance he experienced after 1688.

As we shall see then, the idiosyncrasies of Dryden's Virgil can be attributed to both personal attraction to a picture of an author resistant yet popular, as well as public awareness of an audience in front of whom he wishes to assert his willful critical presence. Public recognition was certainly not out of Dryden's sight while he was translating and enlisting his subscribers, nor was the nationalist implications of his project. In fact, for the interior exile Dryden, the importance of an English Virgil would have appealed to him as he negotiated between his private exile and the English homeland to which he remained attached. Dryden's translation was a very publicized and patronized event, hotly anticipated, and presented from the start as a cultural and literary monument.[29] As is well known, it was also one of the first printed texts by a living author that was largely financed through subscription. John Barnard's meticulous work on the five-guinea and two-guinea subscribers lists (five guineas got the subscriber a dedication on one of the lavish Ogilby plates dispersed throughout the work, two guineas, a name on the list that appeared in the printed edition) shows the wide-ranging political and religious affiliations of the subscribers. These included members of the Whig junto, such as Charles Montagu or Dryden's longtime patron the Earl of Dorset, as well as Catholics and Jacobites such as James Cecil, the Earl of Salisbury, whom Dryden hailed, in the plate dedicated to him, as an English Laocoön, warning direly of the country's impending fate.[30] Poring over the record of the subscription lists serves as a useful corrective to those quick to anoint the Dryden Virgil as a Jacobite text, even though the political affinities of its author are well known.[31] Barnard's work reminds us that the Virgil meant many different things to many different readers, and that attempting to force a coherent and unilateral politics onto the prefaces and poems is reductive. At the very least, we must recognize the diverse and overlapping motives of the subscribers, from personal affinity to and patronage of Dryden to the desire for cultural prestige, from aesthetic curiosity to political interest.

Above the complexity of these localized narratives of the forces that drove and attached themselves to Dryden's translation, however, floated almost all of the subscribers' sense that they were participating in a significant print event that reflected particularly on the cultural achievements of the English nation. The large-paper folio that appeared in 1697 represented, first of all, a culmination of the Tonson line of classical translations that began with the 1680 collection, "by several eminent hands," of *Ovid's Epistles. The Works of Virgil* came onto the market after Tonson, in the 1680s and '90s, had virtually single-handedly created the reading public that would eventually subscribe to and buy a completed works of Virgil. Not only did Dryden's Virgil signify a noteworthy moment in the boom in English translations during this period, it also stood out as the most substantial print event in Dryden's career. As Paul Hammond's analysis of the circulation of Dryden's poetry has made clear, Dryden, unlike Jonson, showed little desire to control and create his own canon. His verse, while he lived, remained scattered in epilogues, prologues, the Tonson miscellanies, and as individual, often anonymous, original poems.[32] His translation of Virgil entailed the most extended, if not public, poetic endeavor of Dryden's print career. *The Works of Virgil* loomed large, for Tonson, for Dryden and for the subscribers who waited eagerly for the return on their investment.[33]

Of course, contributing to the sense of anticipation was Virgil's status as the early modern continental and English exemplar of classical poetic achievement. Since Petrarch and Dante, Virgil had held the mantle of the model poet, a non-Christian whose poetry and times anticipated and predicted the coming of Christ, and whose career embodied the ideal arc of a poet's progression from eclogue to georgic to epic. Now here was England's former Poet Laureate returning to Virgil. In the *Dedication*, Dryden gives his readers an idea of what he saw was at stake in his translation; towards the close, he returns to an evaluation of his translation after another digression, this time on foreign translators: "What I have said, though it has the face of arrogance, yet is intended for the honour of my Country; and therefore I will boldly own, that this *English* Translation has more of *Virgil's* Spirit in it, than either the *French*, or the *Italian*" (*Works* V: 325). Here, Dryden argues for the superiority of his English translation of Virgil, and thus in the tradition of *translatio imperii*, lays an English claim to Virgil himself. For Dryden, and, if Samuel Johnson is to be believed, for his readers, the translation became an issue of national pride.[34] In the accompanying materials to *The Works of Virgil* Dryden repeatedly expresses his hopes that the translation will do honor to his country; Tonson and the subscribers hoped and felt that this honor would be forthcoming as well.[35] The English Virgil would ideally outclass its continental competitors, especially considering the special connection that the English felt to the *Aeneid*, from which they drew their own originary myths.

Part of the nationalistic project in which Dryden engages in the translation relates as well to the improvement of the English language. Even early on in his career, Dryden connected the purity and power of the English language to the health of the state. In the *Defence of the Epilogue* to the *Conquest of Grenada* (1672), Dryden argues that the return of Charles II had spurred an improvement in English conversation since "the desire of imitating so great a pattern, first waken'd the dull and heavy spirits of the *English*, from their natural reserv'dness: loosen'd them from their stiff forms of conversation; and made them easy and plyant to each other in discourse. Thus, insensibly, our way of living became more free: and the fire of the English wit . . . began first to display its force by mixing the solidity of our Nation, with the air and gayety of our Neighbors" (*Works* XI: 216–17). The degree to which Dryden attributes the prosperity of the national literature to the monarch's conversation illustrates sharply the extent to which language and literature were enmeshed in power politics during the seventeenth century. That Dryden linked the refinement of English to the return of monarchy reminds us too that Thomas Sprat and the Royal Society, under the patronage of Charles II, led an effort to improve the native language in order to improve the quality of life, with the assumption that "the purity of Speech and greatness of Empire have in all Countries still met together."[36]

Indeed, in the years after the restoration, members of the Royal Society, as well as a number of other nobles and intellectuals, called for the refinement of what they considered the embarrassingly barbaric English language. Most notably, around 1680, the Earl of Roscommon, inspired by Cardinal Richelieu's prototype, founded an Academy interested in "refining, and fixing the standard of our language."[37] Dryden played an active role in Roscommon's Academy, whose members spent much of the decade translating classical authors into English as part of the refinement of English letters.[38] Roscommon, much like Dryden in the dedication of *Troilus and Cressida* in 1679, believed that these translations would widen the experiential and linguistic base of the language and thus lead to its refinement.[39] As Roscommon observes in his *Essay on Translated Verse* (1684), France after the Fronde turned to translation through the patronage of Louis XIV, and learning spread through the land to make it prosperous:

> From hence our generous Emulation came
> We undertook, and we perform'd the same.
> But now, *We* shew the world a nobler way,
> And in *Translated Verse*, do more than *They.*[40]

Dryden's Virgil comes as a culmination of what Roscommon has envisioned, his translation a monument to the renewed strength and vigor of the English language and nation, as well as an imperial claim to the Roman epic and thus the Roman tradition.

The translation itself shows Dryden articulating together, and to full effect, languages of various origins, relying on the etymologic and onomatopoetic qualities of words, particularly from Anglo-Saxon or Latin roots, to sharpen his translation. For example, at the end of Aeneas's chilling encounter with Dido in hell, Dido has no desire to listen to the hero's entreaties:

> But whirl'd away, to shun his hateful sight,
> Hid in the Forest, and the Shades of Night.
> Some pious Tears the pitying Heroe paid;
> And follow'd with his Eyes the flitting Shade.
> Then took the forward Way, by Fate ordain'd,
> And, with his Guide, the farther Fields attain'd;
> Where, sever'd from the rest, the Warrior Souls remain'd. (VI: 637–45)[41]

The opening lines take advantage of a series of discordant monosyllabic words, obviously Anglo-Saxon in character, to emphasize Dido's sudden and angry movement away from Aeneas. The somewhat harsh, abrupt tone to these early lines, while lingering in the alliterative trail of "flitting," "forward" and "farther Fields," shades over into the more stately Latinate rhyme of the triplet as our attention is drawn to the implacable Aeneas. Our hero continues on his way "by Fate ordain'd," a phrase anticipated in the alliteration in the third line of the Latinate "pious . . . pitying . . . paid" which evokes Aeneas's highest heroic virtue, and the driving force behind his abandonment of Dido. The triplet, however, also recalls Dryden's explanation for his use of this rhyme scheme in the *Dedication*, in which he calls upon Chaucer, Spenser and Cowley, the "Magna Charta of Heroick Poetry," for justification. The triplet becomes a right of Dryden's as an Englishman, since he is "too much of an *English*-man to lose what my Ancestors have gain'd for me" (*Works* V: 331). Overall, the passage combines the local effects of both series of words to heighten the pathos of Aeneas's meeting with Dido. Linguistically, Dryden elevates what he considers the "barbarism" of the monosyllables of Old English, alone unfit for heroic verse, while simultaneously remaking Virgil in English garb.

A nationalistic edition of Virgil that sought to claim this classical author for English honor might seem strange coming from a writer at odds with the current state. What is one to make, finally, of the fact that Dryden's *Dedication* is rife with a strong sense of nationalistic pride that at times borders on xenophobia?[42] We might, first of all, see Dryden's nationalism as a defensive posture from which Dryden can continue to identify with, and claim loyalty to, his country. To some extent, he sought to anticipate his critics and patrons by aggressively, indeed even theatrically, displaying his interest in the glory of the English nation. The defensive repetition of this nationalism seems, thus, an attempt to counteract his own marginalization and removal from such authoritative positions as Poet Laureate and Historiographer Royal, positions from which he could previously determine questions of national literature and history. Moreover, such nationalism from an author writing from exile is not uncommon as they remained engaged, often more vehemently so, with their homeland from afar. As we have repeatedly seen, English exiles in the seventeenth century, while writing from a distant, marginalized position, consistently sought to redefine the homeland they had left behind in order to reorient the disjunctions of exile as faithfulness to a truer Englishness. While Dryden's jibes on French criticism and culture indicate his unusual capacity as an interior exile to remain wholly unconcerned with the international dimensions of the Jacobite cause, and thus the Jacobite's tainted reliance on French power, Dryden, in participating in such a nationalistic project, lays claim to Virgil's *Aeneid* for England, thus laying claim to one of the foundational texts of classical and English learning. That he would have laid "his Author" at the feet of a returning James II betrays his wishes for the translation. Hoping that James would return triumphantly to his epic, yet knowing that William's supporters (and Dryden's subscribers) were expecting their own English Aeneas, Dryden's translation lies somewhere between displacement and home.

Yet more important than the exact politics of the translation would be Dryden's own reclamation of Virgil. Through his idiosyncratic rewriting of his classical forbear for his audience and himself, he imposed his own identity and presence in reaction to the dialectics of exile. As he negotiated the distances of his political and religious removal from the center, his version of Virgil, nationalistic yet resistant to outside pressures and wholly Dryden's own creation, came into focus. This is not to say that Dryden eschewed contemporary political language in translating Virgil. The *Aeneid* – in its own terms a thorough examination of political conflict and legitimacy – lends itself to this infusion; yet the ease with which Dryden's vocabulary so readily shades over into a seventeenth-century context is remarkable.[43] The political overtones of Dryden's translation make themselves immediately apparent in the opening lines of the poem. It is hard to imagine that any reader in 1697 but the most stubborn Williamite would miss Dryden's expansion of the Latin in the opening lines in which Aeneas is "Expell'd and exil'd" from his home but eventually "His banish'd Gods restor'd to Rites Divine,/And settl'd sure Succession in its Line" (I: 7–8). Indeed, at various junctures in the epic, Dryden makes his sympathies especially clear. His Jacobite leanings come through sharply in Book VI where, in the depths of hell, Aeneas encounters those suffering torments for their deeds on earth. Amongst this catalogue are "they, who Brothers better Claim disown,/Expel their Parents and usurp the Throne" (VI: 824–5), lines that find little justification from the Latin and allude clearly and partisanly to the actions of William and Mary, who were often figured in Jacobite propaganda as ungrateful children violating natural, familial laws.[44] The list continues:

> To Tyrants others have their Country sold,
> Imposing Foreign Lords, for Foreign Gold:
> Some have old Laws repeal'd, new Statutes made;
> Not as the People pleas'd, but as they paid. (VI: 845–8)

Dryden's translation draws upon the vocabulary of the Jacobite and country party pamphlets that represented the Jacobite resistance as an English opposition to the corruption and encroachments of a Dutch invader.[45] These Jacobite appeals to conscience maintained the loyalty of the Jacobites to English principles and the ancient constitution, in part to counteract Williamite attacks on French influence over Jacobite political hopes. Dryden surely had such arguments in mind while translating these lines, and by drawing upon their vocabulary sought to remind his readers of just such polemic.

I do not want to dwell further on the Jacobite allusions in Dryden's translation, a topic that has been dealt with thoroughly and adroitly elsewhere. Rather, I would like to emphasize, for a moment, the various other political trajectories that Dryden's translation negotiates. After all, Virgil's epic is not only a story of the destruction of Troy, but also of the foundation of a new empire by a conquering foreign king; and, Dryden's translation is not deaf to the potential application of the Iliadic second half of the epic to the politics of post-Revolutionary England. As much as we might want to emphasize the language of Turnus's decision "To meet in Arms th'intruding *Trojan* Guest:/To force the Foes from the *Lavinian* Shore/And *Italy*'s endangered Peace restore," we must also recall Latinus, several hundred lines earlier, praising Aeneas:

> A foreign Son upon the Shore descends,
> Whose Martial Fame from Pole to Pole extends.
> His Race in Arms, and Arts of Peace renown'd,
> Nor *Latium* shall contain, nor *Europe* bound.
> 'Tis theirs what e're the Sun surveys around. (VII: 142–6)

Tonson's transformation of the Ogilby plates and repeated requests that Dryden dedicate his translation to the present king should certainly have dispelled Dryden's illusions, if he had any, over how his translation could and would be used.[46] Dryden, nevertheless, certainly did not eschew contemporary political language in translating Virgil. In fact, he consistently calls attention to the events of the past sixty years, departing from Virgil's language to transport the episodes of the *Aeneid* into the seventeenth century at almost every turn. In the speeches of Turnus and Latinus, Dryden inserts both the notion of "restoring" Italy's "endangered Peace" as well as the figure of "Europe" in the second passage, encouraging the reader to consider the resonance of these speeches for a Williamite England engaged with the continent. The rendering of Virgil's original in such a manner fulfills his claim to make Virgil speak "as he wou'd himself have spoken, if he had been born in *England*, and in this present Age" (*Works* V: 331). Yet it also shows Dryden conducting a sustained meditation for himself and his readers on the political implications of that most political of classical poets. Dryden had used the Virgilian world to explore issues of political as well as poetic authority with regularity in his career, most famously in his satirical appropriation of Augustan succession in *MacFlecknoe*, and the golden Augustan overtones that highlight the Biblical vehicle at the end of *Absalom and Achitophel*. The ease with which Dryden moves between classical and contemporary worlds in these poems and others is one of their distinctive, most poetically effective, features. In the 1690s, as he turned to translation, he took the opportunity to revisit his old "master" and the complex political arena of Augustan Rome that he envisioned Virgil inhabiting. The language of his translation, with its powerful political resonances, reminds us (and his audience) of the extent to which Dryden had turned to Virgil in his career to comment on English affairs of state, the extent to which Dryden read Virgil to understand what it was to write political poetry.

What we see, then, in Dryden's *Dedication* and translation is the poet returning to the *Aeneid* as part of an effort to re-envision Virgilian authorship at a time when his own notions of public writing were in need of revision. No longer could Dryden speak with the confidence of a poet patronized by the monarch and under specific instructions to write; nor could he speak from the measured and rhetorically powerful position of a moderate, fair-minded citizen, as he had prior to 1688. For his part, Virgil had been constructed by Stuart supporters as the great poet of Augustan empire and patronage. Drawing on the classical legacy of an Augustan golden age in which the gates of Juno were first closed, and the arts flourished, these writers paralleled the return of Charles II with Roman magnificence and Augustan peace. Dryden had also participated in this perception as he celebrated the restoration of Charles II in Virgilian tones that envisioned the return of "arms and arts" with the return of the king, a celebration that linked great poetry with monarchic power and vice versa. In the French criticism upon which Dryden relied so heavily, Segrais, Le Bossu and Ruaeus depict Virgil as writing wholeheartedly in the service of Augustus.[47] According to Segrais, who wrote his translation "avec le privilege du roi," Segrais only parallels Virgil in "mesme zele pour la gloire de V.M. que ce grand homme eut pour la gloire de son Prince."[48]

Yet there existed another tradition of Augustanism, less prominent in seventeenth-century histories and consistently ignored by Stuart apologists, and it is upon this tradition that Dryden drew as he rethought his own vocation from interior exile.[49] From Tacitus, Dio Cassius and other republican-minded classical historians came a far more critical picture of Rome's great emperor that emphasized Augustus's bloody rise to power, his tyrannous rule, rejection of Rome's republican past and the resultant immorality of his court and the Roman nation more generally. In this tradition, Virgil would have to be a propagandist and flatterer of Augustus, writing his epic dishonestly in the service of the state. Writing just as the Tacitean tradition was returning to vogue with the English gentry in the 1620s, William Lisle sees that in the First Eclogue that "Virgil could not have . . . flattered more artificially, than by confessing to have gained liberty by his meanes, who was suspected to have aimed at the destruction and usurpation of the general liberty and immunities of Rome."[50] While Le Bossu and others recognized Virgil's poem as an effort to reconcile the Roman people to Augustus's rule, it was left to the republican-minded, such as Lisle, to criticize him for dishonesty and a betrayal of principles. Dryden seems to take up this Tacitean tradition and use it to his own ends in the *Dedication* as he sketches his own precise vision of Virgilian authorship. This depiction departs noticeably from the familiar Royalist characterization of Virgil as a willing, and wholehearted, propagandist for his patron, while stopping short of criticizing Virgil for blatantly abandoning honesty and truth. In fact, it is Virgil's delicate tact and negotiation of principle and publicity that Dryden sees as most commendable in the *Aeneid*.

To be sure, Dryden's Virgil works in the service of Augustus, indeed, according to a vague, knowing reference in the *Dedication*, even had "obligations" to him (*Works* V: 280). Further, he does not depart from his French predecessors in arguing that Virgil has modeled his Aeneas to reflect the person of his patron. Dryden notes that Virgil wrote for Augustus as a propagandist after he "concluded it to be the interest of his Country to be so Govern'd: To infuse an awful Respect into the People, towards such a Prince" (*Works* V: 281). Virgil's decision to write for the state, according to the account Dryden presents, however, did not come easily, nor without doubts; it is a decision Virgil "maturely weigh'd." In fact, he embarks on his epic panegyric to Augustus only after relinquishing his hope for the timely return of a republican Rome, after he realized "an entire Liberty was not to be retriev'd" in the near future (*Works* V: 281). The Virgil that comes into focus in Dryden's portrait is a reluctant epic poet, one whose private opinions consistently differed from his public pronouncements. Dryden emphasizes throughout Virgil's presence as an independent actor in the construction of his poem. Thus, he alludes to the story that Virgil attempted to have his poem burnt upon his death, but that Augustus disobeyed the poet's orders. Similarly, according to Dryden, Virgil draws upon the myth of Roman origins, because "that it was the receiv'd Opinion, that the *Romans* were descended from the *Trojans*, and *Julius Caesar* from *Julus* the Son of *Aeneas*, was enough for *Virgil*; tho' perhaps he thought not so himself" (*Works* V: 281–2). The myths and stories that the *Aeneid* tells its Roman readers are just that, constructed by a poet who designed them in order to influence public opinion while not necessarily agreeing with them.

Even so, what Dryden sees to be the "true" beliefs of Virgil seep through in the poem. For example, in Dryden's explication, he imagines Virgil in Book V dispensing the prizes and defeats of the Trojan funeral games for Anchises as poetic praise and revenge for the contemporary Roman families that either pleased or angered him. Perhaps most surprisingly, yet consistently, Dryden asserts that his poet was one who "was still of Republican Principles at Heart" (*Works* V: 280). The line that Virgil writes in praise of Cato "Secretosque Pios, his dantem jura Catonem" leaves little doubt that Virgil maintained republican allegiances. Dryden, departing from the French critics he relies on so heavily elsewhere in the *Dedication*, expands on this notion of a resistant Virgil at length in his notes to his translation, where he attacks Ruaeus for misinterpreting Virgil's praise of the republican Cato as praise for Cato the Censor and firmly holds: "Nevertheless I continue in the same Opinion, concerning the Principles of our Poet." As if he has not made himself clear enough, he immediately returns to this topic in the next note after he had seemingly said all he needed (*Works* VI: 823–4). Virgil's republicanism seems a topic that exercised Dryden while he wrote the critical material to accompany the *Aeneis*, indeed, seems even a touchstone for his imaginings of the author. His insistence on Virgil's oppositional politics, in the *Dedication* and notes, should also remind us of his casual mention of Montaigne's republicanism. Read alongside the praise of his anti-Williamite cousin John Driden in 1700, as well as his new-found sympathy for the work of the republican Milton, these observations on the politics of authorship reveal an author exploring the nature of opposition and loyalty in sources far from the dynastic politics now perhaps so distasteful to Dryden.

In the *Dedication*, Dryden envisions Virgil negotiating a precise space between his personal convictions and the desires of the Augustan court, desires that also happen to coincide with the health of the Roman state. Throughout this account, moreover, Dryden confidently sees Virgil in complete control of his circumstances as client, as public poet and as epic visionary. Dryden wants to show: "how dext'rously he mannag'd both the Prince and People, so as to displease neither, and to do good to both, which is the part of a Wise and Honest Man: And proves that it is possible for a Courtier not to be a Knave" (*Works* V: 283). Dryden's praise here of Virgil's wisdom and honesty emphasizes that these values are defined in political terms throughout the *Dedication*. Later in the same piece, Dryden will commend Virgil for honorably drawing the truth of the Punic Wars out of the fictitious account of Aeneas's spurning of Dido, an account that Virgil has included, according to Dryden, to please and fuel popular mistrust of Carthage.[51] The picture of Virgil is not altogether flattering, and has attracted the vitriolic ire of at least one modern Virgil scholar.[52] Because of the Virgil we receive in Dryden's *Dedication* and in other revisions of Virgil around the turn of the century, Alexander Pope can state casually in 1705 that "the *Aeneid* was evidently a party piece, as much as *Absalom and Achitophel*. Virgil was as slavish a writer as any of the gazetteers."[53] If we may step back, however, from such moral judgments, we can also see in Dryden's Virgil a writer who remains steadfast in his political convictions and in control of his poetry; the freight of "honest" in the above passage, that is, carries forward into Dryden's next period, where he imagines a Virgil above the fray of courtly deception and sycophancy. Even though Virgil wrote in the service of Augustus, he continued to maintain his own independent beliefs, while also remaining conscious of the exact political implications of every line of his poem.

In the notes to the *Aeneis*, as Dryden returns to his argument that Virgil remained a republican at heart, he praises Virgil, in similar terms as above, for "judiciously" contriving a criticism of Augustus by veiling it as the opinion of the venerable Anchises (*Works* VI: 824). Virgil's honesty and judiciousness, it seems, derive as much from his ability to moderately and intelligently criticize without being censured as in his ability to praise his patron.

While the attractions of this detailed description of Virgil, at once client yet virtuous independent, may in many ways be self-evident in terms of Dryden's political situation, viewed through the dialectics of "interior exile" we might see Dryden's full investment in the *Dedication* falling elsewhere. Indeed, the Virgil that Dryden reads into the *Aeneid* enables him to construct a version of authorship that comprehends the various public uses, including Williamite, to which his translation could be put, without compromising his private Jacobite loyalties. In fact, just as Virgil "judiciously" inserted his republican sentiments into the epic, Dryden would include Jacobite sentiments in his translation. And, just as Augustus accepted, without censuring, Virgil's anti-monarchic views, so Dryden had the right, as a "free-born Subject" of England, to continue to speak his mind. Yet the relative Jacobitism of Dryden's *Dedication* and translation becomes less the point when we consider the willful self-creation that drives this version of authorship. First of all, the turn to a past master for authorization shows Dryden imagining an exemplary poet writing under the same duress as he wrote. Dryden creates an authorizing precedent that answers to his own experience of writing from the margins and in the process creates a novel version of literary history that goes some way towards justifying loyalty to a lost political cause that has forced these writers into different forms of exile. As an exile, he reorients poetic lineage to construct a marginalized, oppositional tradition into which he can place himself. As he calls upon a past fellow master for poetic legitimacy, he does so in a way that draws attention to the experience of loss and the defeat of political hopes that each author supposedly had in common. Further, for an interior exile such as Dryden, a republican Virgil who judiciously and knowledgeably controls virtually all aspects of the reception of his epic fulfills the exile's own desires for control.

Similarly, where much of the energy of Dryden's *Dedication* lies is in the critical reorientation of Virgil as Dryden digressively leads his readers through his often arcane ruminations. The surprising rewriting of Virgil, the reconsideration of Milton's epic achievement, the more subtle, yet insistent, turn to republican modes of thought – these habitual patterns show Dryden, in his late period, constructing an eclectically personal, yet strongly national and public, voice that seeks to answer to his own psychology of interior exile. In fact, the very eclecticism and digressiveness is one of the primary features of the late Dryden that arises out of this psychology as Dryden drew attention to his own authorial presence in an effort to elide the loss of authority that came with his removal to the political and religious margins of England. For many exiles the performative, be it the public gesture, the fashionable garment and posture, or the published written text, becomes an essential method through which identity is asserted and the disruptions of exile are overridden. For Dryden in the 1690s, this assertion came through most forcefully in his critical ruminations where we are forced to rely upon the author's own personality and associations to understand Virgil and epic, Juvenal and satire. In the long, digressive *Dedication of the Aeneis*, Dryden's historical and political imagination seems especially active, heightened, it seems, by the recent upheavals in the English polity, and his return to the author he had translated, admired and so often deployed to inform his understanding of the complex events of the Civil War and restoration. As a result, the detail with which Dryden paints the actions and motivations of Virgil in Augustan Rome is substantial, the mature work of a mind that understood fully the nature of public writing in seventeenth-century England, and that applied this understanding to the classical authors he translated. While the politically informed language of Dryden's *Dedication* encourages his readers to view recent English events through the lens of Roman history, those readers are also encouraged to notice, at almost every turn, the historically specific origins of Virgil's epic and the powerful sense of periodicity with which Dryden informs the entire project.

 Dryden is the crucial mediating presence between the lost historic specificity of Virgil's epic and the seventeenth-century reader.[54] Towards the end of the *Dedication*, Dryden discusses the inherent difficulties in translating Virgil: "What he says of *Sybil*'s Prophecies, may be as properly apply'd to every word of his: They must be read, in order as they lie; the least breath discomposes them, and somewhat of their Divinity is lost" (*Works* V: 319). The act of translation, Dryden admits, entails a loss of the purity and intent of the original. Yet the presence of Dryden as authoritative historical and critical scholar attempts to restore Virgil's original meaning as the translator clarifies the meaning of various passages. Indeed, Dryden takes particular pleasure in adjudicating the historical controversies and legacy of Virgilian scholarship. He seems intent, throughout the *Dedication*, to uncover the undiscovered origins of passages in Virgil, often drawing attention to the "hidden" or "secret" meanings that lie behind them. Earlier in the decade, writing from a similarly constructed authoritative position, he had discovered hidden and secret meanings throughout his notes to the *Satires of Juvenal and Persius*. For example, in his commentary on the Sixteenth Satire of Juvenal, Dryden concludes that "if it be well observed, you will find he intended an Invective against a Standing Army" (*Works* IV: 245). In uncovering these lost readings, he refocuses the attention of the reader onto the authoritative critic who determines the meaning of the text that he translates for his readers. It is clear from the *Dedication* that the Virgil Dryden's audience received is only made possible through the critical acuity and historical knowledge of his translator. While Dryden's translation enhances the honor of the English nation, in the process it also makes this English Virgil, with all its honors, particularly Dryden's own.

Epilogue

In 1688, around the time that William of Orange was marching his way to the English crown, across the Channel the Swiss doctor Johannes Hofer was writing a medical dissertation that examined the homesicknesses of domestic servants in Germany and Swiss soldiers fighting abroad. Hofer created the term nostalgia (from two Greek roots meaning "a longing for home") to define his newly diagnosed disease of displaced peoples. Hofer's diagnosis of this strange version of homesickness, in which people became incapacitated by sounds, smells and sights that evoked the homeland, helped to identify this existing psychological affliction, as well as encourage its spread across Europe.[1] The confluence of the discovery of the disease of nostalgia and the triumph of William III in England seems to me worthy of a moment's reflection. Just as William's forces, some of whom were fighting in a foreign land, were participating in one of the more epochal political transitions in the grand arc of English history, Hofer was recognizing and pondering the profound impact that these types of transitions, as well as other types of dislocations, had upon individual experience. While nostalgia is often communal and political in its ideological trajectory, spurring invasions or wars much like the one in which William's soldiers participated, because its roots lie in memory and desire its manifestations are often deeply idiosyncratic, affective and personal. What evokes the clearest of memories in one nostalgic might spur an entirely different reflection, or no reflection at all, from his or her closest companion.

Exile, which is largely colored by nostalgic longing, by the memories of the homeland before the moment of departure, is experienced in a complex and deeply personal way. While the renewal of communal and affective bonds certainly is integral to mitigating the exigencies of the removal from home, each exile necessarily carried personal associations of the homeland that shadowed hir or her steps in exile. The "contrapuntal" nature of exile, its negotiation of exile and home, while broadly shaped

by the communal political or religious concerns of a large-scale displacement, was given particular point by the personal shadows of the exile's
memory of and reaction to home. In many ways, the willful acts of the
imagination that I have detailed here show these authors working to order
the particular psychological upheavals of their exiles. So, Milton creates
his purposefully idiosyncratic theodicy both out of a reaction to the high
political drama of the fall of the republican cause and the restoration, and
out of his heterodox memories of what was lost at the moment of defeat
and exile. The idiosyncrasies of each of these creations remind us that the
experience of displacement was felt in the personal details of the exile's
life. To say that these creations were uninflected by continued concern
for larger political, religious or literary events would be naïve, and, as
evidenced by my analyses here, wrong; yet, to say also that these creations
were uninflected by the lived experience and memories, the daily reminders and persistent psychological difficulties of displacement would be
equally naïve and wrong.

In the face of the large-scale displacement of peoples, particularly in the
past one hundred years, it is important to recall the individual traumas
enacted by these movements across the world stage. Ideally, the study and
contemplation of exile necessitates an awareness of and sensitivity to the
profound psychological impact it can have on the individual. Much of
what we have learned, and what is most striking about this experience,
comes from the deeply felt relation of the personal experience of and
reactions to displacement. For the twentieth century, the genre of exile
has been the memoir; these writings have invaluably widened our understanding of this complex experience. Indeed, even in the early modern
period, we can see numerous exiles, including Edmund Ludlow, Margaret
Cavendish, Ann Fanshawe, and John Winthrop, turning to the memoir in
an attempt to comprehend, justify and convey their removal from a
homeland they had once known. It is through these memoirs, both
modern and early modern, that we can locate the quotidian vagaries of
living through the experience of displacement; its attractions to these
writers testify to the profoundly personal, yet also often continuously
public, trajectories of exile.

Throughout this study of the experience and literature of exile in the
early modern period, I have attempted to retain a vision of these various
authors as they lived through and wrote through their displacements. My
analyses have necessarily been grounded in an understanding of the broad
political, religious or literary concerns into which these authors wrote
from the margins. The disputes that caused the exiles that I analyze

here were intractably political and ideological in their origins, and the writings from exile were inflected by these disputes. Yet, as Hofer's diagnosis of nostalgia reminds us, there were numerous people, including Bradstreet and Hobbes, Milton and Dryden, whose lives were irreparably changed because of these disputes, whose worlds were irreparably ruptured. I would like to think that my study can serve as a prompt to consideration of these damaged lives, a reminder that Milton wrote much of *Paradise Lost* while blind and sequestered in his house on Jewin Street; that Hobbes wrote much of *Leviathan* in a sickroom somewhere near St. Germain, France, as the mobs of the Fronde called for the heads of Charles Stuart and his band of exiles; that the act of creation lies somewhere between the politics and ideologies of literary form and the quotidian particulars of everyday life.

Notes

INTRODUCTION: THE "REMANENCE" OF THE PAST:
THE EARLY MODERN TEXT IN EXILE

1 Bandello's city appears in *Novella* I; Randolph Starn speaks about Bandello's vision in his study of exile in sixteenth-century Italy, *Contrary Commonwealth: The theme of exile in medieval and renaissance Italy* (Berkeley: University of California Press, 1982), p. 45.

2 Marco Polo, at the end of Italo Calvino's *Invisible Cities*, after admitting that every city that he talks about is, in fact, his Venice in disguise, ruminates: "Perhaps I am afraid of losing Venice at once, if I speak of it" (*Invisible Cities*, trans. William Weaver [New York: Harcourt Brace Jovanovich, 1974], p. 87).

3 Svetlana Boym, in her reflections on these collections of the fragmentary experience of exile, describes these "immigrant souvenirs" as markers for both the experience of exile and for a "newfound exilic domesticity" in *The Future of Nostalgia* (New York: Basic Books, 2001), pp. 327–36.

4 André Aciman, "Shadow cities," in *Letters of Transit: Reflections on exile, identity, language, and loss*, ed. André Aciman (New York: The New Press, 1999), p. 34.

5 Joseph Brodsky, "A room and a half," in *Less Than One: Selected essays* (New York: Farrar, Strauss & Giroux, 1986), p. 472.

6 Ann Fanshawe, *The Memoirs of Anne, Lady Halkett and Ann, Lady Fanshawe*, ed. John Loftis (Oxford: Clarendon Press, 1979), p. 131. Sir John Suckling met a similar fate, most likely committing suicide in France in 1642; Richard Crashaw, after spending some time in the service of the Catholic court of Henrietta Maria in the late 1640s, wandered to the outskirts of Rome, where, destitute and without significant patronage, he died in 1649.

7 Charles Simic has observed, after spending much of his childhood on the move from his native Czechoslovakia and being asked repeatedly for his identification, that nothing can impress the arbitrary nature of our existence upon us as much as exile ("Refugees," in *Letters of Transit*, p. 124).

8 Paul Tabori describes the story of Sinuhe in detail in *The Anatomy of Exile: A semantic and historical study* (London: Harrap, 1972), pp. 43–5. Sinuhe reconciled himself with the Pharaoh Sesostris I after a lifelong odyssey

through numerous unnamed villages. His reconcilement allowed him to be buried as a servant of the Pharaoh in pomp, and thus allowed us to know the story of his displacement.

9 I take my notion of the written text as constitutive of a social process, as an object whose primary use is "rhetorical and social," from Arjun Appadurai, "Introduction: commodities and the politics of value," in *The Social Life of Things: Commodities in cultural perspective*, ed. Arjun Appadurai (Cambridge: Cambridge University Press, 1986), pp. 29–41. Appadurai discusses the demand for luxury goods as socially determined; the value of the literary text, then, becomes embedded in the circumstances of its dissemination and consumption. For my purposes, Appadurai's formulation has been useful in understanding the text in exile as both constitutive and representative of the formation of new systems of exchange that answered to the exigencies of communal displacement. Hans Robert Jauss in *Toward an Aesthetic of Reception*, trans. Timothy Bahti (Minneapolis: University of Minnesota Press, 1982), pp. 1–57 argues that an effective history of reception must consider the literary text as both originally insightful of and a formative agent in history.

10 This is Dr. Frederic Gottfurt, who participated in an international symposium on exile organized by Paul Tabori. Tabori quotes Gottfurt's reflections at more length in *The Anatomy of Exile*, p. 34.

11 *The Riverside Shakespeare*, eds. G. Blakemore Evans and J.J.M. Tobin, 2nd ed. (Boston: Houghton Mifflin Company, 1997), p. 852.

12 Ralph Verney, *Memoirs of the Verney Family, Compiled From the Letters and Illustrated by the Portraits at Claydon House*, comp. Frances Parthenope Verney, 4 vols. (London: Longmans, Green, 1892–99), vol. II, p. 222.

13 Edmund Ludlow, *A Voyce From the Watchtower: Part Five, 1660–1662*, ed. A.B. Worden (London: Royal Historical Society, 1978), pp. 191, 196.

14 Benedict Anderson details this move to a standardized idiom in his exploration of the origins of national consciousness in *Imagined Communities: Reflections on the origins and spread of nationalism*, new edition (London: Verso, 1991), pp. 37–46.

15 *Memoirs of the Verney Family*, vol. II, pp. 222–31 and Ludlow, *A Voyce From the Watchtower*, p. 196.

16 I detail the particulars of this removal from the standard modes of print circulation below, especially on pages 22–31 for the New England exiles and 66–70 for the royalist exiles. While their removal *may* have been little different from the removal of a remote landowner in northern England, the perception of their removal exacerbated the particular psychological and social difficulties of exile and encouraged specific rhetorical patterns as they wrote back into this distant community. Further, many of these exiles, especially those who continued to write for publication, left behind organized, sophisticated distribution systems of print exchange.

17 Charles Simic, "The golden age of hatred," in *New York Review of Books*, vol. 1, 16 (Oct. 23, 2003), p. 43.

18 David Bethea describes the "aesthetic discourse" of the exile as anathema to the tyrant because it has a memory older than the present social contract in *Joseph Brodsky and the Creation of Exile* (Princeton: Princeton University Press, 1994), p. 38.

19 Ludlow, *A Voyce From the Watchtower*, p. 123.

20 Seidel, *Exile and the Narrative Imagination* (New Haven: Yale University Press, 1986), p. xi.

21 Edward Said, "Reflections on exile," in *Reflections on Exile and Other Essays* (Cambridge: Harvard University Press, 2000), p. 183.

22 Said, "Introduction," *Reflections on Exile*, p. xxi. In "Reflections on Exile," p. 176, Said notes suggestively that all nationalisms develop from a condition of estrangement. My study would tend to corroborate this suggestion, at least as far as it discovers a tendency towards the creation of fictive worlds, intolerance and a willful and insistent didacticism.

23 *The Riverside Shakespeare*, p. 1470. Similarly, in *Richard II*, Gaunt advises his son Bullingbroke on the verge of his banishment to "Think not the King did banish thee,/But thou the King" (1.3.279–80). Interestingly, Ralph Verney, upon leaving for France in 1644, remembered earlier lines from this scene in which Gaunt also advises his son to remain stoic in his banishment and Bullingbroke's firm response: "Call it a travel that thou takest for pleasure/ BULL: My heart will sigh when I miscall it so,/Which finds it an inforced pilgrimage" (I.iii.261–3); see *Memoirs of the Verney Family*, vol. II, p. 206.

24 Eva Hoffman, "The new nomads," in *Letters of Transit*, p. 44.

25 Seidel, *Exile and the Narrative Imagination*, p. 5. Benjamin details the creation of a "fragile, precious reality" in his essay on Proust, "The image of Proust," in *Illuminations*, ed. Hannah Arendt, trans. Harry Zohn (New York: Harcourt, Brace & World, 1968), p. 205. Said, similarly, notes that exiles create worlds over which to rule ("Reflections on Exile," p. 182).

26 George O'Brien, in exploring the representation of exile in Irish literature, notes the importance of the performative to exilic identity ("The aesthetics of exile," in *Contemporary Irish Fiction: Themes, tropes, theories*, eds. Liam Harte and Michael Parker [New York: St. Martin's, 2000], pp. 45–8). O'Brien is chiefly concerned with the trope or theme of exile, even though we certainly should consider the text itself as a form of performance, one of the widely available and expansive forms of performance available to the early modern exile.

27 Boym, *The Future of Nostalgia*, p. 10.

28 Gilroy, *The Black Atlantic: Modernity and double consciousness* (Cambridge: Harvard University Press, 1993), pp. 15–16.

29 Bhabha, "Frontlines/borderposts," in *Displacements: Cultural Identities in Question*, ed. Angelika Bammer (Bloomington: University of Indiana Press, 1994), p. 269.

30 Gilroy, *The Black Atlantic*, p. 4.

31 It is important to add that because English, as an international language, remained little used and much derided, even by native speakers, the

opportunities for international print publication in English in the seventeenth century remained severely limited, and usually only came about through the particular efforts of a community of English exiles or merchants. For the period 1620–1680, according to the *English Short-Title Catalogue* there were 284 new titles printed in English in Amsterdam, by far the largest producer of Continental texts in English. It is difficult to tell how many of these titles were actually produced there and how many were printed in London surreptitiously with false imprints, although Wing has done an admirable job of culling counterfeits from the bibliography. See Keith Sprunger, *Trumpets from the Tower: English Puritan printing in the Netherlands, 1600–1640* (Leiden: E.J. Brill, 1994) for an account of Puritan efforts at Continental publication for an audience primarily located back in the homeland. Henri-Jean Martin and Lucien Febvre in *The Coming of the Book: The impact of printing 1450–1800*, new edition, trans. David Gerard (London: N.L.B., 1976), pp. 230–5, note that during the 1640s the international book trade generally fell into a deep recession, a recession that forced many publishers and printers to turn to local and vernacular markets for their profits rather than chance the higher cost international market in Latin books.

32 Bhabha suggestively calls the text from exile, from displacement, an event that should be looked at independently as it formulates and negotiates its own discourse as it speaks from the margins; see "Frontlines/borderposts," pp. 270–1. J.G.A. Pocock, although from the perspective of the historian of ideas, explores the historiographical implications of considering texts as events, at situating the "action in the midst of conditions and circumstances that will help us understand, first, what the action in fact was and, second, why and how it was performed," "Texts as events: reflections on the history of political thought," in *Politics of Discourse: The literature and history of seventeenth-century England*, eds. Kevin Sharpe and Steven N. Zwicker (Berkeley: University of California Press, 1987), pp. 21–33. Finally, or perhaps originally, in outlining his theory of reception, Hans Robert Jauss also asks us to consider the work of art as an event since there is no link between works not created by the receiving subjects (*Towards an Aesthetic of Reception*, p. 56). While Jauss's reception theory is inevitably more traditional and less troubled by political dynamics than Bhabha's picture of textual negotiations or Pocock's vision of the author as political actor, its rooting in Marxist aesthetics does allow for an understanding of the text as the product (and importantly for Jauss progenitor) of a historical moment and of social change.

33 See, especially, Joad Raymond, "The newspaper, public opinion, and the public sphere in the seventeenth century," in *News, Newspapers, and Society in Early Modern Britain*, ed. Joad Raymond (London: Frank Cass, 1999), pp. 109–40 and his work on newspapers generally in *The Invention of the Newspaper: English Newsbooks 1641–1649* (Oxford: Oxford University Press, 1996); Sharon Achinstein, *Milton and the Revolutionary Reader*

(Princeton: Princeton University Press, 1994), pp. 3–26; and David Norbrook, "*Areopagitica*, censorship, and the early modern public sphere," in *The Administration of Aesthetics: Censorship, political criticism and the public sphere*, ed. Richard Burt (Minneapolis: University of Minnesota Press, 1994), pp. 3–33. Habermas's work is still critical for its synthesis of social, economic and political histories, its understanding of the impact of the materials of an emerging market economy upon the development of a fundamental precondition of modern politics.

34 Nico Israel, in *Outlandish: Writing between exile and diaspora* (Stanford: Stanford University Press, 2000), pp. 1–22, also explores the interplay between the critical terms of exile and diaspora in discussing modern texts produced from one form of displacement or another. Israel's explication of the distinct trajectories that these two terms trace informs my discussion here.

35 Maureen Quilligan, Margrata de Grazia and Peter Stallybrass, "Introduction," in *Subject and Object in Renaissance Culture*, eds. Maureen Quilligan, Margrata de Grazia and Peter Stallybrass (Cambridge: Cambridge University Press, 1996), pp. 1–12.

36 Quilligan, de Grazia and Stallybrass, "Introduction," p. 8.

37 This phrase is from Harold Love's groundbreaking study of early modern manuscript publication, *Scribal Publication in Seventeenth-century England* (Oxford: Clarendon Press, 1993), p. 177. I cite it because Love's manuscript communities, due to their ostensibly closed and private nature, have some similarities with the exiled communities I study here. As is the case with these exiled communities, we may question the extent to which Love's readers remained like-minded as writing and reading, even of manuscripts, became more widespread and implicated in the religious and political conflicts of the century.

38 Miller in *The New England Mind: The seventeenth century* (New York: Macmillan, 1939) especially, and Bercovitch in *The American Jeremiad* (Madison: University of Wisconsin Press, 1978) and *The Puritan Origins of the American Self* (New Haven: Yale University Press, 1975).

39 Bercovitch, *The Puritan Origins of the American Self*, p. ix. Similarly, in *The American Jeremiad*, he flags the "jeremiad" form as the source of an "ideological consensus," a comprehensive, officially endorsed cultural myth that became entrenched in New England and spread throughout the growing nation (pp. xii–xiii). While Bercovitch does note that in his vision of ideological consensus he does gloss over economic, social and psychic tensions, we might also consider that his work also glosses over the uneven ideological development of a nationalism that arose more haphazardly out of Old World forms.

40 Andrew Delbanco, *The Puritan Ordeal* (Cambridge: Harvard University Press, 1989), pp. 1–27.

41 See Spengemann's *A New World of Words: Redefining early American literature* (New Haven: Yale University Press, 1994); Paul Giles, *Transatlantic*

Insurrections: British culture and the formation of American literature, 1730–1860 (Philadelphia: University of Pennsylvania Press, 2001). See also Jim Egan, *Authorizing Experience: Refigurations of the body politic in seventeenth-century New England writing* (Princeton: Princeton University Press, 1998). Egan's work is carefully aware of the transatlantic context in which early American literature was written, and thus is valuable in its ability to identify the transatlantic ideological strains and rhetorical traditions within which early New England writers were writing. Beyond these literary critics, my work on the New England Puritans is most indebted to historians of the early colonies, particularly Ian Steele, David Grayson Allen and Timothy Breen and Stephen Foster. Social historians of the New England colonies, perhaps due to their interest in commercial exchange and institutional influence, have in the past twenty years constructed a more complex and transatlantic picture of the early settlements, generally emphasizing their continuity and indebtedness to the British homeland.

42 Giles, *Transatlantic Insurrections*, pp. 12–14 and 23.

43 The important texts here are Lois Potter's *Secret Rites and Secret Writing: Royalist literature 1641–1660* (Cambridge: Cambridge University Press, 1990); Nigel Smith, *Literature and Revolution in England, 1640–1660* (New Haven: Yale University Press, 1994); Thomas Corns, *Uncloistered Virtue: English political literature, 1640–1660* (Oxford: Clarendon Press, 1992); David Norbrook, *Writing the English Republic: Poetry, rhetoric and politics, 1627–1660* (Cambridge: Cambridge University Press, 1999); Steven Zwicker's *Lines of Authority: Politics and English literary culture, 1649–1689* (Ithaca, NY: Cornell University Press, 1993). There has also been a slew of shorter and longer studies, some of which I detail below, that have followed up on the methodological assumptions of these studies, namely that the literature of this period was intricately and inevitably tied to the political ruptures of the period.

44 Steven Zwicker's *Lines of Authority* also works from the premise of the "polemicization of English literary culture between the outbreak of the civil wars and the Glorious Revolution" (p. 1). Yet Zwicker's study, in its juxtaposition in each chapter of texts from both sides of the ideological divide, invites the notion that these texts spoke to and against one another, that their authors read and reacted to one another, and that they envisioned their work as an entry into the sharply contested, yet very public and diverse (if elite), sphere of print publication.

45 While most critics remain sensitive to the constantly shifting political loyalties of most of the prominent writers in the '40s and '50s, their inclusion of particular texts as exemplary of "royalist" or "republican" literature to me seems often inaccurate. For example, Norbrook, who is one of the more careful readers of civil war ideologies, appropriates Hobbes's *Leviathan* to the republican tradition by discussing the advertisement for Hobbes's work in the Parliamentarian newsbook *Mercurius Politicus*. Yet also advertised was Davenant's *Gondibert* as well as numerous publications

by the supposedly "royalist" publisher Humphrey Moseley. At the same time that Hobbes's *Leviathan* was being released to the London public and Nedham was appropriating parts of Hobbes's older work for his Parliamentarian propaganda machine, Richard Royston, the publisher of numerous blatantly royalist polemics in the 1640s, was printing Hobbes's *De Cive*, translated for the first time into English by Charles Cotton.

46 Hobbes, *Leviathan*, ed. Richard Tuck (Cambridge: Cambridge University Press, 1996), p. 3.

47 Wilcher, *The Writing of Royalism, 1628–1660* (Cambridge: Cambridge University Press, 2001) pp. 322–3.

48 For Milton, see particularly, Christopher Hill, *The Experience of Defeat: Milton and some contemporaries* (New York: Viking, 1984), pp. 298–330; Louis Martz, *Milton: Poet of exile* (New Haven: Yale University Press, 1986), pp. 79–113; Blair Worden, "Milton's republicanism and the tyranny of heaven," *Machiavelli and Republicanism*, eds. Gisela Bock, Quentin Skinner and Maurizio Viroli (Cambridge: Cambridge University Press, 1990), pp. 225–45; Norbrook, *Writing the English Republic*, pp. 433–88. Dryden's work of the final decade has received increased attention in the past few years, most notably in Steven Zwicker, *Politics and Language in Dryden's Poetry: The arts of disguise* (Princeton: Princeton University Press, 1984), pp. 177–205; David Bywaters, *Dryden in Revolutionary England* (Berkeley: University of California Press, 1995); and Paul Hammond, *Dryden and the Traces of Classical Rome* (Oxford: Oxford University Press, 1999), pp. 218–82.

49 Hill, *Writing and Revolution in Seventeenth-century England*, quoted in N.H. Keeble, *The Literary Culture of Nonconformity in Later Seventeenth-century England* (Athens, Ga.: University of Georgia Press, 1987), p. 119. See also Hill, *Milton and the English Revolution* (London: Faber and Faber, 1977), pp. 64–5, 216–18, 405–7. Keeble spends a chapter discussing the methods and manners of censorship upon nonconformists after 1660 in *The Literary Culture of Nonconformity in Later Seventeenth-century England*, pp. 96–119.

50 Loewenstein, *Representing Revolution in Milton and his Contemporaries: Religion, politics and polemics in radical Puritanism* (Cambridge: Cambridge University Press, 2001), pp. 203–39. Norbrook pushes the date for the composition of the majority of *Paradise Lost* back before 1660, thus avoiding the problematic dynamic of the influence of censorship, while noting that the licensor's impression can be seen clearly on the hesitations and admissions to the necessity of tyranny in Michael's historical narrative in the final two books (*Writing the English Republic*, pp. 434–6).

51 See especially Zwicker, *Politics and Language in Dryden's Poetry*, pp. 177–205; Thomas Fujimura, "Dryden's Virgil: translation as autobiography," in *Studies in Philology* 80 (1983), 67–83; Zwicker and Bywaters, "Politics and translation: the English Tacitus of 1698," in *Huntington Library Quarterly* 52 (1989), 319–46; Kirk Combe, "Clandestine protest against William III in Dryden's translations of Juvenal and Persius," in *Modern Philology* 87

(1989), 36–50; Murray Pittock, *Poetry and Jacobite Politics in Eighteenth-Century Britain and Ireland* (Cambridge: Cambridge University Press, 1994), pp. 94–107; and Howard Erskine-Hill, *Poetry and the Realm of Politics: Shakespeare to Dryden* (Oxford: Clarendon Press, 1996), pp. 201–15.

52 Hammond, *Dryden and the Traces of Classical Rome*, pp. 223 and 251–60, especially for his political, Jacobite reading of the poem. Similarly, Tanya Caldwell, who notes some of the ways in which Dryden's translations have particularly contemporary concerns, argues that "Dryden's nostalgia for and adherence to ideologies and convictions he had expressed as early as 1660 are evident in his late translations," *Time to Begin Anew: Dryden's* GEORGICS *and* AENEIS (London: Associated University Presses, 2000), p. 23.

53 Raymond Astbury, "The renewal of the Licensing Act in 1693 and its lapse in 1695," in *The Library*, 5th ser. 33 (1978), pp. 315–17.

54 Buruma, "The romance of exile," in *The New Republic* (February 12, 2001), pp. 33–8.

55 Adorno, *Minima Moralia: Reflections from damaged life*, trans. E.F.N. Jephcott (London: Verso, 1978), p. 39.

56 Kristeva, "A new type of intellectual: the dissident," in *The Kristeva Reader*, ed. Toril Moi (New York: Columbia University Press, 1986), p. 298.

57 Michael Seidel explores the exilic qualities of Defoe, Joyce, Sterne, James and Nabokov in *Exile and the Narrative Imagination*; Terry Eagleton in *Exiles and Émigrés: Studies in modern literature* (New York: Schocken Books, 1970) details the metaphoric transformation of "exile" in the works of Virginia Woolf, E.M. Forster, Aldous Huxley and Evelyn Waugh; Nico Israel reads the works of Conrad, Adorno and Rushdie from the perspective of exile in *Outlandish*.

58 Mann expressed this sentiment in an open letter to Walter von Molo published in the *Augsburger Anzeiger*: "It may be a superstitious belief, but in my eyes, any books which could be printed at all in Germany between 1933 and 1945 are worse than worthless and not objects one wishes to touch. A stench of blood and shame attaches to them. They should all be pulped," quoted in J.M. Ritchie, *German Literature Under National Socialism* (London: Croom Helm, 1983), p. 115.

59 "Alienation" has become a much-used critical term since the 1960s, and can cover Marx's concept of alienation which refers to the artificial separation of man from his labor, and thus man from nature and himself, to more vague Romantic notions of voluntary isolation and creative eccentricity. For Marx's theories, see especially, Istvan Meszaros, *Marx's Theory of Alienation* (New York: Harper, 1970), Richard Schacht, *Alienation* (Urbana, Ill.: University of Illinois Press, 1970), and Schacht, *The Future of Alienation* (Urbana: University of Illinois Press, 1994). In referring to a post-structuralist theory of exile, I am thinking mainly of Julia Kristeva's formulation of our universal exile within language in *Strangers to Ourselves*, trans. Leon S. Roudiez (New York: Columbia University Press, 1991).

CHAPTER 1: NOSTALGIA AND NATIONALISM IN
NEW ENGLAND LITERATURE

1 For the sake of clarity, I have limited my discussion of "the early settlers" of New England to first-generation inhabitants. This first generation, crucially for my purposes, had lived for a time in England, and thus would have known the experience of displacement and migration. The second, "creole" generation, on the other hand, encountered and necessarily responded to a different set of circumstances of their settlement in the New World.

2 Perhaps a full one-sixth of those involved in the "Great Migration" remigrated, either back to England or to elsewhere in the American colonies, Joseph A. Conforti, *Imagining New England: Explorations of regional identity from the pilgrims to the mid-twentieth century* (Chapel Hill: University of North Carolina Press, 2001), p. 23.

3 Ian K. Steele, *The English Atlantic: An exploration of communication and community* (Oxford: Oxford University Press, 1986), esp. pp. 24–50 and pp. 116–53.

4 For much of the information about the exchange of information and written materials in the following account I have relied primarily upon Steele's *The English Atlantic*, pp. 116–53, and David Cressy, *Coming Over: Migration and communication between England and New England in the Seventeenth Century* (Cambridge: Cambridge University Press, 1987), pp. 213–34.

5 Hugh Amory has noted that excluding almanacs, broadsides and session acts, eighty-two distinct titles were produced collectively by Cambridge and Boston, out of 45,500 volumes (Amory, "Printing and bookselling in New England, 1638–1713," in *A History of the Book in America*, eds. David D. Hall and Hugh Amory [Cambridge: Cambridge University Press, 2000], p. 105). See also Thomas Goddard Wright's somewhat crude, but instructive, breakdown of the types of books printed at Cambridge from 1638–70 in *Literary Culture in Early New England, 1620–1730* (New Haven: Yale University Press, 1920), p. 82. Joseph Loewenstein has remarked on the "obsessively conservative" early Venetian press in his *The Author's Due: The intellectual history of copyright* (Chicago: University of Chicago Press, 2002), pp. 70–1. The Venetian printers' output, as far as range of titles is concerned, anticipates the similar conservatism of both the early English and early New England market in books.

6 Perry Miller also made this point over sixty years ago in *The New England Mind: From colony to province* (Cambridge: Harvard University Press, 1953), p. 6. Hall and Amory's recent and extensive work on the history of the book in New England supports this characterization. See *A History of the Book in America*, especially Hall's "Introduction," pp. 1–25 and Amory's chapters, "Reinventing the colonial book," pp. 26–54 and "Printing and bookselling in New England, 1638–1713," pp. 83–116. See also Hall, "The uses of literacy in New England, 1600–1850," in *Printing and Society in Early America*,

eds. William L. Joyce, *et al.* (Worcester, MA: American Antiquarian Society, 1983), pp. 5–45.

7 On the relationships between New England booksellers and London whole-salers, and on the importation of books into America more generally, see Amory, "Reinventing the colonial book," and "Printing and bookselling in America"; James Raven, "The importation of books in the eighteenth century," in *A History of the Book in Early America*, pp. 183–98; Stephen Botein, "The Anglo-American book trade before 1776: personnel and strategies," in *Printing and Society in America*, pp. 48–80. Worthington Chauncey Ford's *The Boston Book Market, 1679–1700* (Boston: The Club of Odd Volumes, 1917) has useful primary material on the early booksellers in Boston, including several shipping lists from the London wholesaler Richard Chiswell to Hezekiah Usher, the most prominent early Boston bookseller.

8 Perhaps the most bizarre alliance made by Winthrop, Jr. was with Sir Kenelm Digby, the eccentric Royalist exile and bibliophile, who in 1647 and 1654 sent chests of books to New England for the fledgling library at Harvard. For Winthrop and others' attempts to procure books from friends in England, see Wright, *Literary Culture in Early New England*, pp. 25–61.

9 Quoted in *The Works of Anne Bradstreet in Prose and Verse*, ed. John Harvard Ellis (New York: P. Smith, 1932), p. lxi.

10 Cressy, *Coming Over*, pp. 213–62. Cressy cites numerous letters from Winthrop's papers and elsewhere as proof and states categorically: "the literate elite in colonial New England waited as eagerly for intelligence about church and state in England as they did for family news from the homeland" (p. 235). See also James M. O'Toole, "New England reactions to the English civil wars," in *New England Historical and Genealogical Register* 129 (1975), 3–17 and Ian K. Steele, "Communicating a revolution to the colonies," in *Journal of British Studies* 24 (1985), 333–57.

11 Nathaniel Ward, *The Simple Cobler of Aggawam* (London, 1647), p. 67. All further citations will be from this edition and cited in the text.

12 The pamphlets on the Antinomian Controversy were numerous and are usefully put into order by David Hall in *The Antinomian Controversy, 1636–1638: A documentary history* (Middletown, Conn.: Wesleyan University Press, 1968). At least partially, the pamphlet boom can be under-stood as an attempt by the colonists to justify their persecution of Hutchinson and her followers as they came under increasing fire from English authorities, spurred by the complaints of Samuel Gorton and the Hingham militia petitioners. However, the title pages and prefaces to these works address the English reader, often specifically offering the Antinomian controversy as instruction for England's "present miseries." See John Winthrop, *A Short Story of the Rise, Reign, and Ruine of the Antinomians, Familists and Libertines* (London, 1644), t.p. and Thomas Lechford, *New-Englands Advice to Old-England* (London, 1644) for example. The colonists' trouble with dissidents and English authorities in the 1640s is detailed

adroitly by Robert Emmet Wall, *Massachusetts Bay: The crucial decade, 1640–1650* (New Haven: Yale University Press, 1972).

13 Larzer Ziff, "Introduction," in *John Cotton on the Churches of New England*, ed. Larzer Ziff (Cambridge: Belknap Press, 1968), p. 27. The Independents also sounded a note of support for Massachusetts Bay's religious policies in *An Apologeticall Narration* (London, 1643). Cotton, Thomas Shepard, and Thomas Hooker were invited to attend the Westminster Assembly in 1642, but refused, thinking the Presbyterian faction too strong.

14 See particularly Miller, *The New England Mind: The seventeenth century* (New York: Macmillan, 1939); Miller, *Errand into the Wilderness* (Cambridge: Belknap Press, 1956); Bercovitch, *The American Jeremiad* (Madison: University of Wisconsin Press, 1978) and *The Puritan Origins of the American Self* (New Haven: Yale University Press, 1975).

15 Said, "Reflections on exile," in *Reflections on Exile and Other Essays* (New York: St. Martin's Press, 2000), p. 174.

16 Anderson, *Imagined Communities: Reflections on the origins and spread of nationalism*, new edition (Boston: Verso, 1991), pp. 47–65.

17 William Spengemann makes a similar argument in *A New World of Words: Redefining early American Literature* (New Haven: Yale University Press, 1994), pp. 33–6.

18 Steele, *The English Atlantic*, pp. 60–1.

19 Quoted in Cressy, *Coming Over*, p. 262.

20 Steele, *English Atlantic*, p. 6.

21 Michael Walzer, *The Revolution of the Saints: A study in the origins of radical politics* (Cambridge: Harvard University Press, 1965), esp. pp. 244–7, 264–7. See also Stephen Foster's *The Long Argument: English Puritanism and the shaping of New England culture, 1570–1700* (Chapel Hill: University of North Carolina Press, 1991). Foster usefully issues the following caveat: "We consign the Puritans to Arcadia; they themselves would no doubt have preferred urban centers and bustling market towns" (p. 18).

22 Roger Thompson, *Mobility and Migration: East Anglian founders of New England, 1629–1640* (Amherst: University of Massachusetts Press, 1994), pp. 184–204.

23 See, first, David Grayson Allen's analysis of four separate New World communities in *In English Ways: The movement of societies and the transferal of English local law and custom to Massachusetts Bay in the seventeenth century* (Chapel Hill: University of North Carolina Press, 1981) and T.H. Breen, "Transfer of culture: chance and design in shaping Massachusetts Bay, 1630–1660," in *New England Historic Genealogical Register* 132 (1977), 3–17. See also Breen and Foster, "The Puritans' greatest achievement: a study of social cohesion in seventeenth-century Massachusetts," in *The Journal of American History* 60 (1973), 5–22.

24 Winthrop wrote to his son in October of 1629, shortly before leaving for New England, asking him to copy Higginson's second letter and to circulate it to those planning the voyage. Thomas Dudley wrote back to his

patron the Lady Arbella, Countess of Lincoln in 1630, encouraging her to pass his correspondence on "for the use of such as shall hereafter intend to increase our plantation," quoted in Cressy, *Coming Over*, p. 15.

25 Higginson's letters are reprinted in *Letters from New England, the Massachusetts Bay Colony, 1629–38*, ed. Everett Emerson (Amherst: University of Massachusetts Press, 1976), pp. 11–38.

26 Quoted in *Letters from New England*, p. xiii.

27 William Hooke, *New Englands Teares for Old Englands Feares* (London, 1641), pp. 20–1. It should not pass without notice that this sermon, of course, was published in London.

28 Higginson's letter starts: "A true relation of the last voyage to new England declaring all circumstances with the manner of the passage we had by sea . . . ," in *Letters from New England*, p. 12. It should be noted that Higginson's letter is known particularly for its unguarded, and often unfounded, optimism for the prospects of the New England settlements.

29 Even with this reassurance from Wilson in the body of the text, Nathaniel Ward, perhaps taking advantage of his now growing reputation in the English print market, stressed Wilson's veracity in his brief prefatory note. See *The Day-breaking if not the Sun-rising of the Gospel with the Indians in New England* (London, 1647), sig. Av.

30 Thomas Shepard, *The Clear Sun-shine of the Gospel Breaking Forth Upon the Indians* (London, 1648). In the first several pages Shepard reassures Eliot and his audience that he has "sent you their own copy and their own hands to it"; that he cannot continue the account further "from my owne eye and eare witness of things"; that "the rest I shall relate to you as I have received from faithful witnesses"; and finally signs the letter: "I have sent you two witnesses beside my own of the truth of the Indian story printed, you may publish them if you please as they have writ" (pp. 3–8).

31 In John Winthrop's *A Short Story of the Rise, Reign and Ruin of the Antinomians*, the title page emphasizes that the work was published "by one that was an eye and eare-witnesse of the carriage of matters there."

32 See William Wood, *New Englands Prospect* (London, 1634), where he claims to have had his work published since he had lived in the colony for four years and could dispel the "many scandalous and false reports passed upon the country, even from the sulphurous breath of every bas ballad-monger" (p. 17). Jim Egan has documented the development of a rhetoric of "experience" in the writings from the New World, including Wood's, that holds an originary place in American rhetoric in his *Authorizing Experience: Refigurations of the body politic in seventeenth-century New England* (Princeton: Princeton University Press, 1998).

33 Nancy Armstrong and Leonard Tennenhouse have noted, in their discussion of Mary Rowlandson's *The Sovereignty and Goodness of God*, how the slightest phrase or marker could signal to an English reader that the text came from the far distant New World, *The Imaginary Puritan: Literature, intellectual*

labor and the origins of personal life (Berkeley: University of California Press, 1992), pp. 205–7.

34 Sharon Ouditt, "Introduction," in *Displaced Persons: Conditions of exile in European culture*, ed. Sharon Ouditt (Aldershot: Ashgate, 2002), p. xii.

35 See Paul Giles's introduction to his monograph *Transatlantic Insurrections: British culture and the formation of American literature, 1730–1860* (Philadelphia: University of Pennsylvania Press, 2001), pp. 5–16, where Giles postulates a similar relationship between colonial subjects and the homeland, one that entails a constant dialogue and debate across the Atlantic. Giles's theoretical model for American and British literatures, as literatures that developed as heretical alternatives to each other, has deeply informed my discussion of the New England texts I discuss in this chapter.

36 A few words here on terminology. The identification of a "Puritan" tradition and communities in early modern England has been vexed by a complex debate over the meaning and use of the very term, a debate that cuts to the heart of the place and attitudes of this nebulous spiritual community vis-à-vis English society at large. The term itself originated as a term of abuse in the late Elizabethan period, as Patrick Collinson has clearly detailed in *English Puritanism* (London: Historical Association, 1983), pp. 7–11. One has only to think of Jonson's Zeal-of-the-land-busy in his *Bartholomew Fair* to see the outlines of the caricature of the typical Puritan hypocrite killjoy. I use the term here, drawing on the seminal work of Patrick Collinson, to refer to a religious community within the Protestant movement that desired greater reformation (see most importantly, Collinson, *The Elizabethan Puritan Movement* [Berkeley: University of California Press, 1967] as well as Peter Lake, *Moderate Puritans and the Elizabethan Church* [Cambridge: Cambridge University Press, 1982]); and that had a rather unique sense of their personal place within this reformation (see Peter Lake, "Defining Puritanism – again?," in *Puritanism: Transatlantic perspectives on a seventeenth-century Anglo-American faith*, ed. Francis J. Bremer [Boston: Massachusetts Historical Society, 1993], pp. 3–29, and John Spurr, *English Puritanism, 1603–1689* [Basingstoke: Macmillan, 1998], pp. 41–8). This community was never satisfied with the reformed state of the Anglican church, and grew increasingly disillusioned with the potential for the fulfillment of their goals, and with the personal and institutional morality of the rest of England. I am particularly interested in tracing a tradition of protestant spiritual and political thought that I and others have termed "Puritan" through the specific writings of individuals, and the transformation of that tradition due to the experience of migration to the shores and woods of New England.

37 For more on Frith and Tyndale see William A. Clebsch, *England's Earliest Protestants, 1520–1535* (New Haven: Yale University Press, 1964), pp. 79–116 and pp. 146–204. Clebsch definitively asserts Tyndale's impact: "Tyndale by a few emendations turned the very Lutheran prologue to the 1525 New

Testament into an explanation of scripture that without exaggeration can be called the *magna carta* of English Puritanism" (p. 167).

38 Walzer, *The Revolution of the Saints*, pp. 114–37. Christopher Hill, *Society and Puritanism in Pre-revolutionary England* (New York: Schocken Books, 1967), p. 492.

39 For an outline of the development of this historiography, see Avihu Zakai, *Exile and Kingdom: History and apocalypse in the Puritan migration to America* (Cambridge: Cambridge University Press, 1992), pp. 24–46. While Zakai does an adroit job of explaining the historiography created by Bale and Foxe, his eventual analysis of the place of Puritanism in England and also of the New England ministers' relationship with their homeland seems a significant shade wrong. Rather than signaling a definitive and incontrovertible break with the Church of England, as we will see, the migration to New England was viewed by the colonists in much more ambiguous terms.

40 John Bale, *The Actes of English Votaryes* (London, 1546), sig. 23v. Similarly, John Foxe, contrasting the pure and apostolic ancient Roman church of Eleutherius with the corruptions of the later Roman and English churches, defiantly states: "So that, as I said, if the papists would needs derive the faith and religion of this realm [England] from Rome, then let them set us and leave us there where they had us; that is, let them suffer us to stand content with that faith and religion which then was taught and brought from Rome by Eleutherius (as now we differ nothing from the same), and we will desire no better," in *The Acts and Monuments of John Foxe*, ed. Josiah Pratt, 4th ed., 8 vols. (London: The Religious Tract Society, 1877), vol. I, p. 308.

41 Foxe, *The Acts and Monuments*, vol. I, p. 9.

42 Foxe, *The Acts and Monuments*, vol. VI, p. 384.

43 One such minister lamented to a fellow exile, "Oh, Zurich, Zurich, I think more of Zurich in England than ever I thought of England while I was in Zurich," quoted in Walzer, *The Revolution of the Saints*, p. 116.

44 Foxe, *The Acts and Monuments*, vol. VIII, p. 601.

45 See, most importantly, Collinson's *The Elizabethan Puritan Movement* and *Elizabethan Puritanism*, as well as "Sects and the Evolution of Puritanism," in *Puritanism: Transatlantic Perspectives*, pp. 147–66. See also the work of Peter Lake, especially, *Moderate Puritans and the Elizabethan Church*, pp. 279–92. A useful overview is provided by Peter Marshall, *Reformation England, 1480–1642* (London: Arnold, 2003), pp. 113–42.

46 For the use of this metaphor see Lake, "Defining Puritanism – again?," in *Puritanism: Transatlantic perspectives*, p. 15. I discuss the New England Puritans' evolving use of the same metaphor below.

47 Alison Games states that up to 10,000 people left England for the Atlantic world alone in 1635. While all of these certainly did not head to New England, the mid-'30s did signal a peak in the migration to the northern colonies. See Games, *Migration and the Origins of the English Atlantic World* (Cambridge: Harvard University Press, 1999), pp. 3–4.

48 T.H. Breen and Stephen Foster detail the individual, various and often haphazard motivations to leave England in "Moving to the New World: the character of early Massachusetts immigration," in *William and Mary Quarterly* 34 (1973), 189–222. See also Breen, "Persistent localism: English social change and the shaping of New England institutions," in *William and Mary Quarterly* 32 (1975), 3–28. The debate over the reasons for the Great Migration has been extended and fierce. Beginning with James Truslow Adams and Samuel Eliot Morison, historians have vigorously debated the primacy of economic (Adams) or religious (Morison) motivations. Breen and Foster have cogently noted that this debate seems a question poorly posed, since the two factors were inextricably intertwined. David Grayson Allen in *In English Ways* gives a balanced and detailed account of the migration of four different groups from different areas of England. Virginia DeJohn Anderson, in *New England's Generation: The great migration and the formation of society and culture in the seventeenth century* (Cambridge: Cambridge University Press, 1991), however, more recently has reformulated a migration both coherent and religious in its origins (pp. 12–46). Cressy, on the other hand, describes a perhaps *too* secular migration in *Coming Over*, where he is right, however, to emphasize the "untidy, fractured and complex," rather than the "rational, purposeful and coherent," nature of the migration (p. 74).

49 Foster, *The Long Argument*, p. 137.

50 Many of the colonists' own statements say as much, listing the reasons for leaving and always including the interests of king and country in the New World as one.

51 In this depiction of a migration still deeply connected to English society, a migration with one eye still on the homeland, I depart from many accounts of the New England migration. Bercovitch, in *The American Jeremiad*, tends to overstate the separatist tendencies of the New England settlers while correctly noting that the Great Migration inherited the feeling that they were both the true Church of England and a truly separate community of elect saints, pp. 37–8. More recently, Zakai, in *Exile and Kingdom*, also emphasizes the firm religious separatism of the Massachusetts Bay founders, pp. 56–68. On the other hand, Susan Hardman Moore, in "Popery, purity and Providence: deciphering the New England experiment," in *Religion, Culture and Society in Early Modern Britain: Essays in honor of Patrick Collinson*, eds. Anthony Fletcher and Peter Roberts (Cambridge: Cambridge University Press, 1994), pp. 257–89 argues adroitly and convincingly for similarly contradictory impulses at the root of the migration.

52 Allen, *In English Ways*, p. 4. Breen similarly states in "Transfer of culture": "The colonists who traveled with Governor John Winthrop replicated with striking success patterns of community life they had experienced in England" (p. 6).

53 Thompson, *Mobility and Migration*, pp. 183–223, details the types of companies that traveled to the New World, as well as the movements of

certain groups after they arrived. Allen's study of Ipswich/Watertown, Rowley, Hingham and Newbury illustrates the specific local characteristics of each of these towns. Each was settled by colonists primarily from one area, and even one town in England.

54 For the classic exposition of the transferal of institutions to the New World, see Sidney Mintz and Richard Price, *The Birth of African-American Culture: An anthropological perspective* (Boston: Beacon Press, 1972).

55 Thomas Lechford's *Plain Dealing from New England* (London, 1642) was reprinted and renamed in 1644 as *New Englands Advice to Old England*, echoing the titles of sermons previously printed, such as William Hooke's *New Englands Teares for Old Englands Feares* (London, 1641). The re-titling of the reprint suggests that the publisher recognized a market for this genre and attempted to place Lechford's comparative political treatise into this market. See also Hooke's *New Englands Sence of Old England and Irelands Sorrowes* (London, 1645).

56 Hooke, *New Englands Teares*, pp. 16–17.

57 Bradstreet, *The Complete Works of Anne Bradstreet*, ed. Joseph R. McElrath, Jr. and Allan P. Robb (Boston: Twayne Publishers, 1981), p. 141. All further citations will come from the McElrath edition and appear in the text. Since Bradstreet's poems appeared without line numbers in 1650, and are reproduced in the McElrath edition in the same manner, I cite page numbers.

58 Jim Egan, *Authorizing Experience*, discusses the refigurations of the body politic topoi caused by the settlement of New England, pp. 14–30.

59 For example, Cotton's *The Way of Congregational Churches Cleared*, *The Keys to the Kingdome of Heaven*, and *Bloody Tenant Washed* and Hooker's *A Survey of the Summe of Church-discipline*.

60 Hooker, *A Survey of the Summe of Church-discipline* (London, 1648), sig. a3r.

61 *A Platform of Church Discipline* (Cambridge, 1649), p. 1.

62 Richard Mather wrote most of the *Platform*, except the Preface. Winslowe, *Hypocrisie Unmasked* (London, 1647), p. 94. Winslowe, in the paragraph immediately preceding his denunciation of national churches, defends the New England churches, including Plymouth, from the charge of separatism.

63 *The Way of Congregational Churches Cleared*, pp. 5, 10. On Cotton's New England Way, see Larzer Ziff, *John Cotton on the Churches of New England*. Ziff notes that despite Cotton's repeated denials of separatism, his own doctrinal statements leaned more and more in that direction, pp. 1–6.

64 Cited in Ewell's historical note to John Winthrop's *The Humble Request of the Massachusetts Puritans*, ed. S.E. Morison (Boston: Old South Association, 1916), n.p.

65 For more on Williams's expulsion from Salem, see Wall's prologue to *The Crucial Decade*, pp. 1–18 and Stephen Foster, "New England and the challenge of heresy, 1630 to 1660: the Puritan crisis in transatlantic perspective," in *William and Mary Quarterly* 38 (1981), 624–60, and for primary material

John Winthrop, *Winthrop's Journal: The history of New England, 1629 to 1649*, 2 vols. (Boston, 1825), vol. I. Indeed, Winthrop displays a worry over the separatist passages in a manuscript Williams circulated in Boston and Salem precisely because of the delicate situation made worse by Endicott's actions (vol. I, pp. 150–8). Even at this delicate juncture, however, Winthrop notes that the General Council decided to "write cautiously" to a benefactor in England that they would punish Endicott, but with "as much wariness as we might" since they had their own hesitations over using the cross as an ensign (p. 150).

66 For example, in 1631, Henry Lynne was whipped for writing letters into England "full of slander against our government," in *Winthrop's Journal*, vol. I, p. 61. In 1637, a Mr. Pratt was brought in for questioning in front of the General Court for spreading a letter in England that described the plantation as nothing but rocks (vol. I, p. 173).

67 For a detailed account of the dispute, see Wall, *The Crucial Decade*, pp. 93–120.

68 John Child, *New Englands Jonas cast up at London* (London, 1647), pp. 8–9.

69 Edward Winslowe, *New-Englands Salamander* (London, 1647), pp. t.p., 10, 23.

70 Child, *New Englands Jonas*, pp. 10–11.

71 For more on Ward's Marprelate influences, see James Egan, "Nathaniel Ward and the Marprelate tradition," in *Early American Literature* 15 (1980), 59–71.

72 There were a series of Marprelate-influenced polemics in the 1640s including *Vox Borealis, or the Northern Discoverie* (London, 1640), Richard Overton's *The Arraignment of Mr. Persecution ... by Young Mr. Mar-Priest* (London, 1645) and his *Martin's Eccho* (London, 1645). Milton's *Animadversions upon the Remonstrants Defence Against Smectymnuus* (London, 1642) could also easily be included in this list with its colloquial punning and purposefully ridiculous logic.

73 See, for example, Ward, *The Simple Cobler*, p. 26.

74 Also in the elegy to Elizabeth: "But happy *England*, which had such a Queen,/O happy, happy had those dayes still been" (p. 155).

75 Ann Stanford, "Anne Bradstreet," in *Major Writers of Early American Literature*, ed. Everett Emerson (Madison: University of Wisconsin Press, 1972), p. 36.

76 Bradstreet's insistent claims to humility and inability to express her praise or subject adequately have rightly attracted significant attention from her modern critics. Eileen Margerum usefully lays out, albeit somewhat negatively, Bradstreet's Renaissance sources for the humility topoi in "Anne Bradstreet's public poetry and the tradition of humility," in *Early American Literature* 17 (1982), 152–60. More sophisticated is Ivy Schweitzer's discussion of the influence of Bradstreet's status as a woman poet upon this expressed humility, and the potential for a more subversive and

self-conscious use of such topoi (Schweitzer, "Anne Bradstreet wrestles with the Renaissance," in *Early American Literature* 23 [1988], 291–312). See also, more recently, Nancy Wright, "Epitaphic conventions and the reception of Anne Bradstreet's public voice," in *Early American Literature* 31 (1996), 243–63, and my discussion below.

77 The coalescence of the concerns of migration and femininity has been remarked upon by Patricia Caldwell in her trenchant examination of Bradstreet's poetry, "Why our first poet was a woman: Bradstreet and the birth of an American poetic voice," in *Prospects* 13 (1988), 27–8.

78 Eileen Margerum, "Anne Bradstreet's public poetry and the tradition of humility," p. 154.

79 Schweitzer, "Anne Bradstreet wrestles with the Renaissance," pp. 291–2.

80 Schweitzer, *The Work of Self-representation: Lyric poetry in colonial New England* (Chapel Hill: University of North Carolina Press, 1991), pp. 146–7, argues that the sheer number of these dedicatory verses identify this text as anomalous, and because from a woman, in particular need of validation from male authors. Yet in fact the number of dedicatory verses in *The Tenth Muse* seems rather to attempt to place it into contemporary practice. The inclusion of numerous prefatory poems in collections of literature had become a commonplace by the late '40s, especially in the print productions of Humphrey Moseley. The Beaumont and Fletcher folio, printed in 1647, had 42 dedicatory verses, while William Cartwright's posthumous *Poems*, in 1651, had 51. This misstep does not, however, blunt Schweitzer's larger point, which is that this prefatory material served to draw attention to the strangeness of the event that was *The Tenth Muse*.

81 See against Margerum's argument, Schweitzer, "Anne Bradstreet wrestles with the Renaissance," and Timothy Sweet, "Gender, genre, and subjectivity in Anne Bradstreet's early Elegies," in *Early American Literature* 23 (1988), 152–74. More generally on her position as a female author writing as a Puritan and a poet in the seventeenth century, see Carrie Galloway Blackstock, "Anne Bradstreet and performativity: self-cultivation, self-deployment," in *Early American Literature* 32 (1997), 222–48; Wright, "Epitaphic conventions and the reception of Anne Bradstreet's public voice"; and Bethany Reid, " 'Unfit for light': Anne Bradstreet's monstrous birth," in *The New England Quarterly* 73 (2000), 517–42.

82 Thomas Weld, *A Brief Narration of the Practices of the Churches in New-England* (London, 1645), p. 7.

83 Mainly in Cotton's address "To the Reader" in *Abstract of the Lawes of New England* (London, 1641), n.p. Cotton drew this draft up after Winthrop and the General Court called upon he and Ward each to come up with an outline of the fundamental laws of the colony. Ward's draft was eventually chosen, yet Cotton's was published both in Massachusetts and in London, and, concerning the ordinances of God, reflected the feelings of many of the magistrates in the Bay Colony.

84 See Hooker, *The Danger of Desertion* (London, 1641), pp. 7–8; Cotton, *God's Promise to his Plantations* (London, 1634), pp. 6–9. Cotton restates this sentiment after his arrival in Boston in *The Keys to the Kingdom of Heaven*, where he argues that the Puritans left England precisely to maintain the "keys of the kingdom" of heaven, which "are the ordinances which Christ has instituted, to be administered to his Church" (Ziff, *John Cotton on the Churches of New England*, pp. 87–8).

85 *The Bay Psalm Book* (Cambridge, 1640), sig. A2r.

86 Hooker, *The Survey of the Summe of Church-discipline*, sig. A3v.

87 John Wilson, *The Day-breaking*, p. 4.

88 *New Englands First Fruits* (London, 1643), pp. 17–18.

89 Thomas Shepard, *The Clear Sun-shine of the Gospel Breaking Forth*, A4r.

90 The phenomenon of the Antinomian controversy, as we shall see, should not be seen as independent of this ideology.

91 Peter Lake, "Redefining Puritanism – again?," p. 15.

92 *A Platform of Church Discipline*, p. 3. This is Richard Mather writing; Cotton also brings out the same metaphor in the Preface.

93 Ward, *Discolliminium* (London, 1650), p. 3. The warning against a contagious leprosy also reappears in this work.

94 *Winthrop's Journal*, vol. I, pp. 76, 87, 160, etc.

95 Hooker, *The Survey of the Summe of Church-discipline*, sig. A2r.

96 The status of Winthrop's *Journal* as a specifically public document remains unclear, although its author's purposes can perhaps be divined from the fact that Winthrop entitled the second book of this journal *A History of New England*.

97 Historians have made much of the great achievement of the New England Puritans in maintaining such stability in the early years of the colony (see particularly, Breen and Foster, "The Puritans' greatest achievement"). Yet we might want to admit that some of what seems to be stability is, in fact, the ideological formation of this stability by early writers. For a picture of the early Massachusetts colony that concentrates on conflict and opposition, see Wall, *The Crucial Decade*.

98 Perry Miller, *Errand in the Wilderness*, pp. 11–12. For a colonial view of this same interest, see Hooke's sermons expressing New England's sorrow and prayers for the troubles of England in the 1640s.

99 *Winthrop's Journal*, vol. I, p. 136.

100 Johnson, *Wonder-working Providence* (London, 1654), sig. A2v.

101 *Wonder-working Providence*, pp. 4–5. I might add that the leaven image that Ward and the Cambridge Synod use also reappears in Johnson's text, as "the sowre Leven of unfound Doctrine" (p. 7).

102 Bercovitch, *The American Jeremiad*, p. 25.

103 John Winthrop, "A modell of Christian charity," in *Collections of the Massachusetts Historical Society* 7 (1838), 47.

104 Caldwell, "The Antinomian language controversy," in *Harvard Theological Review* 79 (1986), 345–67.

CHAPTER 2: EXILE AND THE SEMANTIC EDUCATION
OF THOMAS HOBBES'S "LEVIATHAN"

1 *The English Works of Thomas Hobbes of Malmesbury,* ed. Sir William
Molesworth, 11 vols. (London: J. Bohn, 1839–45), vol. VII, pp. 5–6.

2 *The English Works of Thomas Hobbes,* vol. VII, p. 336.

3 For which, see David Underdown, *Royalist Conspiracy in England, 1649–1660*
(New Haven: Yale University Press, 1960).

4 Juergen Habermas's work on the public sphere in England has
usefully been revisited and revised recently in order to incorporate the
explosion of the pamphlet culture after the lapsing of the Licensing
Act in 1642, and the general increase in very public interest in state
affairs. See especially Alexandra Halasz, *The Marketplace of Print:
Pamphlets and the public sphere in early modern England* (Cambridge:
Cambridge University Press, 1997) although dealing with an even earlier
period; Joad Raymond, "The newspaper, public opinion, and the public
sphere in the seventeenth century," in *News, Newspapers, and Society in
Early Modern Britain,* ed. Joad Raymond (London: Frank Cass, 1999),
pp. 109–40; Sharon Achinstein, *Milton and the Revolutionary Reader*
(Princeton: Princeton University Press, 1994), pp. 3–26; and David
Norbrook, "*Areopagitica,* censorship, and the early modern public
sphere," in *The Administration of Aesthetics: Censorship, political criticism
and the public sphere,* ed. Richard Burt (Minneapolis: University of
Minnesota Press, 1994), pp. 3–33.

5 Indeed, generally, we might be wary of assuming any sort of community of
like-minded readers, even in seemingly the most restrictive situations. For
an enlightening example, see Carlo Ginzburg's *The Cheese and the Worms:
The cosmos of a sixteenth-century miller,* trans. by John and Anne Tedeschi
(Baltimore: The Johns Hopkins University Press, 1980).

6 See, for example, Lois Potter's reading of William Davenant's unfinished
epic, *Gondibert,* which she describes as an act of defiance, and a work that
assumes that its reading public is dead and seeks to reach out only to a
private world (*Secret Rites and Secret Writing: Royalist literature 1641–1660*
[Cambridge: Cambridge University Press, 1990], pp. 94–100). One wonders
why Davenant would publish both his Preface by itself, and the unfinished
poem, if he felt this way. Stella Revard's "The politics of Cowley's
Pindariques," in *Criticism* 35 (1993), 393–410, twists and tweaks Cowley's
at best ambivalent odes on Brutus and Hobbes into royalist defiance. See
also, Robert Wilcher's *The Writing of English Royalism, 1628–1660*
(Cambridge: Cambridge University Press, 2001), pp. 221–307.

7 An older version of this picture, one that David Norbrook, in *Writing the
English Republic: Poetry, rhetoric and politics, 1627–1660* (Cambridge:
Cambridge University Press, 1999), and Nigel Smith, in *Literature and
Revolution in England, 1640–1660* (New Haven: Yale University Press,
1994), have, to an extent, dispelled, implies that only royalists read poetry,

plays, and romances, while Parliamentarians only read sermons, polemic and newsbooks.

8 See, most immediately, David Norbrook, *Writing the English Revolution*, pp. 212–36. Generally, Norbrook argues that the upheavals of the mid-century engendered a full-fledged republican literary tradition that eventually found its fruition in Milton's English epic, *Paradise Lost*. In tracking a consistently overlooked republican poetics of the sublime in authors such as Lucan, May, Marvell and Nedham, Norbrook has invaluably widened our understanding of the literary culture of the entire seventeenth century. See, however, Markku Peltonen's *Classical Humanism and Republicanism in English Political Thought, 1570–1640* (Cambridge: Cambridge University Press, 1995), pp. 54–118 for copious evidence of a vibrant English republican tradition during Elizabeth's reign. Blair Worden has also done considerable work on the advent of English republicanism in the figures of Marchamont Nedham and James Harrington; see Worden's work in *Republicanism, Liberty and Commercial Society, 1649–1776*, ed. David Wootton (Stanford: Stanford University Press, 1994), pp. 45–138.

9 Norbrook, *Writing the English Republic*, p. 212. He is referring to Nedham's plagiarism of portions of the 1650 edition of Hobbes's *Human Nature* in *Mercurius Politicus* in the early months of 1651. It is not out of the question that the printer Thomas Newcombe, who printed Hobbes's *Human Nature*, provided Nedham with copytext. Newcombe took over the publishing of *Politicus* shortly before Nedham began to plagiarize Hobbes. Nedham also acknowledges Hobbes as his source when he appropriates a portion of the 1650 *De Corpore Politico* in the second edition of *The Case of the Commonwealth of England Stated* (London, 1650). It should be noted that both of these works were published without Hobbes's permission.

10 In 1650, two editions of *Human Nature* came out, one in London, one in Oxford; *De Corpore Politico* was published in May in London and two editions of Hobbes's "Answer," to Davenant's Preface came out in Paris. There is evidence that Davenant's Preface and Hobbes's "Answer" made their way over to England, judging from the fact that a contemporary reader bound the Paris 1650 edition with the London 1650 editions of *Human Nature* and *De Corpore Politico* (see William Andrews Clark Memorial Library, shelfmark B1232 1650). Two more editions of *Gondibert*, with Hobbes's "Answer" were published in London in early 1651, along with an English translation of *De Cive*, published by Richard Royston in March. Finally, of course, *Leviathan* was published sometime in April or May of 1651 by Andrew Crooke. Howard Warrender, in his introduction to *De Cive: The Latin version* (Oxford: Clarendon University Press, 1983), pp. 14–15, attributes the publication of Royston's *De Cive* to a lapse in censorship in 1651. However, Thomason's copy is dated 12 March 1651, while censorship does not seem to have lapsed until September 1651.

11 Norbrook details the republican connections of Fisher's poem, *Writing the English Republic*, pp. 234–6.

12 Holden's full bibliography only runs slightly beyond this list, since he was only active from 1649–53 it seems. Yet he was very active during this period. I infer my picture of the contents of Holden's shop from an advertisement for books sold in his shop printed in *Sir Walter Rawlegh's Ghost* (London, 1651), sig. Bv4.

13 Thomas Corns, *Uncloistered Virtue: English political literature, 1640–1660* (Oxford: Clarendon Press, 1992), p. 3.

14 Alexandra Halasz, *The Marketplace of Print*, pp. 14–45.

15 Ginzberg, *The Cheese and the Worms* and Michel de Certeau, *The Practice of Everyday Life*, trans. by Steven Rendall (Berkeley: University of California Press, 1984), pp. 165–76.

16 See Stella Revard, "The politics of Cowley's Pindariques," pp. 393–410 and T.R. Langley, "Cowley's 'Ode to Brutus'," in *Yearbook of English Studies* 6 (1976), 41–52.

17 Marc Robinson, "Introduction," in *Altogether Elsewhere: Writers in exile* (Winchester, MA: Faber and Faber, 1994), pp. xiii, xviii.

18 Robert Edwards, "Exile, self and society," in *Exile in Literature*, ed. María-Inés Lagos-Pope (London: Associated University Presses, 1988), p. 20. For a detailed examination of the specific social, religious and financial difficulties of the royalist exiles on the Continent, see Geoffrey Smith's invaluable *The Cavaliers in Exile, 1640–1660* (Basingstoke: Palgrave Macmillan, 2003). Smith's research on the royalists in exile begins to fill the large gaps in the historiography of these communities. Much of my research, conducted before Smith's work was available, corroborates Smith's own findings.

19 On the material tastes of the Caroline court, see R. Malcolm Smuts, "Art and the material culture of majesty in early Stuart England," in *The Stuart Court and Europe: Essays in politics and political culture*, ed. R. Malcolm Smuts (Cambridge: Cambridge University Press, 1996), pp. 86–112.

20 *Memoirs of the Verney Family, Compiled from the Letters and Illustrated by the Portraits at Claydon House*, comp. Frances Parthenope Verney, 4 vols. (London: Longmans, Green, 1892–99), vol. II, pp. 235, 315.

21 *Memoirs of the Verney Family*, vol. II, p. 228.

22 John Evelyn, *Diary, Now First Printed in Full from the MSS Belonging to John Evelyn*, 6 vols. (Oxford: Clarendon Press, 1955), vol. II, p. 553 and vol. III, p. 12.

23 Quentin Bone, *Henrietta Maria: Queen of the Cavaliers* (Urbana: University of Illinois Press, 1972), p. 155.

24 Evelyn, *Diary*, vol. III, pp. 5–8.

25 *Memoirs of the Verney Family*, vol. II, p. 312. Cardinal Mazarin also comes under fire for his foreignness in a wonderful sentence from Ormonde expressing his opinion that Mazarin will escape from the Fronde unscathed: "the Cardinal, with his Italian suppleness, like oil, will soon float over all this vinegar," Thomas Carte, *A Collection of Original Letters and Papers,*

Concerning the Affairs of England, from the Year 1641 to 1660: Found among the Duke of Ormonde's papers, 2 vols. (London, 1739), vol. I, p. 328.

26 *Memoirs of the Verney Family*, vol. II, p. 231.

27 Philip Knachel's *England and the Fronde: The impact of the English Civil War and revolution on France* (Ithaca: Cornell University Press, 1967), pp. 238–40. Knachel's book has a wealth of material on the royalists' involvement in French politics while in Paris. It is also particularly illuminating for its examination of the flow of news and political ideologies back and forth across the Channel.

28 *Memoirs of the Verney Family*, vol. II, p. 423.

29 See Thomas Carte, *A Collection of Original Letters*, vol. I, pp. 147–56, where Ormonde recounts the confused duels between partisans of Digby and Prince Rupert outside of Paris in 1646. After Rupert challenged Digby directly, Digby responded formally: "The Prince proceeded most generously . . . he would be glad to have waited on his Highness on horseback" (p. 154). See also Ian Roy, "George Digby, royalist intrigue and the collapse of the cause," in *Soldiers, Writers and Statesmen of the English Revolution*, eds. Ian Gentles, John Morrill and Blair Worden (Cambridge: Cambridge University Press, 1998), pp. 87–90.

30 *A Collection of the State Papers of John Thurloe*, 7 vols. (London, 1742), vol. I, pp. 311–12, 449, 647 for examples.

31 See Marchamont Nedham's *The Case of the Commonwealth Stated*, ed. Philip Knachel (Charlottesville: University of Virginia Press, 1969); *The King of Scotland's Negotiations at Rome* (London, 1650); *A Message from the King of Scots* (London, 1651); *The Declaration and Speech of Colonel Massey* (London, 1650); *A Letter from the Lord General Cromwell* (London, 1651); *A Letter from the King of Scots to the Pope of Rome* (London, 1651).

32 Nedham, *The Case of the Commonwealth*, p. 57.

33 Nedham, *The Case of the Commonwealth*, p. 68.

34 Thurloe, *A Collection of the State Papers*, p. 631, and *Mercurius Politicus* (288), 13–20 Dec. 1655.

35 Quoted in Paul Tabori, *The Anatomy of Exile: A semantic and historical study* (London: Harrap, 1972), p. 34.

36 See, for example, *Memoirs of the Verney Family*, vol. II, p. 222.

37 Indeed, after the Licensing Act of 1643, which incited Milton's famous attack on monopolies in the book trade, the Stationers were able to regain control of much of their privileges, but not all of their policing powers; see Joseph Loewenstein, *The Author's Due: Printing and the prehistory of copyright* (Chicago: University of Chicago Press, 2002), pp. 163–70.

38 Lucien Febvre and Henri-Jean Martin, *The Coming of the Book: The impact of printing 1450–1800*, trans. David Gerard (London: N.L.B., 1976), pp. 230–5. Febvre and Martin sum up: "After 1640, with fewer and fewer books coming out in Latin, and more and more in the vernacular languages, publishing was ceasing to be an international enterprise" (p. 234).

39 Robert Darnton, *The Kiss of Lamourette: Reflections in cultural history* (New York: Norton, 1990), pp. 110–13. This circuit includes the author, the publisher, the printer, the shipper, the bookseller and the reader. To these I would add the manifold practices of exchange, both material and oral, that occur once the book is bought from the bookseller.

40 See the letter from October 1646, in which he suggests some corrections to the proofs that he has seen: "I see there is a great danger that he will make similar mistakes in other passages, both because my writing is not clear enough, and because neither of us is there with him," in *The Correspondence of Thomas Hobbes*, ed. Noel Malcolm, 2 vols. (Oxford: Clarendon Press, 1994), vol. I, p. 143.

41 See Hobbes's letter from February 1647, *The Correspondence*, vol. I, p. 153 and Sorbiere's response, p. 154.

42 Warrender, *De Cive: The Latin version*, Plate IV.

43 Interestingly, Hobbes also complained that the inscription would also serve to inflame his own enemies in England, thereby preventing a return to his own country. This letter shows that, even at this early date, Hobbes had begun to consider the possibility of a return to England, *The Correspondence*, vol. I, pp. 155–9.

44 *A Missive of Consolation: Sent from Flanders to the Catholikes of England* (Louvain, 1647), sig. A4v.

45 *The Flaming Heart* (Antwerp, 1652), sig. A2v.

46 Henri-Jean Martin, *The French Book: Religion, Absolutism, and Readership, 1585–1715*, trans. Paul Saenger and Nadine Saenger (Baltimore: Johns Hopkins University Press, 1996), pp. 41–3.

47 Knachel, *England and the Fronde*, pp. 65–6.

48 John Feather, "The country trade in books," in *Spreading the Word: The distribution networks of print, 1550–1850*, eds. Robin Myers and Michael Harris (Winchester: St. Paul's Bibliographies, 1990), pp. 165–84; Paul Morgan, "The provincial book trade before the end of the licensing act," in *Six Centuries of the Provincial Book Trade in Britain*, ed. Peter Isaac (Winchester: St. Paul's Bibliographies, 1990), pp. 31–40; Tessa Watt, "Publisher, pedlar, pot-poet: the changing character of the broadside trade, 1550–1640," in *Spreading the Word*; and Margaret Spufford, *Small Books and Pleasant Histories* (Athens: University of Georgia, 1982), pp. 111–28.

49 James Raven, "Selling books across Europe," in *Publishing History* 11 (1993), 5–19; Giles Barber, "Book imports and exports in the eighteenth century," in *The Sale and Distribution of Books from 1700*, eds. Robin Myers and Michael Harris (Oxford: Oxford Polytechnic Press, 1982), pp. 77–105. The English book market was much better equipped for importing from the Continent. Martin and Febvre note in *The Coming of the Book* that the period of 1620–40 marked a wide-scale recession in the European book markets. English book buyers and sellers increasingly withdrew into the less capital-intensive domestic market during this period. By 1640, the English presence at the Frankfurt book fair was virtually non-existent,

and the growing Leipzig fair catered heavily to the German, Russian and Polish markets (pp. 230–5).

50 See Elizabeth, Queen of Bohemia, *Letters*, comp. L.M. Baker (London: The Bodley Head, 1953), pp. 75, 90, for example. Henrietta Maria, due to the chaos in and around Paris during the Fronde, did not receive news of her husband's death until two weeks after it occurred (Bone, *Henrietta Maria*, p. 229).

51 Benedict Anderson, *Imagined Communities: Reflections on the origins and spread of nationalism* (London: Verso, 1991), pp. 33–6.

52 *The Memoirs of Anne, Lady Halkett and Ann, Lady Fanshawe*, ed. John Loftis (Oxford: Clarendon Press, 1979), p. 115.

53 *Reading in Exile: The libraries of John Ramridge, Thomas Harding and Henry Joliffe, Recusants in Louvain*, comp. Christian Coppins (Cambridge: LP Publications, 1993) has the library inventories of three exiled English Catholics from the 1570s. Ramridge's library was comparable to a typical Cambridge divine's library in size. The introduction provides an intriguing picture of a reading community created by these Oxford exiles, including a lending system based in the English Catholic college in Louvain. It remains unclear how exactly these exiles were able to transport and maintain their large libraries while in exile (p. 30). Marika Keblusek is currently completing a study of royalist reading practices while in exile that details the collecting practices and successful acquisition of books by these exiles while on the Continent. My focus here is on the haphazard and uncertain exchanges with the English print market specifically."

54 Evelyn, *Diary*, vol. II, p. 39.

55 Evelyn, *Diary*, vol. II, p. 636 n.

56 A.I. Doyle, "John Cosin," in *Dictionary of Literary Biography* 213 (1999), 54–5. Cosin was able to obtain a new collection of works while in France, including some English works. Sir Kenelm Digby, certainly not an exemplary figure in any sense, also collected and maintained a rather large collection while in exile.

57 Charles Kay Smith, "French philosophy and English politics in interregnum poetry," in *The Stuart Court in Europe*, pp. 177–209.

58 Lisa Jardine and Anthony Grafton, "'Studied for action': how Gabriel Harvey read his Livy," in *Past and Present* 129 (1990), pp. 30–78.

59 *Traytors Deciphered* (The Hague, 1650), p. 4.

60 *The History of the King's Majesties Affairs in Scotland* (The Hague, 1647), sig. B4r.

61 Wing gives no indication that the imprint is false. I use the term "community of readers" carefully here to refer to an imagined set of readers that the text anticipates and envisions. As Roger Chartier in *The Order of Books*, trans. Lydia G. Cochrane (Stanford: Stanford University Press, 1994) and de Certeau, in "Reading as Poaching," have argued, the anticipation of the text does not completely control or limit habits of

reading. We cannot assume actual communities of readers to be effects of the book. However, we can envision a text as anticipating and responding to practices of reading and the realities of reading communities, as I do here.

62 *A Fountain of Loyal Tears* (Paris, 1650), t.p.
63 *A Fountain of Loyal Tears*, pp. 3, 7.
64 *A Fountain of Loyal Tears*, p. 2.
65 *A Fountain of Loyal Tears*, pp. 6–7.
66 Thomas Hobbes, "The verse vita: a contemporary translation," in *Human Nature and De Corpore Politico*, ed. J.C.A. Gaskin (Oxford: Oxford University Press, 1994), p. 259. The translation of Hobbes's Latin poem appeared in 1680 anonymously. See also *The Correspondence* and the introduction to *Critique du "De mundo" de Thomas White*, eds. Jean Jacquot and Harold Whitmore Jones (Paris: J. Vrin, 1973), pp. 9–102 for more on Hobbes's pursuits while in exile.
67 León Grinberg and Rebeca Grinberg, *Psychoanalytic Perspectives on Migration and Exile*, trans. Nancy Festinger (New Haven: Yale University Press, 1989), pp. 109–12.
68 "The verse vita," p. 254.
69 Lindsay Kaplan, *The Culture of Slander in Early Modern England* (Cambridge: Cambridge University Press, 1997), p. 20.
70 Thomas Hobbes, *The Elements of Law Natural and Politic*, ed. Ferdinand Tönnies, 2nd ed. (London: Frank Cass, 1969), p. 18. All further references will be to this edition and appear in the text as *EL*.
71 Quoted in Howard Warrender, "Editor's introduction," in *De Cive: The Latin edition*, p. 29, n. 2.
72 For more on Hobbes's turn away from humanist principles see Quentin Skinner, *Reason and Rhetoric in the Philosophy of Hobbes* (Cambridge: Cambridge University Press, 1996), pp. 250–93.
73 I take the phrase from the opening sentence of Samuel I. Mintz's *The Hunting of Leviathan: Seventeenth-century reactions to the materialism and moral philosophy of Thomas Hobbes* (Cambridge: Cambridge University Press, 1962), p. vii.
74 Skinner's articles are still the most comprehensive and perceptive work on Hobbes's relationship to the Engagement controversy; see "History and ideology in the English revolution," in *Historical Journal* 8 (1965), 151–70, and "The ideological context of Hobbes's thought," in *Historical Journal* 9 (1966), 286–317. See also his "Conquest and consent: Thomas Hobbes and the Engagement Controversy," in *The Interregnum*, ed. G.E. Aylmer (Hamden, Conn.: Archon Books, 1972), pp. 79–98, which essentially summarizes the conclusions of the two earlier articles. It is important to note that after careful consideration of the ideological context of Hobbes's mid-century works, Skinner still waffles on the exact relationship between Hobbes and the Engagement polemicists. See "History and

ideology," p. 170,   Conquest and consent," p 91 and "The ideological
context of Hobbes's thought," p. 308.

75 Hugh Trevor-Roper, "Thomas Hobbes," in *Historical Essays* (London:
Macmillan, 1957), p. 233. J.P. Somerville fruitfully extends Skinner's discussion backward, outlining the specific constitutional questions that Hobbes
seeks to address while writing *The Elements*, circa 1640 in "Lofty science and
local politics," in *The Cambridge Companion to Hobbes*, ed. Tom Sorell
(Cambridge: Cambridge University Press, 1996), pp. 246–73.

76 *De Cive: The English Version*, ed. Howard Warrender (Oxford: Clarendon
Press, 1983), p. 56.

77 *The Collected Works*, vol. IV, p. 414.

78 Richard C. McCoy, "Old English honour in an evil time: aristocratic principle in the 1620s," in *The Stuart Court in Europe*, pp. 133–55.

79 Hobbes, *Leviathan*, ed. Richard Tuck (Cambridge: Cambridge University
Press, 1996), p. 65. All further citations will be from this edition and cited in
the text, abbreviated *L*.

80 Skinner, *Reason and Rhetoric*, pp. 284–93.

81 Henrietta Maria had to resort to barricading herself in the Louvre in the
latter months of 1648 after her benefactor, her brother, the young Louis
XIV, fled to St. Germain. After Louis XIV had stopped paying Henrietta
Maria her pension due to his flight, the queen refused a similar payment
from the French Parlement, leaving her and her followers in dire need.
It was in this state that the royalist exiles, several weeks after the event,
found out their king had been executed. See Bone, *Henrietta Maria*,
p. 229; Carte, *A Collection of Original Letters*, pp. 213–15.

82 Hobbes, "The verse vita," p. 260.

83 Indeed, even Hobbes's earliest readers felt that his vision of the "state of
nature" was the most remarkable aspect of his theories. As Quentin Skinner
notes, the association of Hobbes with his view of the state of nature was
a commonplace even in the restoration. See Skinner, "The ideological
context of Hobbes's thought," pp. 298–9.

84 Walzer, *The Revolution of the Saints: A Study in the Origins of Radical Politics*
(Cambridge: Harvard University Press, 1965), p. 15.

85 The topic of obedience unsurprisingly held particular interest for many of
the exiles, as they contemplated their defeat, the rise of the Commonwealth
and Protectorate, and their own decision to remain in exile or return to
England to compound and make their peace. For more on the Cavendish
circle and their interest in obedience see James R. Jacob and Timothy
Raylor, "Opera and obedience: Thomas Hobbes and *A proposition for the
advancement of moralitie* by Sir William Davenant," in *Seventeenth Century* 5
(1990), 205–50.

86 The 1647 *De Cive*, with its additional "Preface to the Reader," also shows
a growing concern for audience. Yet, here, Hobbes has a specific
Continental scientific community in mind. The polemical edge of *De
Cive*, thus, is far blunter than *Leviathan*. See Warrender, "Editor's

introduction," in *De Cive: The Latin version*, pp. 23 and 29–30. The *De Cive* was not always to remain this way, however. Richard Royston, the prominent royalist publisher, issued a version that Hobbes seemed to have little, if any, involvement in, titled *Philosophical Rudiments* (1651).

87 See his letter to Sorbiere from 1647, quoted in n. 43, and a September 1649 letter to Gassendi, *The Correspondence*, vol. I, p. 179.

88 Edward Hyde, Earl of Clarendon, *A Brief View and Survey of the Dangerous and Pernicious Errors to Church and State in Mr. Hobbes's Book, Entitled* LEVIATHAN (London, 1676), p. 1.

89 Hyde seems to have had a propensity for suspecting the motives of publishing during the exile. He himself decided against the publication of his history, worrying that it would displease everyone involved in the Revolution. Later, he would attack Abraham Cowley for the same motives as Hobbes, perhaps because of a conciliatory clause in Cowley's "Preface" to his 1656 *Poems*.

90 Annabel M. Patterson, *Censorship and Interpretation: The conditions of writing and reading in early modern England* (Madison: University of Wisconsin Press, 1984); Potter, *Secret Rites and Secret Writing: Royalist literature 1641–1660* (Cambridge: Cambridge University Press, 1990).

91 Skinner, *Reason and Rhetoric*, p. 347.

92 The classic modern statement of this is by Leo Strauss, *The Political Philosophy of Hobbes: Its basis and its genesis*, trans. Elsa M. Sinclair (Chicago: University of Chicago Press, 1984), pp. xiv–xv.

93 Hill, *The Enemy's Country: Words, contexture and other circumstances of language* (Stanford: Stanford University Press, 1991), p. 25.

94 Kevin Dunn, *Pretexts of Authority: The rhetoric of authorship in the renaissance preface* (Stanford: Stanford University Press, 1994), pp. 130–1.

CHAPTER 3: THE EXPULSION FROM PARADISE:
MILTON, EPIC AND THE RESTORATION EXILES

1 Edward Hyde, *The History of the Rebellion and Civil Wars in England*, ed. W. Dunn Macray, 6 vols. (Oxford, 1888), vol. VI, p. 143.

2 John Milton, *The Complete Prose Works of John Milton*, gen. ed. Don M. Wolfe, 8 vols. (New York: Columbia University Press, 1953–82), vol. VII, p. 463. All other citations from Milton's prose will be from this edition and cited in the text, abbreviated *CPW*.

3 Similarly, Edmund Ludlow remarks in his memoirs, upon finding shelter with a royalist acquaintance, that: "It was twielight (as we call it) with us both: with me it was as that of the evening, when it darkens by reason of the departure of the sunne, but with him as that of the morning," in *A Voyce From the Watchtower: Part Five, 1660–1662*, ed. A.B. Worden (London: Royal Historical Society, 1978), p. 109.

4 In a similar comment to Clarendon's, Evelyn saw the miraculous deliverance of the English people as comparable only to God's hand in the escape

from the Babylonian captivity, *Diary, Now First Printed in Full from the MSS Belonging to John Evelyn*, 6 vols. (Oxford: Clarendon Press, 1955), vol. IV, p. 246.

5 For more on the providential explanations of the restoration, see N.H. Keeble, *The Restoration: England in the 1660s* (Molden, MA: Blackwell, 2002), pp. 32–5.

6 See, for example, Keeble, *The Restoration*, pp. 46–56; Richard Greaves, *Deliver us from Evil: The radical underground in Britain, 1660–1663* (New York: Oxford University Press, 1986), pp. 3–19. Edmund Ludlow, perhaps bitterly, noted that the London crowds celebrated as much out of fear as out of affection for their returned monarch (*A Voyce From the Watchtower*, p. 118).

7 Ludlow, *A Voyce From the Watchtower*, pp. 115 and 150. It should be noted that Ludlow's "memoirs" were first published in 1698, although this edition little resembles the original MS recently uncovered in the Bodleian. For the 1698 edition, John Toland appropriated Ludlow's MS and liberally excised, revised and wholly rewrote certain parts to serve the radical Whig cause after the revolutionary settlement. Worden has published a section of the original MS, from which I cite here. For more on Toland's fascinating "revision," see Worden's introduction and Joseph Loewenstein, *The Author's Due: Printing and the prehistory of copyright* (Chicago: University of Chicago Press, 2003), pp. 206–24. I treat Ludlow's manuscript similarly as other texts from exile that were actually published since it seems that Ludlow had an English audience in mind while writing the memoirs in Vevey; see Worden's introduction, pp. 10–16.

8 Ludlow, *A Voyce From the Watchtower*, p. 149.

9 Algernon Sidney, *Court Maxims*, ed. Hans W. Blom, Eco Haitsma Mulier and Ronald Janse (New York: Cambridge University Press, 1996), p. 19.

10 Indeed, shame, in the Continental context, figures prominently in the late-Interregnum and restoration writing of many defeated revolutionaries. This sense of shame on the Continental stage should be understood in conjunction with the feeling, earlier, that God's true reformation of the world had begun in the British Isles.

11 Ludlow, *A Voyce From the Watchtower*, p. 127.

12 Sir Henry Vane, *Two Treatises* (London, 1662), p. 1.

13 For example, in Toland's wholesale revisions of Ludlow's manuscript into a republican, Roman history of the times. See Worden's "Introduction" to his edition of *A Voyce From the Watchtower* for more on Toland's dubious editorial practices and efforts to suppress what he saw to be the unattractive religious enthusiasm of the mid-century revolutionaries' writing.

14 Ludlow, *A Voyce From the Watchtower*, p. 188.

15 Simic, "Refugees," *Letters of Transit: Reflections on exile, identity, language and loss*, ed. André Aciman (New York: The New Press, 1999), p. 128.

16 *The Character of the Rump* (London, 1660), pp. 2–3. See Barbara Lewalski's *The Life of John Milton: A critical biography* (Oxford: Blackwell Publishers,

2000), pp. 375–82 for more contemporary attacks on Milton and on the declining fortunes of his party.

17 David Norbrook, *Writing the English Republic: Poetry, rhetoric, politics, 1627–1660* (Cambridge: Cambridge University Press, 1999), p. 415.

18 Michael Watts, *The Dissenters*, 2 vols. (Oxford: Clarendon Press, 1978), vol. I, pp. 241–2.

19 For the old orthodoxy see especially J.R. Jones, *Country and Court: England 1658–1714* (London: Edward Arnold, 1978), pp. 140–55 and J.P. Kenyon, *Stuart England* (New York: St. Martin's Press, 1978), pp. 181–97.

20 Greaves, *Deliver us from Evil*, pp. 21–84.

21 Jonathan Scott, *Algernon Sidney and the English Republic, 1623–1677* (Cambridge: Cambridge University Press, 1988), pp. 164–83, which details many of the internal disputes between the exiles and their course of action.

22 Worden, "Introduction," *A Voyce From the Watchtower*, pp. 12–13.

23 Keeble, *The Literary Culture of Nonconformity in Later Seventeenth-century England* (Athens, Ga.: University of Georgia Press, 1987); see more recently Keeble's chapter, "The patience of heroic fortitude: nonconformity, sedition and dissent," in *The Restoration*, pp. 137–48.

24 Worden, "Milton's republicanism and the tyranny of heaven," in *Machiavelli and Republicanism*, eds. Gisela Bock, Quentin Skinner and Maurizio Viroli (Cambridge: Cambridge University Press, 1990), pp. 243–4. For a correction, see Laura Lunger Knoppers's work on Milton's polemical engagement with restoration politics in *Historicizing Milton: Spectacle, power, and poetry in restoration England* (Athens, Ga.: University of Georgia Press, 1994). Hers is a notable exception. I will return to the dispute over Milton's engagement in *Paradise Lost* below.

25 Worden, "Introduction," in *A Voyce From the Watchtower*, p. 67 and Keeble, *The Literary Culture of Nonconformity*, p. 72.

26 Coven, *The Militant Christian* (London, 1668), n.p.

27 Ludlow, *A Voyce From the Watchtower*, p. 11.

28 Cf. Knoppers, *Historicizing Milton*, pp. 47–55.

29 Owen Lloyd, *The Panther-prophesie* (London, 1663), pp. 2–7.

30 George Sikes, *The Life and Death of Sir Henry Vane* (London, 1662), pp. 44, 46.

31 For more on the various uses of the ideology of the Church in the Wilderness before and after the restoration, see Christopher Hill, *The Experience of Defeat: Milton and some contemporaries* (New York: Viking, 1984), pp. 298–306.

32 *The Life and Death of Sir Henry Vane*, p. 5.

33 Daniel Baker, *Yet One Warning More to Thee O England* (London, 1660), p. 4.

34 Greaves, *Enemies Under his Feet: Radicals and nonconformists in Britain, 1664–1677* (Stanford: Stanford University Press, 1990), pp. 3–14. For more on the capture of Okey, Barkstead and Corbet, and the Dutch's reluctant involvement with their extradition, see Sir Ralph Catterall,

"Sir George Downing and the regicides," in *American Historical Review* 17 (1917), 268–89. James, in a supreme irony considering his desperate dealings with Louis XIV during his own exile, hostilely responded to suggestions of the English regicides returning at the head of a Dutch army that Englishmen always united when faced with a foreign threat.

35 Vane, *Two Treatises*, sig. A3r.

36 Sidney, *Court Maxims*, p. 2.

37 Blair Worden, "Republicanism and the restoration," in *Republicanism, Liberty and Commercial Society, 1649–1776*, ed. David Wootton (Stanford: Stanford University Press, 1994), p. 154. Scott also notes the growing Tacitean tinge to Sidney's letters, where he sees his persecution by the corrupt court of Charles II as only natural (*Algernon Sidney and the English Republic*, p. 150).

38 Ludlow, *A Voyce From the Watchtower*, pp. 115–16. Worden notes the combination of republican and dissenting rhetoric in Sidney's *Court Maxims* in "Republicanism and the restoration," p. 155.

39 Sikes, *The Life and Death of Henry Vane*, p. 53.

40 Sikes, *The Life and Death of Henry Vane*, pp. 140, 118.

41 I have spoken of Hobbes's similarities with Calvin and their relation to his experience as an exile above, pp. 78–9. See also Michael Walzer, *The Revolution of the Saints: A study in the origins of radical politics* (Cambridge: Harvard University Press, 1965), pp. 14–15, for the resemblances between the two.

42 Sikes, *The Life and Death of Henry Vane*, pp. 19–23.

43 Worden, "Marchamont Nedham and the beginnings of English republicanism, 1649–1656," in *Republicanism, Liberty and Commercial Society*, pp. 53–60.

44 Jones, *Mene Tekel* (London, 1663), p. 1.

45 Jones, *Mene Tekel*, p. 15.

46 Thomas Corns, *The Development of Milton's Prose Style* (Oxford: Clarendon Press, 1982), pp. 60–5, details the shifts in style in *The Readie and Easie Way*.

47 William Riley Parker, *Milton: A biography*, 2nd ed. (Oxford: Clarendon Press, 1996), p. 543.

48 For example, towards the end of the treatise Milton argues that in each chief town the subordinate "Commonaltie" "should have heer also schools and academies" which would "soon spread much more knowledge and civilitie, yea religion through all parts of the land, by communicating the natural heat of government and culture more distributively to all extreme parts" (*CPW* VII: 460). This picture of a republican nation, whose people are well-versed in civic virtue and governance, goes along with Milton's understanding that education necessarily must fix the "fluxible fault, if any such be, of our watry situation" (437), and thus begins to illuminate how far short the nation is of its republican ideal at this moment.

49 All citations to *Paradise Lost* will be from *The Works of John Milton*, 18 vols., ed. Frank Allen Patterson, *et al.* (New York: Columbia

University Press, 1931–8), vols. I and II and cited in the text with Book and line numbers.

50 Laura Lunger Knoppers, *Historicizing Milton*, pp. 67–9.

51 For the censorship argument, see most forcefully, Christopher Hill's *Milton and the English Revolution* (London: Faber and Faber, 1977), pp. 64–5, 216–18; however, the assumption that fears of censorship were critical to the structure of the poem informs numerous readings with often bizarre results. Michael Wilding, for example, in an otherwise exemplary reading in his *Dragon's Teeth: Literature in the English revolution* (Oxford: Clarendon Press, 1987), p. 244, ends up arguing that the poem becomes more open about its politics towards the end of the poem because Milton figured the censor would not read that far. The argument that Milton's poem shows a withdrawal from contemporary politics is somewhat of a critical paradigm at this point.

52 See particularly Knoppers, *Historicizing Milton* and N.H. Keeble, *The Literary Culture of Nonconformity.*

53 For a useful corrective to Milton's own description here, see Stephen Dobranski, *Milton, Authorship, and the Book Trade* (Cambridge: Cambridge University Press, 1999), pp. 1–40, as well as, generally, David Masson, *The Life of John Milton and the History of His Time*, 8 vols. (Gloucester, MA: Peter Smith, 1965), vol. VI, pp. 431–518.

54 To the extent that one of the overriding reactions by contemporary readers to the poem was the feeling that they were reading something sublime and weighty, this strategy seems to have succeeded. See for readers' reactions, Andrew Marvell's commendatory poem in the 1673 edition of *Paradise Lost* as well as Nicholas von Maltzahn's survey of early readers' reactions in "The first reception of *Paradise Lost* (1667)," in *Review of English Studies* 47 (1996), 479–99, and "Laureate, Republican and Calvinist," in *Milton Studies* 29 (1992), 181–98.

55 Peter Lindebaum, "*Paradise Lost* and the republican mode of production," in *The Yearbook of English Studies* 21 (1991), 106.

56 Nicholas von Maltzahn, "The first reception of *Paradise Lost*," 481–90.

57 Sharon Achinstein, *Milton and the Revolutionary Reader* (Princeton: Princeton University Press, 1994), pp. 177–82. See also Achinstein's *Literature and Dissent in Milton's England* (Cambridge: Cambridge University Press, 2003), pp. 115–30, for an exploration of the poem as addressed to an audience of like-minded, persecuted religious dissenters.

58 Hugh Amory, "Things unattempted yet," in *Book Collector* 32 (1983), 54–5.

59 Quoted in Nicholas von Maltzahn, "Laureate, republican and Calvinist," p. 189.

60 See above, p. 84.

61 See John Rumrich, *Milton Unbound: Controversy and reinterpretation* (Cambridge: Cambridge University Press, 1996), pp. 1–8, although Rumrich is more interested in debunking an "invented Milton" comfortable in his Christian orthodoxy and establishing him as an eccentric and

heterodox poet, Victoria Silver. *Imperfect Sense: The predicament of Milton's irony* (Princeton: Princeton University Press, 2001), esp. pp. 3–14, 41–55; Jeffrey Shoulson, *Milton and the Rabbis: Hebraism, Hellenism, and Christianity* (New York: Columbia University Press, 2001), particularly his notion of a "bounded hermeneutics" in *Paradise Lost*, pp. 39–44; and Peter Herman, *Destabilizing Milton: PARADISE LOST and the poetics of incertitude* (New York: Palgrave Macmillan, 2005), throughout but esp. pp. 1–59. Herman sums up his approach at the end of his introduction: "I use 'incertitude' because I believe that, in the aftermath of the Revolution, the critical sensibility that Milton championed throughout his career led him to engage in a wholesale questioning of just about everything he had argued for in his earlier prose works, and *he does not come to a conclusion*" (p. 21) [italics in original]. While Shoulson and Herman also emphasize the importance of the failure of the Revolution to the uneasiness of Milton's poem, my exploration of Milton as an "interior exile" outlines more specifically the impact of defeat and restoration on Milton's thought.

62 For more on the traditions of Lucanian epic form see David Quint, *Epic and Empire: Politics and generic form from Virgil to Milton* (Princeton: Princeton University Press, 1993), pp. 268–324; see also more recently David Norbrook's narrative of a continuing republican poetics of the sublime arising from Lucan in *Writing the English Republic*.

63 Richard Helgerson, *Self-crowned Laureates: Spenser, Jonson, Milton and the literary system* (Berkeley: University of California Press, 1983), pp. 238–42.

64 Helgerson, *Self-crowned Laureates*, p. 240.

65 Quint, *Epic and Empire*, p. 8.

66 William Spengemann, *A New World of Words: Redefining early American literature* (New Haven, Yale University Press, 1994), p. 113; and David Armitage, "John Milton: poet against empire," in *Milton and Republicanism*, eds. David Armitage, Armand Himy and Quentin Skinner (Cambridge: Cambridge University Press, 1995), p. 216. J. Martin Evans explores the colonial implications and trajectories of Milton's narrative voice in *Milton's Imperial Epic: PARADISE LOST and the discourse of colonialism* (Ithaca: Cornell University Press, 1996), pp. 112–40. Sharon Achinstein also notes that wandering and exploring mark the sign of a fallen nature in *Milton and the Revolutionary Reader*, p. 213.

67 William G. Riggs, *The Christian Poet in PARADISE LOST* (Berkeley: University of California Press, 1972), pp. 19, 25. Riggs concludes: "He is after the contrast, but he does not wish to gain it by slighting the similarities. On the contrary, the more clearly he can see and project similarities between the poet and Satan, the more sure he can be that he has not been blinded by pride" (p. 25).

68 Anne Ferry, *Milton's Epic Voice: The narrator in PARADISE LOST* (Cambridge: Harvard University Press, 1963), pp. 34–5.

69 The laughter of God here also reminds us of the wandering search for truth by the devils in Book II after the council at Pandemonium when the fallen

angels: "reason'd high/Of Providence, Foreknowledge, Will, and Fate,/Fixt Fate, Free will, Foreknowledge absolute,/And found no end, in wand'ring mazes lost" (II: 558–61).

70 See Blair Worden, "Marchamont Nedham and the beginnings of English Republicanism, 1649–1656," in *Republicanism, Liberty and Commercial Society*), pp. 56–60 for Milton's disappointment with the English government in 1648–9; Martin Dzelzainis, "Milton and the Protectorate in 1658," in *Milton and Republicanism*, pp. 181–205, and Blair Worden, "John Milton and Oliver Cromwell," in *Soldiers, Writers and Statesmen of the English Revolution*, eds. Ian Gentles, John Morrill and Blair Worden (Cambridge: Cambridge University Press, 1998), pp. 243–64, detail his projected falling out with Cromwell's regime in the later 1650s.

71 John Rogers, *The Matter of Revolution: Science, poetry and politics in the age of Milton* (Ithaca: Cornell University Press, 1996), pp. 122–43 depicts, in the poem, a tension between the scientific hopes of the early books of the poem and the authoritarian, Calvinist turn of the later books.

72 See Stephen M. Fallon, "'Elect above the rest': theology as self-representation in Milton," in *Milton and Heresy*, eds. Stephen B. Dobranski and John P. Rumrich (Cambridge: Cambridge University Press, 1998), pp. 94–6.

73 William Empson, *Milton's God* (London: Chatto and Windus, 1965).

74 See Victoria Silver, *Imperfect Sense*, pp. 71–93; Jeffrey Shoulson, *Milton and the Rabbis*, pp. 93–9 and 107–13; and Peter Herman, *Destabilizing Milton*, pp. 107–25. Michael Bryson in *The Tyranny of Heaven: Milton's rejection of God as king* (Newark: University of Delaware Press, 2004) argues that Milton's God, the unappealing monarch of heaven, is the poet's attempt to illustrate the inherent and absolute corruption of monarchy generally. According to Bryson, Milton believed the depiction of God as a monarch originated from human custom, not divine authority, and in *Paradise Lost* he sets out to show the wrongness of such a depiction (pp. 42–76). However, in my view, Bryson does not adequately take into account the frequently disturbing and unappealing versions of the divine that we see elsewhere in Milton's poetry. That is, Milton is not attempting to teach his *readers* about the nature of divinity, but rather agonizing over his own disturbing imaginings of the divine at moments of personal crisis.

75 John Rogers, "Milton's Circumcision," in *Milton and the Grounds of Contention*, eds. Mark R. Kelley, Michael Leib and John T. Shawcross (Pittsburgh: Duquesne University Press, 2003), pp. 204–6.

76 John Rumrich takes issue with Fish's notion of Milton's theodicy in *Milton Unbound*, pp. 1–23. Of course, Fish would deny that pathos was even on Milton's Puritanical mind while he wrote his epic. However, in Fish's reading we must end up denying that Milton's lament "O for that warning voice" at the opening to Book IV, for example, can carry any emotion once the reader applies the Fishean paradigm. Milton evokes the pathos here only

to lead the reader astray, since, according to Fish, really no voice would have been able to prevent the fall.

77 Michael Seidel, *Exile and the Narrative Imagination* (New Haven: Yale University Press, 1986), p. 5.

78 Nicholas von Maltzahn, "Milton's First Readers," p. 191.

79 David Norbrook, *Writing the English Republic*, pp. 420–1.

80 Later, after Adam asks him to relate the creation of the world, Raphael repeats the same worry: "though to recount Almightie works/What words or tongue of Seraph can suffice,/Or heart of man suffice to comprehend?" (VII: 112–14).

81 David Loewenstein, *Representing Revolution in Milton and his Contemporaries: Religion, politics and polemics in radical Puritanism* (Cambridge: Cambridge University Press, 2001), p. 230; see also Roger Lejosne, "Milton, Salmasius, Satan and Abdiel," in *Milton and Republicanism*, pp. 106–17; Armand Himy, "*Paradise Lost* as a republican 'Tractatus theologico-politicus,'" in *Milton and Republicanism*, pp. 118–34; Robert Fallon, *Divided Empire: in Milton's political imagery* (University Park: Pennsylvania State University Press, 1995); Mary Ann Radzinowicz, "The politics of PARADISE LOST," in *The Politics of Discourse: The literature and history of seventeenth-century England*, eds. Kevin Sharpe and Steven N. Zwicker (Berkeley: University of California Press, 1987), pp. 204–29.

82 In *Destabilizing Milton*, Peter Herman has insightfully explored the preponderance of "or" in the poem and its various incarnations, pp. 43–59. Herman's emphasis on the incertitude that accompanies this preponderance informs my discussion here. However, while Herman solely emphasizes the "aporia" that result from Milton's "poetics of incertitude," I wish to consider this poetics alongside Milton's epic claims and gestures towards encyclopedic inclusion, as both arising out of the experience of "interior exile."

83 Quoted in Corns, *Milton's Language* (Oxford: Blackwell, 1990), pp. 1–2.

84 Corns, *Milton's Language*, pp. 1–9.

85 Corns, *Milton's Language*, pp. 83–113. For more on the importation by Milton from various languages, see John Hale, *Milton's Languages: The impact of multilingualism on style* (New York: Cambridge University Press, 1997).

CHAPTER 4: SYBIL'S LEAVES: DRYDEN AND THE
HISTORIOGRAPHY OF EXILE

1 In the early 1690s, John Toland, writing under the pseudonym of "Ludlow," a name Toland wanted associated with the exiled regicide Edmund Ludlow, borrowed extensively from *Eikonoklastes* in a series of pamphlets attacking Charles I's authorship of *Eikon Basilike* and, as a result, his legitimacy as king. For more on these pamphlets, and Toland's liberal rewriting of Ludlow's memoirs, see Blair Worden, "Introduction,"

in *A Voyce From the Watchtower*, ed. A.B. Worden (London: Royal Historical Society, 1978); and, for their specific borrowings from Milton, George Sensabaugh, *That Grand Whig Milton* (Stanford: Stanford University Press, 1952), especially pp. 143–55. Toland also was responsible for the *Life of Milton* in 1699. Charles Blount was perhaps the most dedicated of Milton's plagiarists, borrowing extensively from *Areopagitica* at various junctures in his pamphlet career. For more on the plagiarisms and revisions of Milton in the 1690s and its impact on nascent forms of authorial property and authorship, see Joseph Loewenstein, *The Author's Due: Printing and the prehistory of copyright* (Chicago: University of Chicago Press, 2002), pp. 206–24.

2 In earlier accounts, Milton's epic looms ominously over the last decades of the former Poet Laureate's career as a defeated Dryden resorted to translation after 1688 and after, supposedly, a tacit recognition of his inability to write such an epic poem. Steven Zwicker has reminded us, however, of the possibility that the anxiety did not merely go one way in this relationship, that, in fact, Milton shows his own unease at the precocious success of his younger contemporary in the attack on the slavish reliance on rhyme in Milton's note on "The Verse" of *Paradise Lost*; see Zwicker, "Milton, Dryden and the politics of literary controversy," in *Culture and Society in the Stuart Restoration: Literature, Drama, History*, ed. Gerald Maclean (Cambridge: Cambridge University Press, 1995), pp. 137–58. For the most forceful accounts of Dryden's meek and submissive turn to translation and away from "creative" work, see David Bruce Kramer, *The Imperial Dryden: The poetics of appropriation in seventeenth-century England* (Athens: University of Georgia Press, 1994), pp. 116–38, and Paul Davis, "But slaves we are: Dryden and Virgil, translation and the 'Giant Race,'" in *Translation and Literature* 10 (2000), 110–27. I will have more to say on Dryden's turn to translation as it relates to his loss of the laureateship and minority status below.

3 *The Works of John Dryden*, eds. Edward Niles Hooker, H.T. Swedenberg, Jr., 20 vols. (Berkeley: University of California Press, 1956–2002), III: 208. All other references to Dryden's work will be to this edition and cited in the text, unless otherwise noted.

4 It should be noted that Dryden failed to maintain this elevation consistently in his other criticism. In the *Dedication of the Aeneis*, for example, Dryden dismisses Milton from the pantheon of epic poets (*Works* V: 276).

5 Dryden's oft-quoted, and overused, distinctions between "metaphrase," "paraphrase" and "imitation" appeared in 1680. The distinctions remained far from clear as Dryden ruminated on translation in the next twenty odd years, which allowed various combinations of the terms to seep into his descriptions of certain authors or poems. Judith Sloman calls Dryden's distinctions not "programmatic" but merely a "starting point" in her *Dryden: The poetics of translation* (Toronto: University of Toronto Press, 1985), p. 8.

6 The discussion on the scales in or *Works* V; 316–17. It should be noted that one area in which Dryden never came around on Milton was their differences over rhyme. In the *Discourse of Satire*, Dryden, even while giving the praise I quote above, could not resist smirking that Milton wrote not in couplets because "Rhyme was not his Talent" (*Works* IV: 15). Later, in the *Dedication of the Aeneis*, Milton lingers behind Dryden's digression, a digression to which "he is strangely tempted," that notes that those who write well in rhyme can certainly "write better in Blank Verse" (*Works* V: 324).

7 Bywaters, thus, posits that Dryden's turn away from partisan satire to playwriting and translation does not constitute a turn away from politics, but a new direction in Drydenian polemic, David Bywaters, *Dryden in Revolutionary England* (Berkeley: University of California Press, 1991), pp. 104–62.

8 On the intriguing alliance that formed the "country party" between English Jacobites and the oppositional Whigs, see Paul Monod, *Jacobitism and the English People, 1688-1788* (Cambridge: Cambridge University Press, 1989), pp. 38–45 and Eveline Cruickshanks, *Political Untouchables: The Tories and the '45* (New York: Holmes and Meier, 1979); J.C.D. Clark in *Revolution and Rebellion: State and society in England in the seventeenth and eighteenth centuries* (Cambridge: Cambridge University Press, 1986) notes that by the 1710s the alliance specifically derived from the convergence of concerns of Whig intellectuals such as John Toland and Joseph Molesworth, with a strong Tory nostalgia for monarchy rooted in the landed gentry (pp. 112–15). Interestingly, James II relied almost exclusively upon radical Whigs, specifically Charlwood Lawton and Robert Ferguson, to make arguments for the Jacobite cause in print during the 1690s; see Paul Monod, "The Jacobite press and English censorship, 1689–95," in *The Stuart Court in Exile and the Jacobites*, eds. Eveline Cruickshanks and Edward Corp (London: The Hambledon Press, 1995), pp. 133–7.

9 Elizabeth Duthie, "'A memorial to my own principles': Dryden's 'To My Honour'd Kinsman," in *ELH* 47 (1980), 682–704.

10 Jay Arnold Levine, "John Dryden's epistle to John Driden," in *JEGP* 63 (1964), 461–3.

11 See, for example, Dryden's letter to John Dennis in 1693, *The Letters of John Dryden*, ed. Charles Ward (Durham: Duke University Press, 1942), p. 73, where Dryden somewhat defiantly notes that his "Principles of State" need no explanation: "I believe you in yours follow the Dictates of your Reason, as I in mine do those of my Conscience. If I thought my self in Error, I would retract it; I am sure that I suffer for them; and Milton makes even the Devil say, That no Creature is in love with Pain."

12 The parallel has been made before, both by William Frost in his introduction to Dryden's translation of the *Aeneid* in *The Works of John Dryden*, vol. VII, p. 848, as well as by Steven Zwicker, "The Politics of Literary Controversy," p. 157.

13 The two collections were *John Dryden: Tercentenary Essays*, eds. Paul Hammond and David Hopkins (Oxford: Clarendon Press, 2000) and *John Dryden: A tercentenary miscellany*, eds. Susan Green and Steven N. Zwicker (San Marino, CA: Huntington Library Press, 2001). Hammond's *Dryden and the Traces of Classical Rome* (Oxford: Oxford University Press, 1999) and Caldwell's *Time to Begin Anew: Dryden's* GEORGICS *and* AENEIS (London: Associated University Presses, 2000), while not occasioned specifically by the tercentenary, both came out in the months surrounding the essay collections.

14 For example, Murray Pittock, articulating what is the standard logic behind these Jacobite readings, argues that "Dryden's *Aeneid* deliberately cloaks its politics in translation, a translation which expresses its typology through hint and allusion in order to speak it publicly, in *Poetry and Jacobite Politics in Eighteenth-century Britain and Ireland* (Cambridge: Cambridge University Press, 1994), p. 14; see also his analysis of Dryden's Virgil at pp. 94–107. The work on covert Jacobite commentary in Dryden's translations has been plentiful and fruitful in the past decades. See, to start, Zwicker, *Politics and Language in Dryden's Poetry: The arts of disguise* (Princeton: Princeton University Press, 1984), pp. 177–205; Thomas Fujimura, "Dryden's Virgil: translation as autobiography," in *Studies in Philology* 80 (1983), 67–83; Zwicker and David Bywaters, "Politics and translation: the English Tacitus of 1698," in *Huntington Library Quarterly* 52 (1989), 319–46; Kirk Combe, "Clandestine protest against William III in Dryden's translations of Juvenal and Persius," in *Modern Philology* 87 (1989), 36–50; and Howard Erskine-Hill, *Poetry and the Realm of Politics: Shakespeare to Dryden* (Oxford: Clarendon Press, 1996), pp. 201–15. Pittock's is the most thoroughgoing and intransigently Jacobite reading of the translation. For a divergent reading of the manifestation of Dryden's Jacobitism in the later work, see William J. Cameron, "Dryden's Jacobitism," in *Restoration Literature: Critical approaches*, ed. Harold Love (London: Methuen, 1972), pp. 277–308.

15 Lawrence Lipking uses the term "cabalistic reading" to refer to the search for Jacobite sympathies in various restoration and eighteenth-century writers in "The Jacobite plot," in *ELH* 64 (1997), 847.

16 Richard Kroll, for example, in his reading of one of Dryden's last efforts for the public stage, *Don Sebastian*, argues that the play sustains a series of moral doublings that arise from Dryden's committed Catholicism yet moderate loyalism and that "caused him to view both William and James – that is, kings as such – with a profound and yet an imaginatively constitutive ambivalence," "The double logic of *Don Sebastian*," in *John Dryden. A tercentenary miscellany*, p. 54. Similarly, Sean Walsh rightfully emphasizes the difficulty of assigning strict Jacobite meanings to the poems in *Fables* and notes that in these poems "the limits of perceiving Dryden merely as a Stuart loyalist and Catholic become evident, while the subtlety of his late thought on culture and politics emerges," "'Our lineal descents

and clans': Dryden's *Fables Ancient and Modern* and cultural politics in the 1690s," in *John Dryden: A tercentenary miscellany*, p. 176. It should be noted, however, that Walsh limits his readings of the complexity of the late Dryden to *Fables* and seems to revert to a simpler understanding of the author's translations when he notes in passing that Dryden was "committed to finding new ways of talking" including "the exploitation of translation as a form of subversive expression in his Virgil and Juvenal" (p. 176). Walsh's argument that the *Fables* represent a statement of poetic and literary relationships over and above the political in some ways replicates David Bywaters's thesis in *Dryden in Revolutionary England*. Caldwell, as well, while noting the "open-endedness" of Dryden's translation (p. 124), tends to revert too quickly to the cabalistic reading of older critics, particularly as she moves through Dryden's Dedication to and translation of the *Aeneid*. Too often in her readings, Dryden emphasizes Aeneas's immorality to criticize William while he expands those passages that detail the hero's displacement and exile in order to focus on the disruptions to the Stuart succession (pp. 107–22).

17 Paul Hammond in *Dryden and the Traces of Classical Rome* describes Dryden's translation of the *Aeneid* as the poet's contemplation of "tragic loss and alienation" (p. 220), while also deftly detailing the shifting politics of the *Dedication* and translation (pp. 220–8). My analysis of Dryden's *Dedication* recognizes that, in fact, Dryden's psychological positioning as an "interior exile" was exactly what drove the irreducible and shifting politics of his *Dedication* and translation. While Hammond is more interested than I am in Dryden's turn to this epic about displacement as a turn to Virgil and to the story of Aeneas for solace, I am attempting to understand his complex politics, to which Hammond is quite attuned, more clearly as arising out of his "interior exile," and specifically out of the nature of public expression from such a position. Our analyses do converge in their depiction of Dryden's translation as an idiosyncratic space which Dryden imaginatively inhabited.

18 Paul Monod, "Jacobitism as court culture and popular culture," paper presented at Northeast American Society for Eighteenth-Century Studies, Sept. 1996, quoted in Kathryn King, *Jane Barker, Exile: A Literary Career: 1675–1725* (Oxford: Clarendon Press, 2000), p. 135.

19 In speaking of the "patronage" accorded Dryden's translation, I refer primarily to the subscribers to the edition, subscribers solicited by, among others, Tonson and Dryden. Dryden was surely aware of the wide-ranging political affiliations of his subscribers to this volume and his indebtedness to them. For a detailed account of the subscription list, and Dryden and Tonson's involvement with locating subscribers, see John Barnard, "Dryden, Tonson, and the patrons of *The Works of Virgil* (1697)," in *John Dryden: Tercentenary Essays*, pp. 174–230.

20 Marc Robinson, "Introduction," in *Altogether Elsewhere: Writers in Exile*, ed. Marc Robinson (Winchester, MA: Faber and Faber, 1994), p. xiv.

21 James Anderson Winn details the facts known about Dryden's move to Soho sometime in 1688–90 in *John Dryden and his World* (New Haven: Yale University Press, 1987), pp. 436–8.

22 On the influence of Dryden's recusancy upon, and his corresponding attachment to the domestic, the private and the feminine in, his later verse, see Anne Cotterill, "'Rebekah's heir': Dryden's late mystery of genealogy," in *John Dryden: A tercentenary miscellany*, pp. 201–26.

23 Daniel Szechi, *The Jacobites Britain and Europe, 1688–1788* (Manchester: Manchester University Press, 1994), pp. 60–1; Frank McLynn, *The Jacobites* (London: Routledge & Kegan Paul, 1985), pp. 81–2; for the Catholic community in England generally during this period, see John Bossy, *The English Catholic Community, 1570–1850* (New York: Oxford University Press, 1976), ch. 4.

24 See above, pp. 19–20, for my discussion of the term "alienation" and the modern critical models for more theoretical and metaphoric forms of exile.

25 For more on Dryden's digression as aggression, see Anne Cotterill, "The politics and aesthetics of digression: Dryden's *Discourse of Satire*," in *Studies in Philology* 91 (1994), 464–95.

26 Nico Israel discusses the exile's interest in literary history, anthropology and philosophy in similar terms in his somewhat clumsy application of Greenblatt's theories on self-fashioning to the exilic experience. See his otherwise laudable, *Outlandish: Writing between exile and diaspora* (Stanford: Stanford University Press, 2000), pp. 14–15.

27 For the argument that for the most part nostalgia drove Dryden's engagement with Virgil, see Howard Erskine-Hill, *The Augustan Idea in English Literature* (London: Edward Arnold, 1983), pp. 228–32. There are of course other explanations, economic primarily, that can be put forth and that certainly played a role in the decision to translate Virgil in full.

28 For which see Davis, "But slaves we are," especially.

29 The most comprehensive work on the circumstances of the production of the Dryden–Tonson Virgil is by Barnard, "Dryden, Tonson, and the patrons of *The Works of Virgil* (1697)."

30 Barnard, "Dryden, Tonson and the patrons of *The Works of Virgil* (1697)," pp. 188–97. See also Zwicker's analysis of the Jacobite leanings imbedded in many of the plates in *Politics and Language*, pp. 190–6.

31 The easiest corrective is the fact that the other driving force behind the Virgil, Tonson, was a steadfast Whig and member of the Kit-Kat Club who thought it appropriate, and not altogether out of the realm of possibility, to ask Dryden to dedicate the translation to William, a request, of course, Dryden refused.

32 Paul Hammond, "The circulation of Dryden's poetry," in *The Papers of the Bibliographical Society of America* 86 (1992), 379–409.

33 In the *London Gazette* in June 1697, Tonson announced to the London reading public that copies for subscribers would be ready in a week (Frost, *The Works of John Dryden*, vol. VI, p. 845).

34 Johnson states that "the nation considered its honor as interested" in Dryden's translation in *The Lives of the English Poets*, ed. George Birkbeck Hill, 3 vols. (Oxford: Clarendon Press, 1905), vol. I, p. 448.

35 He communicates this hope towards the end of the *Dedication* (*Works* V: 325) and would also repeat it in the "Postscript" which appeared at the end of the volume, where he rather confidently states that "what I have done, Imperfect as it is, for want of Health and leisure to Correct it, will be judg'd in after Ages, and possibly in the present, to be no dishonour to my Native Country" (*Works* VI: 807).

36 Sprat, *The History of the Royal Society of London*, in *Critical Essays of the Seventeenth Century*, ed. J.E. Spingarn, 3 vols. (Oxford: Clarendon Press, 1908), vol. II, pp. 112–13. Timothy J. Reiss notes, more generally than I do here, this recurring connection between language and a successful state, citing Davenant, Dryden and Sprat among others, in his essay, "Power, poetry and the resemblance of nature," in *Mimesis: From mirror to method, Augustine to Descartes*, eds. John Lyons and Stephen Nichols (Hanover, NH: University Press of New England, 1982), pp. 215–47.

37 Quoted in Winn, *John Dryden and his World*, p. 387.

38 Greg Clingham has recently posited that the Dryden–Tonson translations represent an effort to put into action the theories of Roscommon's Academy concerning translation and the refinement of the English language. See his "Roscommon's 'Academy,' Chetwood's manuscript 'Life of Roscommon,' and Dryden's translation project," in *Restoration* 26 (2002), 15–27. Clingham also has provided a transcription of Knightly Chetwood's "Life of Roscommon," in *Restoration* 25 (2001), 117–38. See also Stuart Gillespie, "The early years of the Dryden–Tonson partnership," in *Restoration* 12 (1988), 10–19, for more on the participation of the Roscommon circle, and specifically Dryden, in the early Tonson miscellanies that appeared in the 1680s.

39 Clingham, "Roscommon's Academy," p. 16. Dryden, in the dedication to *Troilus and Cressida*, seems to imagine an Academy in conjunction with Roscommon's (*Works* XIII: 221–2).

40 John Dillon, Earl of Roscommon, *An Essay on Translated Verse* (London, 1684), p. 3.

41 *Works* V: 550. All further citations of Dryden's translation of the *Aeneid* will be from this edition, cited with Book and line numbers.

42 A few examples: "I shall say perhaps as much of other Nations, and their Poets, excepting only Tasso: and hope to make my Assertion good, which is but doing Justice to my Country" (*Works* V: 287); "To love our Native Country, and to study its Benefit and its Glory, to be interested in its Concerns, is Natural to all Men, and is indeed our common Duty. A Poet makes a further step; for endeavouring to do honour to it, 'tis allowable in him even to be partial in its Cause" (*Works* V: 298); and on the French: "Our Men and our Verses overbear them by their weight; and *Pondere non Numero*, is the British Motto" (*Works* V: 322).

43 Hammond, *Dryden and the Traces of Classical Rome*, p. 227.

44 Probably most extensively in Arthur Mainwaring's poem, *Tarquin and Tullia* (London, 1694).

45 See, for example, James Montgomery, *The People of England's Grievances* (London, 1693); William Anderton, *Remarks Upon the Present Confederacy* (London, 1693); Robert Ferguson, *A Brief Account of Some of the Late Incroachments and Depredations of the Dutch* (London, 1695).

46 Of course, Dryden resisted Tonson's overtures, and even on the eve of publication wrote to Chesterfield that he had delayed the dedication as long as possible, "in hopes of his return, for whom, and for my Conscience I have sufferd, that I might have layd my Author at his feet," in *Letters*, pp. 85–6.

47 Peter White, *Promised Verse: Poets in the society of Augustan Rome* (Cambridge: Harvard University Press, 1993), pp. 95–109. White astutely notes that Dryden, in his depiction of Virgil, has dropped the part of the moral in Le Bossu that pertained to Augustus, without following up the implications of this observation, p. 106. Richard Thomas, *Virgil and the Augustan Reception* (Cambridge: Cambridge University Press, 2001), also discusses the French theorists and their influence on Dryden's *Dedication* and translation, pp. 134–44.

48 Quoted in Thomas, *Virgil and the Augustan Reception*, p. 142.

49 For which, see Howard Weinbrot, *Augustus Caesar in "Augustan" England: The decline of a classical norm* (Princeton: Princeton University Press, 1978), pp. 49–85 and on Virgil specifically, pp. 120–30. Weinbrot discusses Dryden's depiction of Virgil specifically on pp. 122–4 and places him clearly in the growing Tacitean camp.

50 Lisle, *Virgil's Eclogues* (London, 1628), p. 18.

51 The same freight attaches itself to "judicious" at times as well. Dryden praises Virgil's "judicious" decision to make the seat of the high priest of the Trojans vacant in Book II so that Aeneas, and thus Augustus, can ascend to it (*Works* V: 285).

52 Thomas, *Virgil and the Augustan Reception*, where his judgments tend toward the following: Dryden "converted Virgil into a flatterer, with the way he viewed Virgil and Virgilian poetry through the lens of his own times, whether Jacobite or Williamite, and consequently made Virgil's poem something that it had once not been" (p. 95).

53 This quote is from a recounting by Joseph Spence in *Joseph Spence: Observations, anecdotes, and characters of books and men collected from conversation*, ed. J.M. Osborne, 2 vols. (Oxford: Clarendon Press, 1966), vol. I, pp. 229–30. Dryden participated in this revaluation and, due to the prominence of his translation, almost certainly spurred the depiction of Virgil as propagandist and flatterer. Pope's evaluation remained in vogue well into the twentieth century. As recently as 1961 Robert Graves, in a lecture at Oxford University, could characterize Virgil as the "anti-poet" who exemplified "pliability, subservience ... narrowness ... lack of originality,"

quoted in Douglas Stewart, "Among the Politician," in *Virgil: Modern critical views*, ed. Harold Bloom (New York: Chelsea House Publishers, 1986), p. 103. A long needed revaluation of Virgil's politics and the tone of his poem has occurred in the past forty or so years, beginning with Adam Parry's seminal, "The Two Voices of Virgil's *Aeneid*," in *Arion* 2 (1963), 66–80 and finding its fullest, most eloquent expression in W.R. Johnson's *Darkness Visible: A study of Virgil's* AENEID (Berkeley: University of California Press, 1976).

54 I take this notion of Dryden as an authoritative mediating presence from Thomas Greene's account of authorial imitation in *The Light in Troy: Imitation and discovery in Renaissance poetry* (New Haven: Yale University Press, 1982), pp. 10–17.

EPILOGUE: THE REMANENCE OF EXILE

1 Hofer's story and the beginnings of nostalgia, as a term, are detailed in Svetlana Boym, *The Future of Nostalgia* (Boston: Basic Books, 2001), pp. 3–5.

Index